WINDOWS
FOR Mac Users

Cynthia Baron and Robin Williams

Peachpit Press

Berkeley ■ California

Windows for Mac Users

Cynthia Baron and Robin Williams
©1999 Cynthia Baron and Robin Williams

Cover art and production by John Tollett
Interior design by Robin Williams
Production by Barbara Sikora and Robin Williams
Indexed by Robin Williams
Edited by Nancy Davis and Robin Williams
Production management by Lisa Brazieal

PEACHPIT PRESS

1249 Eighth Street
Berkeley, California 94710
800 283-9444
510 524-2178
510 524-2221 (fax)

Find us on the World Wide Web at www.peachpit.com
Peachpit Press is a division of Addison Wesley Longman

ISBN 0-201-35396-2

10 9 8 7 6 5 4 3 2 1

Printed and bound in the United States of America

To Shai for love and technical help
To Nancy Davis for calm support
To Robin for the experience
—*Cyndi*

To Isabella Melanzana,
who hung in there
to the very end.
—*Robin*

Contents

Part Seven
THE STUFF AT THE END

Why two Mac evangelists wrote this book

We didn't write this book to convince you to switch platforms. Both Cyndi and Robin unabashedly prefer Macs. But unfortunately, even if you'd rather eat bugs than own or use a PC, Windows is everywhere. Whether you're being pressured to change platforms or merely using a network or emailing files, sooner or later you'll have to know something about how the other (more than) half lives. The more you can fit your Mac into the Windows world, the longer you can joyfully keep using your Mac while the rest of the world struggle with their PCs.

This book probably tells you more than you need to know right now. Use the table of contents and the index to figure out how to fix what's buggin' you today, then keep the book on your desk and when you bump into something that makes you crazy, we can almost guarantee it's made us crazy too so we made a point of telling you what you can do about it.

Although this book is quite complete from a Mac user's point of view, a seasoned PC user will notice there are Windows elements we don't cover. We hope you'll read a comprehensive book like *The Windows Bible* from Peachpit Press if you reach the level where you've got to understand nasty system stuff (like the Registry) or non-critical accessories and utilities that only a full-time, permanent PC owner needs.

For the passionate Mac user who has to use a PC sometimes (or often), don't worry—there are several advantages to learning to use Windows: You will feel even more superior to PC owners as you see how much of Windows has been copied from the Mac (you know what they say about imitation); PC owners will take what you say about the Mac more seriously if they know you also understand Windows and are not bragging out of ignorance; you'll be able to educate PC users about how incredibly cross-platform the Macintosh is (and has been) as you bounce back and forth between the two operating systems.

So jump in, learn to use the dumb thing, and move forward empowered!

Robin and Cyndi

Part One

Choosing and Using

For a successful technology,
reality must take precedence
over public relations,
for Nature cannot be fooled.

— Richard Feynman

Richard Feynman never had to use Windows.

— Cynthia Baron

Preparing to do Windows

It's always easier to work exclusively on one platform; that is, on one sort of computer. You can be more productive if your operating system is second nature to you, but for many reasons it may not be possible to limit your work to one platform. Once you've decided you need to use Windows, the more difficult decision may be how far to take that investment—in money, time, and emotional commitment.

In this chapter, we'll look at that decision. What criteria should you use to decide whether or not to take the plunge? What's it really going to cost? What are your options? You may discover you can solve your cross-platform needs simply and inexpensively without being more than an occasional Windows user. And if you discover that you need total immersion, at least you'll be sure that you made the right decision.

Do you really need to "do Windows"?

There are many occasions when the pressure to switch from your Mac to a PC seems strong, but it's coming down on you for the wrong reasons. You probably don't need to change operating systems if:

- The company you work for wants you on their network, and says their system doesn't support Macs.

  Any networking environment can support Macs with the addition of some software. Windows NT comes Mac-ready. Netware has a special Macintosh module that makes it Mac-savvy, plus software you can install to identify your Mac as a Netware client. There is third-party software for your Mac which will make it look and act like a "normal" Windows client.

- You're on the company TCP/IP network, but the printer doesn't recognize AppleTalk protocols.

  Again, there are other ways besides Mac-centric methods to enable you to print over a network. Most of the software that does this magic is considerably less expensive than the purchase of a new computer, and it can be expensed immediately (which bean counters like).

- You need to share files created on cross-platform applications with Windows users.

  See Part Five, Going Back and Forth.

- You do lots of Internet development for a living.

  Since many of the computers in the world aren't Macintoshes, you'll need to deal with different platforms, browsers, and displays. Fortunately, software emulators and add-in cards will let you run any version of Windows and browsers that you need. Only if you need to deal with DirectX, ActiveX, and a lot of other X-filed things are you forced to own a PC.

- Your nine-year-old just showed you the computer game "Tomb Raider," and you're both dying to play it.

  You can add an Orange Micro card to your Mac (see page 27). It does a pretty good job with Windows game software, and if you have a reasonably fast Mac you'll be satisfied with the results.

You probably do need Windows if . . .

- The company you work for flat out refuses to let you use a Mac in the office.

  There isn't too much wiggle room here, unfortunately, unless the company really needs and values your unique abilities.

- Your company has an approved list of standardized software, and most of it doesn't exist on the Mac.

- You work in a specialized market with software customized for its needs.

  Before you give up, visit **www.bizproweb.com/pages/shareware/ mac.html.** *From general accounting to specific operations or human resources software, this web site carries specialized and affordable business software. The rest of the site is a pretty impressive resource of business shareware for Windows.*

- You are becoming seriously involved in 3-D animation.

  This is the one graphics area in which Windows unquestionably rules. If you need a render farm (multiple computers linked so they can map textures to moving wireframes) and capable software that doesn't die at inconvenient intervals, you'll need a Windows NT system.

- You work in Redmond, Washington.

Is your Macintosh ready?

There's a difference between "crossing platforms" and "working cross-platform." If you've decided to leave the community of Mac users and don't expect to have to use Mac files at all, you are "crossing platforms"; if you have kept your Mac but share files with people who use PCs, or you need to use a PC in addition to your Macintosh, you are "working cross-platform."

If you have to make a permanent switch from Mac to PC, you might only work cross-platform for the amount of time it takes you to set up the new computer and transfer files. In that case, a lot of the issues in this chapter won't apply to you, except for the PC-buying guidelines.

On the other hand, if you do anything short of this radical step, you'll have to prepare your Macintosh before you deal with the PC. If you ignore these steps, the actual Windows experience will be much more unpleasant than it has to be.

1. Upgrade your Mac to the most recent operating system.

operating system: The most basic software running on your computer; it manages hard drives and files, provides the Desktop you use, and basically runs your computer.

Operating system upgrades are a good thing in general, but when you're dealing across platforms, they're critical. Apple made some significant compatibility improvements in OS 8.1 which they have built upon in OS 8.5. Not only will you have fewer system crashes and more features, but your Mac will be an active partner in helping file and media transfers go smoothly. We'll go into more detail on this subject in Part Five, *Going Back and Forth.*

2. Upgrade every Mac software program that you'll open PC files with.

If there is any single piece of advice that every cross-platform gottabe should take, this is it. Whenever a software company blesses us with a major upgrade, new features and functions appear in it. Resaving files in earlier formats is the standard strategy for creating a readable file for an older software version, but it can result in files losing important elements. Mac users running different software versions already experience this— imagine the havoc when files must move through revisions on both platforms!

There are lots of good reasons to bite this bullet:
- Even if the older program version you've been using on the Mac serves you well, you won't be able to find its older match

on a new Windows machine. If you do manage to dig up something that has the same version number, there's no guarantee the files will read cross-platform. Most presentation software, for example, was so radically different on the two platforms that you'd think the same application was written by different companies. Much smoke and many mirrors were necessary to transfer files.

■ Whenever Windows users give you files created with their brand-new software, you'll have to ask them to resave the files in an earlier format so you can work with them. They might smile at first and be nice about it, of course, but eventually they'll resent the extra work. And lots of times you won't have the slightest idea who prepared the file or in what version it was created, so you won't even be able to ask.

■ With very few exceptions (most of them belonging to Microsoft, alas), the newer the software, the more likely it is that it will automatically create files that cross seamlessly between Macs and PCs. Do you really want to send along a file format and *protocol sheet* each time you hand your disk to a Windows user?

protocol sheet: A cover sheet that accompanies the file describing the software version used and other compatibility information.

If you're not sure whether a software upgrade must be made immediately, take your cue from the current version on the Windows side. Although most major developers release both versions simultaneously—in fact, more and more it's the Windows side that's upgraded first—there are still smaller companies with fewer resources whose graphics packages premiere on the Mac. If the only new version is for the Mac and you need to share files, you're better off hanging onto your older version until the same revision number of the software exists on both platforms.

3. Consider upgrading your Mac hardware.

If you plan to use a software solution to run Windows applications on your Mac, make sure you have a big enough hard disk, a fast enough processor, and plenty of memory. The two leading "emulation" packages (that make your Mac act like a PC temporarily) want at least a Power Mac with 24MB of RAM and around 200MB of available hard disk space. The software will run on those minimum specs, but only barely; double the minimum specifications, at least, if you don't want to regret your decision. Think of this investment as part of the initial cost of the Windows system.

How should you do Windows?

Once you've taken care of business on the Mac side of the office, turn your attention to Windows. You have three ascending choices of cost and complexity, each one explained below:

- Software emulation
- PC expansion card
- Stand-alone PC computer

Software emulation

The term "emulation" refers to another Macintosh software program that makes your Mac think it's a PC for a while so you don't have to invest in additional hardware. If you want the bare minimum of PC involvement, you may find software emulation to be your best bet. Files are shared between the Mac and PC with drag-and-drop ease. If you suffer from hardware phobia, this is the only solution that doesn't require you to deal with tools and connections at all.

Software emulation will work for you if:

- You only need to run Windows briefly because of a consulting contract or other short-term project. You can even dump it off your drive afterwards without feeling the hole in your pocketbook.

- You have more time than money. The software itself is very cheap, and it uses all the Mac's existing hardware so there are no hidden costs.

- You need to run a Windows program while you're on the road and don't want to give up your PowerBook. Carrying two portable computers is silly.

- You occasionally create web pages and want to check out how they'll look in a Windows browser.

- You're being forced into working in Windows because the Mac doesn't support one specific software package. Emulation is the cheapest and least intrusive solution for that one nasty but necessary application.

- You're a parent who's tired of hearing your child whine that their friends can play games that they can't.

Unfortunately, if you need to be consistently productive in Windows, software emulation can get old very quickly, and you with it. Using emulation, any applications from Microsoft and most other office packages will perform well, but don't expect satisfaction using Photoshop filters on 20MB files. This is particularly true if your Mac isn't very fast, since the emulation software draws its speed directly from the Mac's processor. Any application that's a memory hog in Windows—from CAD software to large-scale database programs—will act like it's on Valium on any Mac slower than a *G3*.

You'll also want to skip the emulation solution if you'll need to use a scanner, film recorder, graphics tablet, or Midi on the PC side. None of your chained SCSI devices or your PCI cards will be recognized while in simulation mode, either.

PC expansion card

At the time of this writing, there's only one company selling PC expansion *cards:* Orange Micro. Apple has discontinued its PC Compatibility Card, and there are no longer other hardware competitors.

Orange offers two different types of solutions. They have a very inexpensive card which is a combination of hardware components and software emulation. Its Intel processor is upgradable and independent of the Mac, so it works quickly and independently, but it uses all the Mac's hardware the way the software emulators do. You can add memory chips to the card directly, without conflicting with your Mac's own memory function. This expansion card is a much better solution for older Power Macs than the software-only emulators. The card makes your Mac act like a fast Pentium MMX, so most Windows applications run without difficulty. You can use it on a network, and you can print.

Orange Micro also makes other cards that are PC *motherboards* masquerading as PCI expansion cards. Besides their own processor and memory, these cards have standard PC input and output ports (places to plug things in) and their own sets of cables. This separation means you can have memory-intensive actions, including printing or backing up, taking place on the Mac and the Orange Micro PC card (called OrangePC) at the same time without compromising either side.

G3: The most recent (and fastest) generation of Power Macintosh computers.

SCSI device: A SCSI (small computer system interface, pronounced "scuzzy") device is hardware designed to attach to a computer through a special kind of connection.

PCI cards: An alternative method to SCSI for attaching peripherals. See page 33.

cards: plastic cards, or boards you insert into your PC to make it do more things.

Pentium MMX: One class of Intel processors (the *processor* is the main chip that runs the computer; it's also called the CPU, the central processing unit). MMX is faster than a Pentium but not as fast as a Pentium II.

motherboard: The main card, or board, inside the computer box that holds the CPU (see above definition).

An expansion card is a good solution for you if:

- Any of the emulation reasons apply, but you need better performance and are short on patience.

- You need to use the Windows side of the computer as much as the Mac side.

- You want or need to connect PC *serial* or *parallel* devices to your computer.

- The computer on your desk is shared with other people, some of whom use Windows, some of whom do not.

serial or parallel:
Different ways to send information to and from devices. See Chapter 3.

So what could possibly be the downside for going with the full-fledged card? Price is one factor. The spiffiest *OMPCs* are quite competitive with mid-range Pentium systems, but they cost almost as much, too. You might have a tough time explaining why your company should shell out $1500 for an internal Macintosh board when they can put a comparable Windows system with keyboard, mouse, and monitor on your desk for about the same price. The only good argument you have, besides wanting to hold onto your Mac as your primary computer, is the desktop real estate one.

OMPC: Orange Micro PC Cards, as described on the previous page.

Setting price aside, PC cards just won't do the job if you are a power user on the Mac (desktop video, 3-D graphics, multimedia development) who also needs to be a power user on the PC. Cards aren't meant to be high-end graphics solutions.

Stand-alone PC computer

You might decide you need to invest in an entire Windows system. Or your CIO came to that conclusion for you. You've got to have a separate Windows computer if:

- All of the expansion card reasons apply, but you want the flexibility of two separate systems.

- Your applications are very memory-intensive, and you'll be using them at least as often on the PC as on the Mac.

- You're a developer, and you have to be certain that anything you create will work equally well on both Macs and PCs.

- Your work comes to you in PC format and goes out from you that way as well, and it's actually taking you more time trying to juggle the cross-platform material.

- Your home office is cold. A second computer will help raise the room temperature. Plus it will depreciate over three years.

Unless the PC will be your office machine while you continue to use your Mac at home, the decision to purchase a new piece of hardware might mean other expenses. If the PC will substitute for your Mac, you will have to buy almost all new peripherals (things like monitor, Zip drive, printer, modem, scanner, etc.) as well; see the following several pages.

A hybrid solution

Before you buy a new PC with all the trimmings, think about how you can leverage what you already own. It's possible to share parts of your existing Mac with the PC, allowing you to keep both computers alive and at your desk.

Sharing a monitor

If you own a *multisync* monitor, it's possible to share it between the Mac and the PC, saving valuable desk space. To do this, you'll need:

- **A Mac video adapter:** They come with some multisync monitors, but if you don't have one already, you can find one for under $10.

- **A monitor data switch box**: These run in the vicinity of $20–$40. You connect both computer cables to the switch box, and the box has a dial that switches the image on the screen between the two computers.

- **An extra monitor cable:** You can get these for under $20 as well, but you should consider getting one of the more expensive ones instead. To prevent *ghosting*, the best cables have each wire in the cable wrapped separately to shield the signal.

- **A monitor cable gender changer:** These are very inexpensive, little connectors. At least one of the plugs and cables between the monitor and the computers won't match up correctly, so you'll need this "gender changer" to adapt one of the plugs.

- **Two *surge protectors* (power strips)** so you can keep the Mac and PC power cables separate.

See the following page for an illustration of how to connect the two different computers to the same monitor.

This is an example of a surge protector. There are various kinds—make sure you get one that will help protect computers and not just televisions.

multisync monitor: A monitor that can be used with many types of computer video inputs because it's capable of changing video frequencies.

ghosting: An extra, shadowy image on the screen.

surge protector: A power strip with special features to protect your computer and other devices from surges in electrical power.

Connecting the monitor

Connect the monitor's own cable to the port labeled **I/O** on the back of the data switch box, then connect the other two cables from the switch box to the computers (see the illustration below). You'll need the video adapter on the Mac side because the monitor cable won't plug into the Mac's monitor port without it. Power up the two systems, and switch between them as you work using the A and B switches on the switch box. There shouldn't be more than a one- or two-second delay between the switch and the monitor redraw.

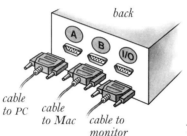

The switchbox is small—you can put it anyplace on your desk, or even on top of the computer. This box is switched to the B line, which is currently feeding the Mac's video signal to the monitor, based on the cabling shown in the illustration of the back side.

Sharing a keyboard and mouse

It's possible to share a keyboard and mouse between the two systems as well, but it's a lot more complicated and a few hundred dollars more expensive because you'll need an adapter that translates between the different Mac and PC ports, as well as a data switcher. So to make it easier (and cheaper) on yourself, get a keyboard and mouse for each system, even though you share the monitor. The PC needs that two-button mouse, anyway.

Sharing peripherals

You can transfer or share some *peripherals*. Most new SCSI devices (see Chapter 3 for details on SCSI), such as scanners and external hard disks, will work on both Macs and PCs as long as you have separate sets of cables, the right PC *driver*, and a SCSI interface card on the PC that is compatible with the hardware. Some peripheral devices have both PC parallel ports as well as SCSI connectors which allow you to connect both the PC and the Mac at the same time.

Choosing your Windows hardware

If there's no getting around it and you have to invest in a full PC system, you should at least make sure the system you end up with will actually do what you need, be as easy as possible to set up, and be loaded with the version of Windows that's right for you. To do that:

Consider your software

The most important requirement of your computer is that it be able to run your necessary and favorite applications. If this is your own computer, research the minimum space and memory requirements for your software. Follow the same rule when buying a PC as you would for a Mac: use the minimum requirements to determine what isn't good enough, then make sure you have at least twice the minimum in hard disk space and in memory. If you've been using the Mac version of an application, you know how much memory and speed you need to work successfully—you definitely won't need less on a PC.

Plan for expansion

Any computer is probably out of date two weeks after you buy it (which doesn't meant it won't work for you for several years). If you can, buy bigger than what you need immediately, and look for a computer with lots of expandability (one that you can add more memory to, a bigger hard disk, perhaps even a faster processor). PCs need more *expansion slots* than Macs do to accomplish the same things.

expansion slots: The long, skinny openings in the motherboard where you can plug in additional cards or memory chips.

Unless you're starting from ground zero and plan to use USB (Universal Serial Bus, the new iMac standard that Microsoft also strongly supports), you've probably got SCSI scanners, SCSI external drives, SCSI CD recorders, and the like (see Chapter 3 for details about working with SCSI devices). Most Windows PCs don't come with SCSI connectors, so you'll want to make sure to have them installed on your new system. You don't want to get stuck doing this yourself—SCSI is great for Mac users, but really nasty to retrofit into a PC.

USB: A new method of connecting peripherals to the computer, similar to SCSI or PCI.

If your new PC will be a laptop, expansion will be even more of an issue. Many laptops don't come with a SCSI interface option, so you're stuck with standard PC connections. If you use a port for one thing, you'll have to swap externals to use something else, and you have to shut down the computer to make the swap. For example, the port a printer uses is the same port you need for an external hard drive, so you can either print *or* use the extra hard disk, but not both at the same time.

Know what you really use and make sure it's there

Make a checklist of everything you already use on your Mac and will still need. Macs come with modem ports and their own basic sound. Newer models also offer sound- and video-in and on-board *Ethernet*. If any of these things sound like something you want or need on your new PC, specify them in your initial purchase.

Ethernet: A universal method of connecting computers and peripherals to each other so they can send information back and forth.

Think about hard drives

You'll probably be thinking about how big the hard drive is and maybe how fast it is. But on PCs you also have to think about **drive types:** Until recently, Mac drives have all been SCSI. On PCs (and the PowerMac G3), you have a choice between SCSI and IDE. The IDE drives of all types—hard disks, CD-ROMs, etc.—are cheaper, which means they're standard on less-expensive PC packages.

There are several good reasons to hold out for SCSI drives. One is that they're faster. Also, SCSI drives are more familiar. As a Mac user, you've probably had lots of experience troubleshooting SCSI devices and won't want to learn a whole new set of troubleshooting procedures on a PC.

There are two significant drawbacks to using SCSI hard drives on a PC. One is cost: any SCSI hard drive will be significantly more expensive than an IDE. You can get an 8GB IDE drive for what you'd pay for a 4GB SCSI drive. Availability is another factor: no pre-built computers come with SCSI drives inside, so if you shop in discount stores for your computer you're almost certainly buying an IDE drive.

If you can, buy only Plug-and-Play (PnP) adapters

Plug-and-Play is the technology that supposedly allows Windows to recognize new hardware (*adapters*, printers, scanners, external hard disks) without the user having to program the computer. Macs have always been plug-and-play—you plug it in and it works. But this is a new concept for PCs.

adapters: another name for cards or boards, those plastic pieces that get inserted into the computer to make it do more things.

Following the guideline of "Only buy Plug-and-Play adapters" can be trickier than you'd think. The system you've decided to purchase may just not have enough PnP slots for everything you want to use. But even if it does, there's a lot of slightly sleazy advertising on the Windows shelves. The only cards which are really PnP are PCI cards with a Windows 95/98 logo on them. Cards whose software has been altered to "somewhat" conform to Windows usually say things like, "Windows *ready*" on the box. As far as we can tell, this means they'll have the correct software interface, but not that they'll work for you right out of the box.

PCI card: PCI stands for Peripheral Component Interconnect, the latest expansion card (adapter card) technology.

Even if you're planning on using Windows NT (where PnP is just a dream) buying PCI is still a good idea. When the next version of NT appears, future installations and additions will be easier. And remember that PCI devices are usually "platform independent"; that is, many of them, with minor changes, may work on your Mac as well as your PC. For more information on Plug-and-Play, see Chapter 2.

Check the video specifications

Mac users expect a certain base level of color and resolution on even a low-level monitor. If you want a full-color desktop at 800 x 600 resolution (the traditional Mac standard), you'll want a 4MB *video card* installed in your PC. If you need the same quality at a resolution of 1024 x 768 or above, look for a system that offers 8MB graphic cards (most computer systems that ship with 17-inch monitors will feature either 4MB or 8MB graphic cards). If you work with 3-D graphics, want super-high quality, or need a large monitor (19-inch or above), look for a 16MB card (you may have to order a customized system to get a 16MB video card).

video card: Very few PCs have the ability to see and display color images on a monitor. To give PCs this ability, you need to plug a special video card into a slot inside the computer box. The port (plug) for the card sticks out the back end of the computer, and you plug the monitor cable into that port. The MB (as in 4MB) refers to how much special memory is on the card just for the video display.

If you are buying a laptop computer, your choices will most likely be between a 2MB or 4MB graphics option. Choose 4MB if you need to hook your laptop up to a high-quality projector for multimedia presentations.

To tell if the computer you're considering has enough video memory, look at the "graphic" specifications listed on the box, in the ad, or on the web site. An 8MB video card will be described as something like "8MB PCI graphics accelerator," or "AGP graphics with 8MB SGRAM." All PCs sold as complete systems will come with a graphics card.

Buy a complete package

If at all possible, make your first Windows computer a custom purchase. Get everything already physically installed and configured. Ideally, all you should do is unpack, plug in your cables, and turn on the machine. If you continue working with Windows, eventually you may have to handle some installations yourself. By that time, there will be more add-on hardware that installs simply, and you will be more knowledgeable and confident enough to do it yourself.

What is Windows (really)?

Someone once said, "Know your enemy." We ask, "How well?" This chapter is a massively abbreviated orientation to the technical aspects of Windows and how they'll affect you. No enthusiastic pages of Windows flattery here—just the basic facts to help you understand what you can expect.

The once and future Windows

Today's Windows versions—Windows NT and Window 95/98—look and feel nothing like the earlier ones. For a Mac user who has to deal with them, this is a very good thing.

graphical user interface:
A way of working with a computer that uses icons and menus and other visual features to make the computer do what you want, instead of having to write boring ol' programming codes.

Early versions of Windows were just grafted on top of DOS (see below), and ran both inefficiently and undependably. They also had pretty laughable attempts at *graphical user interfaces* (called GUIs; GUI is pronounced "gooey"). That is not true of NT and 95/98. Like it or not, Windows has caught up, in part by practicing "creative adaptation" of many of the Mac's features. We aren't saying that Windows is just the Mac OS on a different platform; if that were the case, you wouldn't need this book. But it is possible for someone with a solid background on the Mac to apply some of that knowledge to NT and Windows 95/98.

What is DOS, and is it still in Windows?

Some say MS-DOS stands for Microsoft Seeks Domination of Society.

The acronym DOS, or MS-DOS, stands for Microsoft Disk Operating System. This DOS was created to handle file management, input, and output. It was certainly never designed to support a graphical user interface (GUI) like the Mac's. Because of DOS's inherent limitations, it wasn't until 1990 that computer advances in speed allowed Microsoft to provide a working GUI at all.

It wouldn't be accurate to say Windows still runs on DOS, but it feels that way sometimes. Let's just say that Cyndi, who started out in DOS and ran happily into the Mac's open arms, sees many unpleasantly familiar DOS things in the underlying Windows structures.

backward-compatible:
New, updated software that can still work with older versions of itself.

Microsoft explains they couldn't get rid of the old DOS code in Windows because it had to be *backward-compatible* for their loyal users. But Windows NT was written without the constraint of backward compatibility, and it supports DOS conventions like disk letters and batch files.

What does all this mean for you? If you don't have to upgrade or maintain the computer, maybe nothing, except having to learn Windows' file management and disk system (and memorizing the phone number for tech support). If this is your very own computer, it means the time may come when you'll have to learn something about text-line editing and data, batch, and device drivers. (You can improve your chances of never having to do these things if you follow our purchasing suggestions in Chapter 1, avoid old hardware, and pay qualified people to install new hard drives and adapters for you.)

Some Windows basics

A lot of Windows features don't owe anything to a senile OS — or to the Mac, either. You'll want to know about these because they will affect you, some more obviously and directly than others. Most of these features are found in both NT and Windows 95/98. We've indicated anything that's only found in one Windows version.

What is 16-bit vs. 32-bit?

When programmers write software, they write it specific to the operating system it will be used on. During the DOS/Windows 3.x period, programmers wrote what are called "16-bit applications." For Windows 98 and NT, they write "32-bit applications." The number of bits refers to how much data can be transferred in one chunk, called the "data transfer rate." Obviously, a program that can work with 32-bit chunks will be able to do more and do it faster than a program with a 16-bit limitation.

This data transfer rate is so basic to how a program runs that 16- and 32-bit programs are totally incompatible. Although Windows 95/98 is designed to run 32-bit applications, not 16-bit ones, it creates a little DOS island for those older applications so you can safely run them.

Windows NT doesn't bother to accommodate 16-bit. If you load a 16-bit program on an NT system, NT will lock it into what's called a "protected memory space," which basically means that it won't let the whole system go down if the 16-bit application crashes, which it probably will. A very few well-designed 16-bit applications can survive in NT, but there's no way to determine if the one you need to use will work without installing and then trying to run it.

These incompatibilities can be very frustrating. Neither NT nor 95/98 runs very well on older PCs, and older programs don't run very well on newer operating systems. If you will be inheriting a system or software from someone else, you'll have a much tougher time making everything work and keep working than you would with an older Mac. If you plan to use the PC much, you should probably look at investing in a new one — don't buy an old machine from a newspaper want ad, even if it's really cheap. You get what you pay for.

Multitasking

We like to think of the Mac as a multitasking computer, which means that it will allow you to keep several programs running at the same time. However, the Mac is only a partially multitasking machine. Some functions, particularly those that use basic parts of the system, take over the computer until they're done. We see this whenever we format a disk or apply a Photoshop filter to a large file.

Windows really does multitask. This means you can have a program rendering a file or recalculating a spreadsheet in the background at the same time that you, in the foreground, are downloading files from the Internet. NT even allows you to preset the priority of foreground and background applications so you can make sure the rendering doesn't suffer while you download software.

Properties

One of the underlying (and non-Macintosh) concepts in the design of today's Windows GUI (graphical user interface) is the idea that all objects—icons, hardware, programs, even the desktop—have *properties*. Properties modify actions and alter descriptions of objects. An icon, for example, could have the properties of color, size, and image, as well as represent some specific kind of file.

Whenever there are properties, or attributes, there are ways to change those attributes. Just like the Mac, Windows lets you change the color and size of an icon, or substitute one icon picture for another one.

On the Mac, you change attributes, or properties, through control panels, in the Desktop preferences, and from menus. In Windows, you change the attributes of an object through menus on the Desktop and through dialog boxes and "property sheets" that refer to the selected object. Throughout the rest of this book we'll be showing you how to change the attributes of various elements as we discuss each of them.

Multisystem booting

You can run Windows directly on your Macintosh in two ways, as discussed in Chapter 1: with software emulation or with a second processor. On a PC, you can run almost any combination of operating systems on the same computer. All that's necessary is to own installation disks for both systems and have enough disk space to be able to run a separate *partition* for each operating system. In most cases, if the software you use is able to run on both versions of the OS, it will be shared between the two systems.

Setting up this kind of thing used to be incredibly tricky, but it's become easier lately because there are software solutions for keeping the operating systems safe from each other and for making it easy to switch between them. In fact, there are many people who "dual-boot," which means they set up their computer to run either Windows NT or 95/98, depending on what they plan to do. NT even has a configuration window that lets you determine which is the default system and gives you the opportunity to change your mind before it starts up.

If you read Chapter 1 and still can't decide which operating system to use, or you try one OS and decide you should have chosen the other, dual-booting is probably a good solution for you.

booting: **Starting the computer.**

partition: **You can separate one hard disk into several parts called** *partitions.* **Each partition acts like a separate, independent hard disk.**

Plug-and-Play (Windows 95 and 98 only)

Before Windows 95, users had to be very technically knowledgeable to install new computer hardware. Microsoft included **Plug-and-Play (PnP)** technology in Windows 95 to make it easier for average users to make changes to their computers. PnP allows Windows 95/98 to recognize hardware (adapter cards, printers, external hard drives, scanners) without any special programming by you. Macintosh users aren't as impressed by PnP technology as Windows users are because Macs have always been plug-and-play. Windows NT doesn't offer Plug-and-Play technology yet.

Microsoft tells you that installing hardware on your Windows system will be just as simple as it is on your Mac. And sometimes it really is. Unfortunately, Plug-and-Play only functions properly (meaning you really can plug it in and almost instantly play with it) if every piece of hardware in your computer was designed for Windows 95/98.

Why is this so? Before Windows 95, there weren't any hardware standards for PCs, so manufacturers pretty much did as they pleased. And since there were a lot of peripherals built before Windows 95 was released, there's still a lot of non–Plug-and-Play "legacy" hardware (hardware that is left over, or left behind), such as pre-1996 scanners, printers, and network cards. They still work, and people don't want to make a new investment.

Unfortunately, legacy hardware will haunt you even if you buy new computer parts tomorrow. Lots of shrink-wrapped hardware on the PC shelf is not designed to take advantage of Windows' Plug-and-Play.

It's pretty obvious to a Mac user that making hardware fit the operating system is the only sensible thing to do. Alas, what's obvious to us is not so obvious to many Windows users, probably because they've never seen how easy things can be on a Mac when consistent standards are followed.

To PnP, use PCI cards

PCI is the only type of adapter card that's guaranteed to be Plug-and-Play. (PCI is the same type of card that new Macs use instead of the previous technology called NuBus.)

Cards fit into special little slots inside of the computer. These slots are on the *motherboard*. PCI adapters can only fit into special PCI slots, so computer manufacturers should install at least four PCI slots—for video, audio, network, and SCSI—on their motherboards to support Plug-and-Play properly. Open up the average PC, however, and you'll usually see no more than three PCI slots. The other slots you might see are for ISA boards, the older adapter card format. (You can tell the ISA slots because they're black and have two segments, one longer than the other.)

But the persistence of ISA slots is not just nostalgia for all that ancient technology. Peripherals designed to use PCI slots to connect to your computer are more expensive than their ISA alternatives. If you've just spent $1000 for an entire computer, you might have a hard time justifying to your corporate accountant another $200 for a Plug-and-Play modem card when you can buy an ISA one for $80.

What's in *your* computer?

Some cards in your computer are more likely to be Plug-and-Play than others. Your video card will be PCI. An Ethernet card should also be Windows 95/98-ready, which means PCI. Since PCI is a premium feature, most manufacturers will proudly state on the package or ad that their sound or modem cards are PCI technology.

A low-end audio card or an internal modem, however, is probably ISA. If you buy a discount computer, it will probably have ISA devices to keep the manufacturer's costs down. Unless PCI is specifically mentioned, you should assume that these devices are ISA.

The existence of an ISA device or two doesn't mean you shouldn't buy a discount model. A properly installed ISA device doesn't usually cause problems until you try to install another ISA device. What's really important is whether the computer has PCI expansion slots that you can use for new hardware in the future.

If there's nothing on the package about expansion slots, ask the salesperson how many unused slots the computer has and how many of those are PCI. The price of the computer increases as the proportion of PCI slots to ISA slots goes up. You'll spend a little more for future ease of use.

PCI: **Peripheral Component Interconnect, the latest expansion card (adapter card) technology.**

motherboard: **the board, or card, in the computer that holds the main memory and the CPU (central processing unit, the chip that runs the computer).**

ISA: **Industry Standard Architecture**

adapter, card, board: **often used interchangeably to refer to the same item.**

Windows versions, pros and cons

Since Microsoft is the source for all forms of Windows, the pros and cons of the various versions of Windows provide a lot less *flame bait* than the pros and cons of Mac vs. Windows. For someone with no prior investment in DOS or older Windows applications, choosing the right Windows operating system can be reduced to a feature checklist.

flame bait: A reason for getting into a raging argument.

Windows NT

server: A large computer that stores the bulk of a company's information and resources and "serves" it up to other computers, through the network, as they need it.

Windows NT was originally conceived of as a *server* platform, so it's loaded with security features to protect the system and its data. But servers also need to be very dependable—no one will be happy with a server that crashes every day. So Windows NT is also delightfully stable. Any system will crash when pushed to its limits or loaded with the wrong bunch of software, but a clean NT system, properly loaded and maintained, is as solid as a rock. That makes it useful not only for networking, but for high-end graphics applications, particularly 3-D animation or modeling programs. Windows NT is not cheap; a workstation version costs about $200, and a server version $500.

Windows 95/98

Windows 95/98 was designed for "the average PC user," a person Microsoft identifies as one who cares more about being able to run older programs and hardware than whether the system occasionally crashes. That's why Windows 95/98 is completely backward-compatible with MS-DOS and Windows 3.1 applications. To do this, Windows 95/98 must perform an intricate switching dance, so sometimes things do go wrong, rather spectacularly. Because Windows 95/98 is not a corporate network client like NT, there aren't many security failsafes in 95/98 to prevent a rogue application from hogging resources, which can cause computer crashes or prevent memory-intensive applications from working effectively. On the other hand, Windows 95/98 is more "Mac-like" in handling hardware installations and is easier to troubleshoot and bring back from the dead than is Windows NT.

Most PCs you buy off the shelf in a warehouse store or office supply store today are pre-loaded with Windows 98 (but you may run across some that are still loaded with Windows 95).

Choose Windows 95/98 if:

- **You want or need the widest range of software.**
  Although lots of Windows 95 software will actually run on NT, not all of it will. Lots of shareware and utility programs won't. You'll also have problems with older software versions. For example, if you have a copy of QuarkXPress 3.3x that you want to use with Windows NT, you'll have to give up using PostScript fonts because Quark 3.3x will only work successfully with TrueType fonts on an NT system.

- **You don't have the money for a high-end graphics station, but you want to run two monitors.**
  Windows 98 is the first Windows system that will recognize two separate monitors. (You can get this function with NT by purchasing a customized, publishing-savvy computer like Intergraph's ExtremeZ, but you're looking at a hefty price tag to do it.) And on NT you won't be able to mix different types of cards or run two monitors at different resolutions.

- **You'll have to use existing PC peripheral hardware.**
  All fairly recent PC hardware will work on Windows 95/98, but not all of it will work on NT. Unless the documentation specifically states that a peripheral is NT-compatible, you should err on the side of caution and load 95/98 instead.

- **Gaming is important to you.**
  Games push the edge of computer programming technology, and often speak directly to the CPU and motherboard to deliver faster, more dazzling effects. As part of its backward-compatible design, Windows 95/98 doesn't stop individual software from taking control of the hardware in pursuit of speed, so it's a very game-friendly operating system. Windows NT is not. In the name of stability, Windows NT tries to prevent software from bypassing its control—it would rather die than let an application past its security—so most Windows games crash on Windows NT.

  Because software must be writen very differently to avoid NT death, only a small percentage of the thousands of computer games written for Windows 95/98 have been released with NT versions. If you want the latest and greatest releases as well as the old favorites, stick with Windows 95/98.

Choose Windows NT if:

- **You work in high-end graphics.**

  Windows NT is faster and more inherently stable than Windows 95/98, since it doesn't have to maintain compatibility with DOS software from 1986. If you have to live and work with the system every day, you'll see fewer crashes. It's a lot trickier to set up peripherals in NT than in 95/98, but you only have to do that once in a while. If you are a power user who needs to manipulate large and complex files, NT is the only viable Windows choice.

- **You want to network with Macs.**

  NT can recognize and play nicely with Macs in ways that Windows 95/98 can't because it was designed as a multi-platform networking solution. In fact, NT servers are beginning to show up in places where all the networked computers are Mac because they're so good at handling network traffic and so very fast and stable.

- **You need background processing.**

  NT has real multitasking: the ability to run several different programs at the same time without any one of them preventing the others from using the system resources.

Setting Up Your PC

If you're sitting in front of a Mac using Windows emulation, you can skip this chapter with a sigh of relief. If you are using a Mac with a PC card installed, you'll find some of the explanations here useful. But if you're sitting in a room with a bunch of computer boxes stamped "Intel Inside," this chapter is for you. You need to know what makes a PC physically different from a Mac, and what that means when you are putting it together. We'll build on your Mac knowledge when possible and explain the differences when it's not.

Look at the back of the computer

Any reputable manufacturer will provide instructions and some basic diagrams. The problem is, they'll assume that you know what you're looking at. If the instruction booklet says, "Attach mouse to mouse port or use adapter to connect to serial port," how do you know which port is which?

Let's begin by comparing the back end of a PC with that of a Mac. The first thing you'll notice is that the connectors (the spots where you plug things in, also known as "ports") all look very different. Next you'll notice that most of the PC connectors are actually on "cards" in the *expansion slots* (which means they are poking out through the back of the computer, through those rectangular openings), not on the computer box itself. PCs have fewer standard options and depend on the "à la carte" concept: If the computer doesn't have a modem port, you buy a modem card, open up the computer box, install the card, and then the port (which is on the card) sticks out the back of the box. If you want to attach a scanner or CD recorder, you have to buy a SCSI card, open up the computer box, and install the card so you can connect the device. If you want to connect to a network, you buy an Ethernet card, open up the computer box, and install it so you can connect the Ethernet cables.

expansion slots: The narrow openings aligned in rows on the back of the computer. Inside, a plastic card has been added to expand the capabilities of the computer.

Apple put all the connectors you'd need directly into your Mac so you don't have to do much to customize it. That's one of the reasons everything on a Mac works together so seamlessly. That's also why most Mac users can survive with only three expansion slots in a Mac (and you may never even need those) while a PC user might need double that amount, depending on what kind of work needs to be done: If you add a modem card, a sound card, and a SCSI card, a three-slot PC is full. If you then need an Ethernet card or a second graphics card for another monitor, you'll have no place to put it.

The other nice thing about Mac ports (connectors) is they're easy to figure out, even if the layout varies from model to model. And they're all labeled right on the case. This is not so with a PC: some manufacturers label their ports, some don't. If some do, the labeling is not consistent between brands.

peripherals: Any piece of hardware that is outside of the computer, but connected to it (actually, some peripherals are on cards). Your printer is a peripheral.

PC ports can be positioned anywhere, depending on how the manufacturer has designed the machine. And several different types of *peripherals* use the same kind of connectors.

Keyboard and mouse connectors

The easiest connectors to recognize are those for the keyboard and mouse because they're two round "PS/2 ports" (shown below) which look like Mac ADB ports.

PS/2 ports: **Round connectors, ⅜-inch across with 6 thick pins (only on PCs).**

ADB port: **Apple Desktop Bus port, a special connector for input devices (only on Macs).**

PCs used to have only one round port for the keyboard cable because for a long time mice weren't considered standard equipment on PCs, the way they always were on Macs. There are still older PC mice around that can't use the PS/2 port and instead use one of the other peripheral ports. Eventually, computer manufacturers "borrowed" the Mac idea of treating the keyboard and mouse as special kinds of input and created the ports accordingly.

Note: On a Mac, it doesn't matter which ADB port gets the mouse and which the keyboard. **On a PC, these two ports are not interchangeable even though they look exactly the same!** The mouse must plug into the mouse port, and the keyboard into the keyboard port. If you switch them, nothing will explode, but neither one will work. There is usually a label of some sort to indicate which port is which.

Serial, parallel, SCSI, and USB

There are four kinds of peripherals: those that use **serial ports,** those that use **parallel ports,** those that use **SCSI ports,** and those that use **USB ports** (see page 51).

Serial devices are generally slow because they only handle one bit of information at a time. Parallel devices are much faster because they can send and receive several bits of information "in parallel," which means at the same instant. Parallel and serial devices are completely different in design from each other so you can't use one on the other's connector port, nor can you turn a serial device into a parallel one.

The Mac and PC versions of these connectors go by such different names that you'd never guess they're related. The Mac has serial ports, but they're named for what they do—printer and modem. Their plugs are different so, for example, you can't use a PC serial modem on a Mac without buying a Mac-compatible cable (and of course you'd need the right software, too).

The Mac uses a special kind of parallel connector called SCSI, which stands for Small Computer System Interface and is pronounced "scuzzy." It's much faster than the PC parallel connector and is completely incompatible with PC parallel devices. For years no one made SCSI devices for the PC so it was impossible to share peripherals between the two platforms. Things have changed; now most manufacturers make SCSI peripherals that can be used on either platform if you have the right kind of SCSI cable and software.

Serial ports

PC serial ports are used by printers and modems, but can also be used by scanners, *tablets*, and other peripherals. Once they're in use, they're dedicated to whatever you've plugged into them. You can't *daisy chain* serial devices.

Every PC has two to four ports on the back of the computer, clustered together. The serial ports (also known as RS-232 ports) should look like this:

Serial port.

Sometimes they're labeled COM1 and COM2 (COM = communications). Other times they're labeled with the icon shown below, with the number 1 or 2 next to them. Occasionally the serial ports aren't labeled at all, which is extremely inconsiderate of the manufacturer.

Serial port icon, although many manufacturers don't label the serial port at all.

Here's something to notice about hardware names on the PC: For every sensible, easy-to-remember name on a Windows device (like "serial port"), there's bound to be a more complicated alternate name to make identifying the object difficult when talking to PC tech support people, as in, "Are you sure you used an RS-232 with a DB9 connector?" That probably means, in English, "Was it the plug for your modem and did it have 9 little pins on the end?"

tablet: A flat electronic "board" you draw on with an electronic pen, called a stylus. You can use a tablet and stylus instead of a mouse.

daisy chain: A method of connecting many devices to a computer through one computer port. The first device connects to the computer, the second device connects to the first, the third device connects to the second, and so on.

Parallel ports

There are no parallel ports on Macs because Macs dedicate a serial port to the printer and provide a SCSI (pronounced "scuzzy") connector for most other input and output things (see the following page for SCSI information.) Even the newest Mac models don't have parallel ports, but substitute USB ports for SCSI ones (see USB, opposite page).

The long, skinny connector on the back of the PC is the parallel port. It is also called a "Centronics-compatible" port. A parallel port has 25 slender sockets (holes) divided into two rows like this:

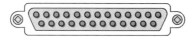 *Parallel port.*

This port is primarily used for printers (yes, the PC has two completely different types of ports for printing), but can also be used for certain other output devices. The parallel port might be identified by a printer icon, or with the letters LPT (Line PrinTer).

Parallel ports are not very fast, compared to SCSI ports. In fact, they're very slow and inefficient, but because they come standard on a PC and always have, there are a lot of parallel devices around. There are even devices you can run on a parallel port that you really shouldn't, like Zip drives, which really belong on a fast SCSI port (see next page about SCSI).

Keeping serial and parallel straight

What if the back of your computer only has long, two-row parallel ports and none of the smaller serial ports? We've described the most sensible layout of PC computer ports that you might find, but it's possible to run into a computer *whose parallel and serial connections are shaped the same.* We'd like to think the different types of ports are labeled, but if they're not, you can usually tell them apart because parallel ports have sockets and serial ports have pins. If you still can't tell, check the manual that came with your computer.

Warning: You can plug a *parallel device* into a *serial port* without anything terrible happening—the device just won't work. **Unfortunately,** if you plug a *serial device* into a *parallel port*, you can fry the port. This is a bad thing to do. If you have to figure things out by experimentation, use a parallel printer as a test device.

USB ports

Newer computers may have one or two USB (Universal Serial Bus) ports. Both Microsoft and Apple are very enthusiastic about USB ports and see them as the future of connectivity. Since the USB port is the only connector on the Apple iMac, there has been an increase in the number of these peripherals available.

Microsoft would like to see the USB port replace both serial and parallel ports on the PC because it is faster than either of them and inexpensive to produce (although it's not as fast as the newer versions of SCSI). USB is also very flexible and easy to use.

You can't daisy chain individual USB devices, like you can SCSI, but you can buy a "hub" and connect numerous USB devices into the hub. If you need to attach even more devices, you can daisy chain the hubs; that is, you can connect another hub to one of the ports in the hub, then connect another hub into that one, and theoretically connect 127 USB devices to one computer. And you'll never need to install an adapter card.

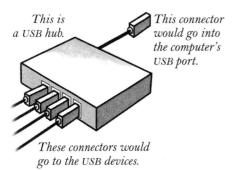

This is a USB hub.

This connector would go into the computer's USB port.

These connectors would go to the USB devices.

This is what USB ports look like. This illustration shows two separate USB ports.

SCSI connections, if you have them!

This is the standard symbol that labels a SCSI port.

If you want to connect SCSI devices to your PC, you need a SCSI adapter card. If your computer has a SCSI adapter installed, you'll find its port sticking out of an expansion slot on the back of the computer. SCSI ports now come in several sizes and shapes, depending on what type of SCSI they are (SCSI-2, Fast SCSI, SCSI Wide). No matter what type you have, it should display the universal SCSI icon for easy identification, shown to the left.

Despite the fact that output devices perform much more quickly and efficiently if they're SCSI, that cheap-but-ever-present parallel port is usually the standard on a PC. If you didn't specifically order a SCSI adapter card when you ordered your PC, there's almost no chance that it's in your computer as a bonus.

But what if your PC has an internal **SCSI hard drive?** When Mac users look at the specifications for a PC computer package, we usually think in Mac hardware terms so we logically assume that having a SCSI drive built into the PC means we can probably also plug in other SCSI devices. Wrong. A SCSI hard drive doesn't have anything to do with SCSI connectors.

If you do have a **SCSI adapter card** installed with a port sticking out of the expansion slot in the back, you'll connect things to it in the same way you would on a Mac. If you need to connect more than one SCSI device, you can daisy chain them (plug each device into the back of the other). Just like on a Mac, the last device in the SCSI chain must be *terminated*.

terminate: To close an electrical circuit. Most new SCSI devices today come with "active termination," which means they figure out if they're the last device in the chain and terminate themselves if they are.

Also just like on a Mac, all SCSI devices have what's called a "SCSI ID" or a "SCSI address," which is a number assigned to the device. Each device must have a different number or nothing will work. Internal SCSI devices have preset IDs, but you can change the ID of any new device you get—there is always a tiny little control where you can change the ID number. But don't change that number until you know the addresses of all the other SCSI devices! See next page.

To find out which SCSI addresses are available for your use

- Click the Start button at the bottom of the Windows screen.

- Slide your mouse up to "Settings," then out to the side and click on "Control Panel." When the Control Panel window appears, find the icon labeled "SCSI Adapters," and double-click it to open the dialog box. You'll see this:

adapter: The card that controls a device. One SCSI card controls up to eight SCSI devices.

Click "Devices" to bring the list forward.

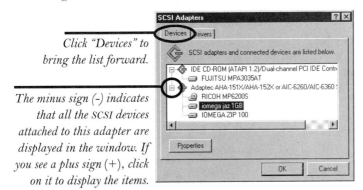

The minus sign (-) indicates that all the SCSI devices attached to this adapter are displayed in the window. If you see a plus sign (+), click on it to display the items.

The illustration above shows two adapters. One adapter has one drive attached to it, and the second adapter has three drives (CD-ROM, Jaz, and Zip) attached to it. Your property sheet may only show one adapter, if that's all you have. To see the actual devices and their ID numbers, follow the directions on the following page.

To see the actual SCSI devices and their IDs

- Double-click on any SCSI adapters listed in the control panel (shown on the previous page). Any SCSI devices the adapter card controls will be displayed below the adapter name. Notice that a plus sign (+) next to the adapter name indicates there are more options (single-click the plus sign to display the options), and a minus sign (-) indicates that all the adapter options are displayed (single-click the minus sign to hide them).

- Double-click on one of the SCSI devices listed, and you'll get a property sheet with two sections. Click the tab for the "Settings" section and you should see this:

This is the "Settings" property sheet for a SCSI device. The device's SCSI ID is the number to the right of "Target ID."

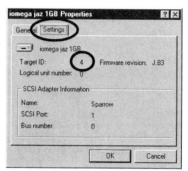

There's no way to see a list of all the SCSI IDs at one time. To see which addresses are available, you need to follow this process for every SCSI device in the list, one at a time.

You've noticed from this experience that PCs can (and frequently do) have more than one SCSI adapter card installed, as long as both SCSI adapters are the "new" SCSI type called SCSI Wide. Each card can control up to eight separate devices for a possible total of 16 SCSI peripherals. That's an awful lot of SCSI stuff (more than you can put on a Mac), but it wouldn't be too hard to envision an ultra–high-end setup where you might want to do this. If you don't have a SCSI Wide adapter, you'll still be limited to a maximum of eight SCSI devices in your computer.

Expansion card connections

Your PC will need a video card for the monitor, a sound card of some sort for even the most basic system alerts, and some kind of connection to the outside—an *Ethernet* card, a modem, or both. Each of these cards will occupy a separate slot on the PC. Here's how to recognize which expansion cards are already installed in your computer by looking at the ports on the back of the computer case.

Video cards

A PC video *card* has two differently shaped *female* receptacles, and each one has fifteen holes. These two receptacles don't allow you to attach two different monitors to your PC—they're alternate connectors so you can attach different types of monitor cables. (If you want to connect two monitors to your PC, you'll need Windows 98 or a very specialized configuration of hardware and software in Windows NT.)

If you've purchased both your video card and your monitor from the same manufacturer (like Dell, IBM, Gateway, Intergraph, etc.), you shouldn't have to do anything except plug the monitor cable into the correct connector on the video card that sticks out of the back of the computer box. If you've mixed and matched products from different manufacturers, you'll need to either load the *video driver* software that comes with your graphics card, customize your monitor setup, or both. For more information on customizing your monitor setup, see Chapter 12, *Display Settings.*

Warning: The smaller of the two connectors on the video card looks a lot like a serial port (see page 49). Look carefully—video ports are usually female (with sockets); serial ports are usually male (with pins). You don't want to plug a serial device into a video port, or a video/monitor cable into a serial port. If the computer is well-made, it shouldn't be possible to do either, but there are lots of PC clones out there; although there are conventions that many manufacturers follow, there are no standards.

Ethernet: A local area network that uses cables to connect computers so they can share information.

male and female connectors: If a connector (plug) has a prong that pokes into something, it's considered a *male* connector. If the plug has a hole waiting to put something inside, it's considered a *female* connector.

Board, card, and adapter are three different terms for the same thing. (An adapter might come in other forms besides a card or board.)

video driver: Software that enables the computer to recognize and use the video card.

Sound cards (audio cards/boards)

Sound cards are probably the easiest cards to recognize since they have universal jacks for speakers and a microphone. Remember that a PC without a sound card won't even give you alert sounds, so every PC package now ships with a sound card already installed. If you haven't asked for anything specific or if you bought a ready-made computer package at the store, you've probably been stuck with the cheapest possible card, the one that sounds like an old Mac SE after a bad night out. If this is the case, don't be surprised if installing an audio card is one of your first experiments with PC hardware installation.

ISA: **Industry Standard Architecture.**

PCI: **Peripheral Component Interconnect, the latest expansion card technology.**

Unfortunately, your audio card will almost definitely be an *ISA* board unless you've bought a high-end system and specified your needs. *PCI* audio boards (sound cards) are relatively recent additions to Windows computers, and they're pretty expensive. See Chapter 1 for information about ISA and PCI cards and how to tell which one you have.

Ethernet and modem cards

If you ordered an Ethernet card, you'll recognize it by its connector on the back of the computer that looks like an oversized phone jack. Modem cards have two smaller phone jacks, a tiny little speaker, and look somewhat similar to an Ethernet card at first glance.

If you ordered the cards with your system, the software drivers that allow the cards to be recognized by the computer are already installed. If you install the cards yourself, you need to install these drivers before you can connect the Ethernet card to your particular network or the modem to your particular Internet Service Provider (ISP).

Joysticks

Game Controllers

Look in "My Computer" for the Control Panel folder. You'll probably find a generic joystick control panel like this.

Many PCs come with a joystick port, which looks like a wide serial port with a few extra pin connectors. Sometimes it's on the front of the case, sometimes it's on the back. Many times a joystick port is on the sound card since sound is such an integral part of the gaming experience.

To install a joystick, just turn the computer off, plug the joystick into its port, start up the computer again, and set the joystick's settings in the Control Panel. Microsoft included drivers for some of the most popular models in the Joystick Control Panel, and many other joysticks will install successfully using the general settings. Most joysticks are so easy to install that they don't even come with special software.

Starting Up and Using Disks

One of the most annoying things about Windows to a Mac user is how Windows handles the simplest issues: starting up, shutting down, and mounting disks. This chapter gets you through these basic mechanics.

Starting up in Windows

Although Macs have a Power button somewhere on the computer box, we usually ignore that button and use the keyboard to turn on the computer. Although some PCs have a power switch on the keyboard, the vast majority turn on with a button on the computer itself.

There should be a Power button on the front of the computer with a small universal power symbol icon right near it: ⏻. Check for this symbol first; if you don't see it, your Power button is probably an obvious color or large size.

Reset button: **Restarts the computer without turning off the power, a gentler way to recover from a crashed or frozen computer.**

Many PCs have a *Reset* button as well as a Power button. Some manufacturers make these two buttons the same shape and keep them both equally accessible on the front of the case. Like the Restart button on Macs, the PC Reset button won't turn your computer on.

Once you've found the correct switch, turn the computer and monitor on. If everything is plugged in correctly, you'll get a green light on the front case of your computer. What happens next and how long it takes will depend on which Windows operating system is loaded, as well as how powerful and fast your hardware is.

The booting process

You've probably already started up (booted) your machine and have watched it go through the process described below. If you want to know what it's actually doing, read on.

Notice there are some points in the process when Windows NT and Windows 95/98 each load a little differently. Fortunately, there are more similarities than there are differences.

Note: **If you're working on a Mac with virtual or hardware emulation,** your startup will follow the standard Windows script described below. With your software or hardware, you should have documentation which provides very specific instructions on how to set up, how to load the Windows version you've chosen, and how to toggle between your Mac and Windows environments.

- Fade up on a black screen with white letters. At the very top of the screen you might see a line with some copyright information and a logo. These belong to the company that created the system BIOS (Basic Input/Output System)—the hardware's program code—which loads before any operating system software.

- Just below the logo line, you'll see a counter with numbers flying past. That's the computer's *RAM* check. Whether you've installed memory or had your retailer install it for you, the final number this counter displays ought to match your memory chips. If your computer is very fast, this counter may move too quickly for you to catch the end. Don't worry, you can check this number later, inside Windows (see Chapter 14 on accessories).

RAM: **Random Access Memory, also known as just "memory."**

- If you're using **Windows 95** or **98,** you'll see a full-screen logo for the next few seconds. It will be replaced briefly with a black BIOS screen with more information that you probably aren't interested in, and a "DOS prompt." (That's **C:\>** on one line.) Don't worry—you aren't expected to do anything at this prompt, and it will go away quickly.

  If you're using **Windows NT,** you won't see a logo. Instead, you'll see two or three other black screens in quick succession. Eventually, the screen changes to electric blue and you'll see a message telling you the computer is loading the OS (operating system). The blue screen might linger on your monitor, as a line of white dots builds on the screen. This lets you know that the computer is still working. Not quite the same as the happy Mac symbol and the parade of colorful extensions, but it does the job.

- Finally, **all versions of Windows** will replace the black screens with the default Windows background color (usually a deep teal blue), with the Windows splash screen centered in the middle. Expect to see the Windows logo in most of the same places that the Apple logo appears on a Mac, and then some.

Launching Windows 95/98

- If you're launching (opening) Windows 95/98 system for the first time, you'll see a "Welcome to Windows" dialog box. It might be tempting to take the Windows tour, but it may not be worth your while. Most Mac users find that it covers general computer topics you already know, deals with portions of the operating system that you as a Mac user may not even want to use, but misses topics you'll really care about. You might want to read through the fifty tips, then uncheck the box at the bottom of the screen that says "Show this Welcome Screen next time you start Windows."

Tip: **If you decide you want to take the Windows tour, you can always click the Start button, then choose "Run." In the edit box that appears, type "welcome," then click OK.**

Logging in to Windows NT

- **If your computer is on a network,** you'll see a screen asking you to **log in,** which connects your computer to the network. Someone at the company should have given you a user name and initial account password to type in here, as well as specific log-in instructions.

   The only way you can see a networked hard drive or share a drive or data with other people and systems is to log in. The specific dialog box for your network log-in will vary, depending on the networking software being used. The two most prevalent networking environments are Windows NT Server and Novell's Netware.

- **If this is your very own system which is not attached to any network,** you'll still get a log-in screen. Windows NT is a very security-conscious operating system which was designed specifically for high-powered network use. It won't let you do anything at all until you prove you have a right to use it.

So:

- Wait until the log-in screen appears. It starts up with a default identity of "Administrator," which sounds very official and off-putting, but don't worry because *you* are the Administrator.

- Ignore the password box. "Administrator" won't have any password assigned to it unless you decide you want to set one. Just use the mouse to click the OK button and your system will finish loading.

The Windows Desktop

With log-in and the welcome wagon behind you, you'll get a screen that looks a lot like this one:

The Windows Desktop

Notice that the Desktop icons appear in a column on the left. You might see a lot more icons on your Desktop. Don't worry—we'll show you how to manage them.

In the lower-right corner, this illustration shows some small icons. If you have extra cards or special features on your machine (sound card, video card, antivirus software), their little icons will blink on one by one.

If you are running Windows 98, you'll also see a group of icons on the bottom-left of the screen, next to "Start." These are the Quick Launch buttons; see pages 141 and 142.

The missing menu bar

Since this is the Desktop and you are a Mac user, you might be expecting a menu bar across the top, right? Wrong. Windows doesn't use a global menu bar; instead, every window has its own menu bar. See Chapter 7 for all the details.

Inside "My Computer"

My Computer

You can rename the alias of this icon (see page 67). We won't tell you what Robin renamed hers.

In the upper left of the Desktop you see an icon labeled "My Computer." This is not just a cute name Windows gives to your hard disk. "My Computer" isn't a hard disk at all—it's a separate window for all the storage devices (floppy disks and hard disks) attached to the computer, and it's also the link to all input and output devices.

Double-click the "My Computer" icon to open it. Its window will look something like this:

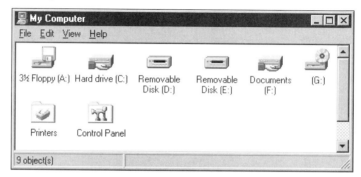

Double-click on the icon labeled "My Computer" to see this window. These icons represent all the storage media options (the disk drives) that the computer currently has installed. This machine has a floppy disk drive (A:), an internal hard drive (C:), a couple of removable drives (D: and E:), an internal hard drive partition (F:), and a CD-ROM drive (G:).

It's hard for a Mac user to understand why "My Computer" is even necessary. It mostly acts as a holding space for the drives, which, from our point of view, would be much more accessible and sensible if you didn't have to open a dang window to see them. See page 248 for a tip on making aliases (called "shortcuts" in Windows) of these drive icons and arranging them on your Desktop to look more like your Mac.

Disk drive letters

If you've never been exposed to a PC before, you might be puzzled by the letters in parentheses in the disk icon labels. These letters are the "real" names for drives and disks on a PC. The rest of the icon label is not the name of the drive, it's just the description of what Windows sees so you can easily identify which letter refers to which drive. If you click on one of these labels, it will highlight, but you won't be able to change the name by just typing, as you would on a Mac.

The colons (:) that follow the drive letters are not decorative; they're part of the drive name. Any time you need to identify a drive by its letter (and you will have to do this sometimes in Windows), you'll need to add the colon or the system won't recognize the letter as representing a disk. It will just think you're typing random text.

What do these letters stand for? **Drive A:** (or **B:** if you have one) always represents a diskette (floppy disk) drive. **Drive C:** is the main computer hard drive; the system files are usually kept in Drive C:. If you have applications already loaded on your system, you'll usually find them on the C: drive as well.

There is no guideline for how your system will determine your computer's letter codes beyond the standards A: through C:. In fact, if your PC has been programmed to boot with more than one operating system, the same physical setup can look very different in Windows 95/ 98 and Windows NT. A drive labeled D: may be a second partition on the hard drive, or it may be a completely separate piece of hardware.

Then there are network and shared drives. If you are on a network, the server's drives could have almost any letter attached to them. Letters from the end of the alphabet are usually servers, which makes them easier to spot. But if your company is running an NT network which lets you share drives between computers the same way Macs do, you could have computer letters popping up all over the place with different drive letters at different times, depending on which ones get shared first.

Hard drive
(C:)

This is the icon for your main hard drive.

Drive icons: what's what?

If you have drives in "My Computer" with letters other than C: and A:, you might want to check them out to see what's on them and what Windows will let you do with them. Their icons help you identify what types of drives they are. Below is a list of icons matched with the most common types of disks.

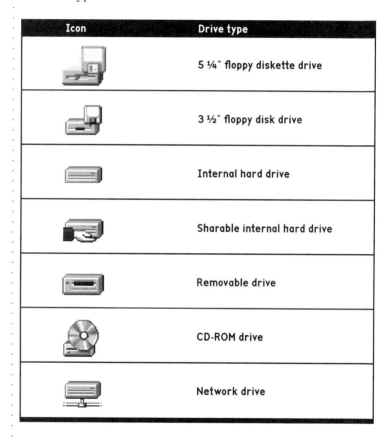

Icon	Drive type
	5 ¼" floppy diskette drive
	3 ½" floppy disk drive
	Internal hard drive
	Sharable internal hard drive
	Removable drive
	CD-ROM drive
	Network drive

All removable drives use the same disk icon. Windows doesn't make a visual distinction between Syquest, Zip, Jaz, or any other brand unless the manufacturer arranges for the icon to be loaded as part of the installation.

Drive C: and the Windows system folder

Let's open the C: drive. If the window for "My Computer" is not open on your screen, first double-click the icon for "My Computer." In that window, double-click on the C: drive icon. The C: drive window contains several folders and even more files, some with names like "autoexec.bat" and "boot.ini." These are the critical system files that actually set the Windows environment and launch Windows itself.

Hard drive
(C:)

The names of the files tell their ancient origin: .bat (pronounced "dot bat") stands for "batch." Batch files were mini-programs like Apple-Scripts, that were used to load applications or handle disk maintenance. "Autoexec" was the mother of all batch files, the one that launched DOS. The ".ini" files are leftover from earlier versions of Windows. These were configuration files, similar to preferences and control panel settings on the Mac. Windows 95/98 and NT are all supposedly using the *Windows Registry* for all system settings instead of these old text files, but it's surprising how many .ini files still hang out on the C: drive. Don't delete them; Windows still uses those files for older programs and sees them as part of the system, even if it never has to actually use them.

Windows Registry: A kind of database of system information. It keeps track of every hardware driver, extension, and Windows setting. If the Registry is damaged or deleted, Windows will not load on your system.

Unless someone has come in and customized its icon, the **system folder** on your C: drive is pretty anonymous. It's either called Windows or WinNT, and it looks like any other generic folder on the desktop. Unlike the Mac, the icon for the PC system folder doesn't have any connection to whether the computer sees it as the Windows system folder or not.

Windows

This is what Windows 9598 considers to be its system folder.

Mac users are accustomed to opening up and changing our System Folders. We dump preferences, drag in extensions, delete extra printer profiles, and set startup files and shutdown files. You can't do any of this with a Windows system folder, or at least you shouldn't. People with lots of prior system experience sometimes tinker, but it's a dangerous sport. Unlike a Mac, you can't cheat and keep a copy of an old System Folder around to copy over if something goes wrong. As far as a typical user is concerned, the Windows system folder doesn't exist.

To carry out the kinds of functions Mac users perform directly in the System Folder, a Windows user works within the Control Panel folder, right-clicks files to access their property sheets, buys special utility software, or—if they're very Windows-savvy—edits the Windows Registry. Editing the Registry is more like programming than it is like using the Macintosh *Extensions Manager*, and is much more dangerous to the integrity of the system if you make an error.

Extensions Manager: A Mac Control Panel that helps you manage all of your extensions.

Where's the disk?

Insert a floppy disk in the 3½″ drive that Windows calls Drive A:. But don't bother watching the Desktop waiting for the disk icon to appear— it won't.

This is one of the biggest differences between Macs and PCs. When you put a disk or cartridge into a Mac, the operating system automatically recognizes that it's there and *mounts* it for you. PCs don't automatically mount any kind of media that's not permanently and physically attached to the computer.

mount: **Recognize a disk so it can be used. When you see the disk icon, you know the computer has *mounted* the disk and you can use it.**

So then how do you mount a disk and see its icon?

To see the disk icon so you can get to its contents, you need to open the window for "My Computer": double-click on its icon in the upper-left of the screen. The "My Computer" window (as shown on page 62) displays the **drives** themselves—it doesn't see any individual disk or cartridge that you've put in the drive. If you really did insert a floppy disk, then double-click the floppy drive icon and the window for that disk will appear. The title bar of a floppy disk window looks like this:

Windows 98: title bar from disk window in the A: drive.

Windows 95 or NT: title bar from the disk window in the A: drive.

Make a shortcut to your disk drive!

alias: **an icon that represents a file; you double-click the alias icon and it finds the real file and opens it.**

See Chapter 17 for more information about shortcuts!

If you are familiar with *aliases* on the Mac, then you will be pleased to know you can create the same thing on the PC; it's called a **shortcut.** You can make a shortcut to any disk drive and put the shortcut icon on your Desktop. Then when you insert a disk, simply double-click the drive shortcut to open the disk's window.

To make a shortcut

1. Open the window for "My Computer."
2. Click once on the drive icon that you want a shortcut for.
3. Hold down the Control and Alt keys, then drag the selected icon to the Desktop. It will look like this, with a tiny arrow:

   You can rename the shortcut icon: select the text and type, just as you do on the Mac.

Shortcut to Removable Disk (D)

Disk names

Does the disk in the A: drive have a name? You can't tell. The title bar of its window, as shown on the previous page, has a generic label telling you you're looking at a disk in the A: drive. Duh. The only exception to this rule is your CD-ROM drive. When you insert a CD and double-click on the CD-ROM drive icon, you might get the software manufacturer's icon for the drive, as shown in the margin to the right, instead of the generic one. If you open the CD itself, though, the title bar of its window will still display just the generic letter.

So how can you tell if a disk has a name that gives you a clue what's on it, and how can you give a disk a name if it doesn't have one?

Photoshp (G:)
Photoshop CD icon

Name the disk here.

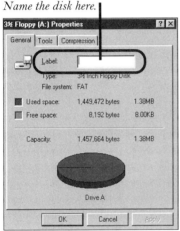

You can use caps or lowercase, but you're limited to eleven characters.

1. Open the window for "My Computer," if it isn't already.

2. Right-click the floppy disk icon in the window.

3. From the pop-up menu, choose "Properties."

4. Click the "General" tab to see the disk's "Label," which is what we would call its "name."

5. If the Label field is empty, the disk doesn't have a name. Go ahead and type a name in here.

6. If you want to change its existing name/label, just select the one that's in there and type the name you want. Click OK (don't click the X in the upper-right corner of the box!).

Tip: If the Label box is gray and you can't type in the Label field, the disk you've chosen isn't mounted, which can easily happen if you've right-clicked on one of the removable drive icons before you've actually put in a cartridge.

Just because Windows only sees drive letters doesn't mean giving a disk or drive a name isn't worth doing. You still want to name your disks and cartridges to keep track of them.

Mounting Macintosh disks in Windows

If you're using a Mac with software emulation or a PC card, you won't experience anything unusual when you try to mount PC disks—they mount as A: or B: drives, and all other disks or removable cartridges mount as shared *volumes*.

volume: Another name for disk, or for a partition of a hard disk.

But have you tried to mount a Macintosh disk in your Windows computer yet? A real PC treats any Mac-formatted disk as if it came from Mars. "Your disk is not formatted," it will tell you. Then the PC will either ask if you want to format the disk, or it will automatically open the Format dialog box. As you know, formatting a disk permanently destroys everything on it, so you probably don't want to do that.

If you must mount a Mac disk directly on your Windows computer, you'll need to buy third-party software. (Intergraph Systems includes the necessary software as part of their ExtremeZ publishing system, but they're very much the exception.) Make sure the software works for your version of Windows—all mounting software runs on Windows 95/98, but support for NT is not consistent.

Some mounting software makes a distinction between different kinds of Mac media. You probably have a Zip drive, but if you are using Syquest cartridges or optical drives it will be very important to have mounting software that reads any SCSI media. You'll also want to make sure the software will format and write Mac disks, as well as read them. Cyndi's favorite solution is DataViz's MacOpener, which was one of the first programs to support Windows NT. It's completely mindless to install and use, and it reads just about anything you throw at it.

If you don't think you'll need to open Mac disks on the PC very often, you can use the Mac's ability to read and write PC-formatted disks instead. Read Chapter 21 to learn how to write to PC disks on the Mac, and Chapter 22 on how to prepare the files properly so they'll be recognized in Windows.

Clues in the File menu

As you've surely noticed by now, there is no menu bar across the top of the entire Desktop—every window has its own menu bar (discussed in detail in Chapter 7). The options in those menu bars change in each window according to what options that window allows.

The File menu is useful in helping you figure out what kind of Desktop element you're looking at and what you can do with it. What's in the File menu changes according to what kind of object is selected.

1. Double-click the icon "My Computer" to open its window, if it isn't already open.

2. Click once on the C: drive icon or on a file icon.

3. Click on the File menu.

   The choices in the File menu are a combination of what comes with your version of Windows, what you've loaded on the computer yourself, and which icon you've selected. The computer Cyndi's using has anti-virus and Mac-mounting software loaded, so their options have been automatically added to the File menu, as you can see below. The options in your File menu are probably different.

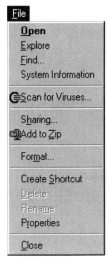

*This is the File menu in "My Computer" window with **a hard drive selected**. Notice the options, which include "Format."*

*This is the File menu in "My Computer" window with **a file selected**. It has different options in the menu because you can do different things to a file than you can to a disk drive.*

Initializing and erasing disks

There will be times when you need to erase or initialize (format) a disk. New disks usually come pre-formatted, but if you want to reuse a disk you should erase its old material and start fresh. This is particularly important if you want to recycle a Mac disk for Windows use.

Formatting floppies and removable hard disks

Formatting a floppy disk or removable hard disk is pretty simple. Once the disk is mounted:

1. Open "My Computer."

2. Locate the icon for the drive the disk or cartridge is in and *right-click* on it.

3. From the pop-up menu that appears, choose "Format..." to get the formatting dialog box.

   The exact dialog box you'll get will depend on the type of disk, but generally you'll want to leave all the default settings which appear. Name the disk here in the Label box, if you want.

4. Click the "Start" button.

   You can return to whatever you were doing before. Both Windows 95/98 and Windows NT format disks in the background, so you don't have to wait around for the process to finish.

right-click: Use the right-hand button on the mouse to click with. On a PC, the right-hand button makes different things happen. In this case, you will get a menu.

Formatting a hard disk

Frankly, formatting a hard disk on a PC is a tricky proposition. It's different in Windows 95/98 than in NT, and it matters what kind of hard disk you have and what kind of formatting you're trying to do.

In any case, this isn't something that a Windows *newbie* ought to try. If you must do it, find a friend with this kind of technical knowledge. If you don't know anyone, invest in one of the massive Windows references for your operating system, like Peachpit's *Windows 98 Bible.* If you're willing to try something like this, you've probably made a permanent, serious commitment to the Windows side of things, and you'll use that book more than just this once.

newbie: Someone who is new to a certain kind of technology.

Ejecting: it's not a drag

On the Mac, when you want to eject a disk from a drive, you can drag the disk icon to the trash. On the PC, drag a disk icon to the Recycle Bin (the PC equivalent of the trash) and its transparent "ghost" icon is covered by a big, black "not" symbol.

The international forbidden symbol.

This is another important difference between the way the Mac and the PC mount and unmount disks. Since the PC doesn't see the disk as being mounted in the first place, it thinks you're trying to throw away the whole disk drive.

To eject a floppy disk or removable cartridge

1. Open "My Computer."

2. Right-click on the drive icon whose disk you want to eject.

3. Choose "Eject Disk" from the menu that pops up.

   OR:

1. Close the window of the disk by clicking on the tiny **X** in the upper-right corner of the window.

2. Push the eject button next to the drive slot.

No matter which method you choose, there's no confirmation on your screen that the cartridge is ejected. In fact, the system is so blind that it doesn't even notice if you eject a disk when its window is still open on the screen—it's so dumb it sometimes leaves the window open on the Desktop even though the disk has been ejected. But if you try to click on something in the ejected disk's phantom window, you get this message:

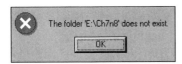

It would be much nicer if the message would at least tell you the disk is no longer mounted. If you're not keeping track of which window belongs to which drive, a message like this can scare you unnecessarily.

Depending on your point of view, this method of dealing with disks is either a feature or a problem: It eliminates those awful times when disks are held hostage in a system crash; but on the other hand, you have no visual clue that tells you something is mounted, so you have to remember to eject the disks before you walk away from a computer. Check any PC lab or service bureau, and you'll find plenty of orphaned disks.

Restart, sleep, or shut down

Whether you want to restart the computer, put it to sleep (stand by) temporarily, or shut it down, you'll use the Shut Down command (typical Microsoft logic).

To restart, put the computer to sleep, or shut down

1. Quit all programs.

2. Click the Start button (bottom-left of the screen), and choose "Shut Down."

   You'll see one of these dialog boxes, depending on your version of Windows.

"Shut Down Windows" screen in Windows 98.   *"Shut Down Windows" screen in Windows* NT.

Here's what each of these options means:

- **Restart** doesn't need much explanation, since it's just like the Mac restart. You'll mostly use it after having installed utility software that changes the Windows system.

- Windows 98 adds a new option, **Stand by,** which is the same as "Sleep" on the Mac. It's a low-power mode. To wake up the machine after you've put it on stand by, either click any key on the keyboard, or push your computer's special "wake up" button.

- As a Macintosh user, there will be very few times, if ever, that you choose the option of **Restart in MS-DOS mode.** MS-DOS is a "text-based, command-line operating system" which, as we mentioned in Chapter 2, is at the base of Windows 95 and 98. And it's really boring.

- **Log on as different user** sounds like you're being asked to go undercover, but it's actually quite useful if you aren't the only user of the computer. You may have special privileges that you don't want to share, or personal files that other people could gain access to if you just walk away. This option lets you leave the computer on for the next person, which can be a nice gesture when it takes so long to boot.

  Windows 98 no longer puts this option in the Shut Down dialog box because it allows you to log in and out through the Start Menu.

- **Shut down** is the same on the PC as on the Mac. It closes any programs you may have left open and backs out of Windows.

  Click the button next to "Shut down," then click the Yes/OK button (or hit the Enter key). But don't expect the almost instantaneous process you get from a Mac. The complex load sequence when you started up the computer takes place in reverse at shut down because the system needs to put Windows itself away.

Here's what should happen when you **shut down:**

- The Desktop stays on the screen for a few additional seconds, then the monitor flashes and the icons disappear, leaving a blank background. You may or may not get a message saying, "Please be patient while the system writes unsaved data to the disk." If you had any unsaved files left open, you will be asked if you want to save them or not.

- Hang in there and don't walk away thinking you're finished. Eventually any messages will be replaced with a new one that tells you it's safe to turn off the computer. Some computers will then turn off the power for you; others will wait for you to do it. If you're using Windows NT, you'll definitely have to hang around to turn the power switch off yourself.

It's nice that Windows allows you to customize so many options as part of the the restart and shut down process, but it would be even nicer if these options were menu choices, as they are on a Mac. On some machines, Windows retains whatever option you last chose in this dialog box—it's very easy to forget to change the setting next time you want to shut down and be forced to hang around while the system restarts instead.

If you have a computer that doesn't automatically power off when you shut down for the day, a little shareware can help. There are several possibilities, but Cyndi's favorite is called "Shutdown NOW!" which you can find at download.com or shareware.com. It has options to eject disks at shut down, to shut down and restart, and to turn the power off. It also has a shut down scheduler so even if you forget to shut down before you leave for the day, your computer and the environment won't suffer for it. It won't work on all hardware, but it's certainly worth trying.

Don't leave a disk in a drive at shut down

If you don't eject everything before you shut down, your computer might not boot up again properly, especially if you leave a non-startup disk in the A: drive (the floppy drive). The poor computer (Robin says "stupid computer") will find a disk in the A: drive and assume you're trying to override the C: drive system. As you know, if a Mac doesn't find a System Folder on a disk in any drive, it ejects the disk and keeps searching. When DOS doesn't find what it's looking for, it gives up, even though the operating system is intact on the hard drive. If this happens, you'll get a "Non-System disk or disk error" message. Remove the disk and hit any keyboard key.

The Keyboard

Half of what makes us productive computer users is keyboard control. Mousing is great, but it's hard on the hands. Hang around for this chapter, and you'll feel comfortable (well, less uncomfortable) with the PC's keyboard shortcuts and different keyboard layout.

Special keys

You've probably discovered that your PC keyboard lacks a start-up button (Power key). All things considered, this is a minor lapse since you only use it once or twice a day. There are other variations in form and function between PC and Mac keyboards which are less obvious but more likely to affect your work habits. As anyone who has ever tried to use a *Dvorak keyboard* can tell you, it's hard to adapt to a keyboard change, even in the name of efficiency. And if efficiency isn't even in the offing . . . well, judge for yourself.

Dvorak keyboard: A more efficient keyboard layout that allows for quicker typing and less trauma to the hands than our present standard arrangement, which is called QWERTY.

The Control key

The Windows Control key (Ctrl) is in the same position as the Control key on a Mac keyboard, but it's far more important on a PC. You'll use it as often on a PC as you use the Command key (⌘) on a Mac.

The Control key is indicated in menus by the abbreviation "Ctrl" or sometimes by the caret symbol: ^

General guideline: If you're working in a program you know very well on the Mac and want to use the keyboard commands that have made you fast and productive, just try substituting the Control key for the Command key. You've got a better-than-average chance the keyboard shortcut will work.

The Alt key

The Alt key (Alt stands for Alternate) is next to the Spacebar on the PC keyboard and functions somewhat like the Mac Option key. The Alt key is used in some application keyboard shortcuts, but there's no way to predict when it might be used instead of the Ctrl key. Getting used to the Alt key is the single most difficult thing about working with software which is otherwise identical on both platforms.

You can also use the Alt key to pull down menus instead of using the mouse. For instance, Alt F displays the Find menu, Alt E displays the Edit menu, Alt V the View menu, and Alt H the Help menu.

Once you display the menu by using the Alt key, you can use letter keys to choose options.

This is very useful on a PC where there are far fewer keyboard shortcuts, and you frequently have to pull down a menu to work. Once you've brought up the menu with the Alt key, take a look at the underlined letters, called "active" letters. Press the letter key (without the Alt key) on the keyboard to choose that option in the menu. In the example to the left, press the letter L to view the contents of the window as a List.

For more information on using Windows menus, see Chapter 7.

The Windows key

The Windows key is between the Control and Alt keys. It's fairly new to the PC keyboard so you might not have one on yours.

This is the Windows key.

The Windows key is simply a shortcut to the Start Menu, that menu that pops up on the lower-left of your screen (discussed in Chapter 8). On a PC, application windows can sometimes obscure the Start Menu button and the Taskbar. When that happens, you lose easy access to most of the Windows goodies and have to dig through layers to unearth them. Think of the Windows key as a patch to fix something that wasn't well thought out in the first place.

The Menu key

Some new PC keyboards have a key on the bottom right-hand side, between the Windows key and the Control key, called the Menu key.

This is the Menu key.

The Menu key is an alternative to right-clicking with the mouse button. In case you haven't used the right button on your mouse yet (discussed in Chapter 6), just know that the PC uses it quite a bit. Right-clicking brings up menus you can't get to otherwise, and the menus it brings up depend on what's selected on the Desktop. Since using the Menu key requires that you move your mouse to the correct place on the screen first, it's of limited value — if you have to position your mouse there anyway, why not right-click?

Chances are you'll use the Menu key mostly by mistake, by hitting it while searching for the Windows key.

Print Screen

One other key is worth mentioning, the Print Screen key (it might be labeled something like Print Scrn). It's in the far-right group of keys at the top of the keyboard. If you hit this key, you'll snap a picture of your entire computer screen. You won't see or hear any clue that a picture was snapped, but the screen shot is put into the Clipboard. You can see it in the Clipboard viewer (see Chapter 14 on accessories).

Keyboard shortcuts:
in Command or in Control

The good news is that most Windows shortcuts have been "adapted" from the Mac, which makes memorizing them a breeze. The bad news is that there aren't a lot of PC keyboard shortcuts, compared to the drop-down menu choices.

Some PC users will object strenuously to that statement. "There's a keyboard shortcut for every action," they'll tell you. Their definition of a keyboard shortcut and ours don't really match. For Mac users, a keyboard shortcut is a group of keys that are all hit at the same time—one action. We also contend that a keyboard shortcut shouldn't require you to open a menu first.

Here's an example of a Windows keyboard "shortcut." Say you want to make a new folder. On the Mac, you select the window in which you want a new folder, then press ⌘ N. In Windows 98, you select the window in which you want a new folder, press Alt F4 to get the File menu, let go of the Alt key and type N for New, then type F for Folder. That takes one keyboard shortcut, then two sequential keys.

active letter:
The underlined letter in a menu, as shown on page 76 and below.

These keyboard "shortcuts" aren't too difficult if the *active letter* is the first letter in the word, but often it isn't—generally you have to open the menu, then search for the correct letter.

You can work with the keyboard instead of the mouse if you prefer, although except for the most frequent actions, you'll probably find that you might as well just use the mouse.

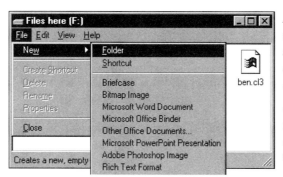

Alt F, then N F is the keyboard sequence to make a new folder in Windows 98.

Windows 95 (shown here) and Windows NT use Alt F, then W F.

Frequently used shortcuts

Speaking of frequent actions, you'll be up and running with these real keyboard shortcuts almost immediately:

Action	Macintosh	Windows
Cut	⌘ X	Ctrl X
Copy	⌘ C	Ctrl C
Paste	⌘ V	Ctrl V
Select All	⌘ A	Ctrl A
Find	⌘ F	Ctrl F
Close a window	⌘ W	Alt F4
Quit / Exit a program	⌘ Q	Alt F4
Force quit	⌘ Option Esc	Ctrl Alt Del
Restart	⌘ Ctrl Powerkey	Ctrl Alt Del (twice)
		(Windows NT) Ctrl Alt Del S R
Picture of screen	⌘ Shift 3	PrintScreen
Picture of active window	CapsLock, ⌘ Shift 4	Alt PrintScreen

Windows does not make any distinction between **Close** and **Quit** (we'll talk more about that in Chapter 7). Some applications, particularly those with Mac counterparts, do recognize that Close and Quit are different actions and provide a Ctrl W keyboard shortcut in their File menu to close the active window. However, check the menu before you use it!

If you use **Alt F4** to close a window (and you probably will), make sure the window you want to close is **selected.** If you type Alt F4 when there is no window selected, you'll get the shut down dialog box.

The **Ctrl Alt Del** combination is a holdover from DOS which is very useful. On a system that's having performance problems, it will cause a **break,** bringing up a log-out screen or confirmation that you want to shut down. On a system that's just crashed and burned, it will usually restart and reload Windows. Frankly, it does a better, more consistent job than the Mac does of closing down a misbehaving application without taking down the whole computer. But then, the DOS/Windows environment had more experience with crashing in its infancy than the Mac did, so it's had the opportunity to get it right.

active window: The window that is in front of all others. Its title bar will be darker than any other window's title bar.

Alt PrintScreen takes a snapshot (a screen capture) of the *active window.* You might take a screen capture of the contents of your Zip disk, then copy that screen capture from the Clipboard (see Chapter 14) into the Windows Paint accessory and print it out. This makes a great record of the contents of the disk.

Application keyboard shortcuts

New: Control N
Open: Control O
Save: Control S
Print: Control P
Cut: Control X
Copy: Control C
Paste: Control V
Undo: Control Z

Fortunately, cross-platform applications that were first on the Mac tend to bring most of their keyboard combinations with them to Windows, so you can count on the following commands to work in the programs you're already familiar with just by substituting the Control key for the Command key: New, Open, Save, Print, Cut, Copy, Paste, and Undo.

If the program you're working with never had a Macintosh version (or had one a long time ago but discontinued it), all "shortcuts" are probably those Windows underlined-letter versions. And you won't necessarily be able to count on the same letters being used for the same action from one application to the next, unless the software is all from the same company. Every developer sets their own rules in Windows.

Customizing the keyboard

You can control the PC keyboard settings in a Keyboard Control Panel, just as you can on the Mac. This is how to open the Control Panel:

1. Click the Start Menu button (or tap the Windows key).

2. Slide up to "Settings," then over to "Control Panel"; click on "Control Panel."

3. In the Control Panel window, double-click on the Keyboard icon: Keyboard

4. Change the keyboard layout, the key repeat speed, or even the keyboard language.

5. Click the Apply button to test your changes. When you're satisfied, click the OK button.

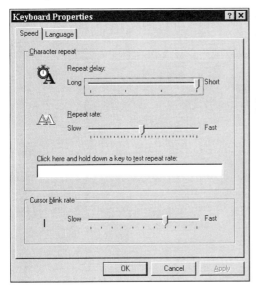

Many of the Control Panels are similar to the Mac's. If you are not yet familiar with the Macintosh Control Panels, you should read The Little Mac Book, *by Robin.*

PC keyboard emulation on a Mac

If you're working on a Mac using a software emulation package or a hardware add-on board, you need to know how to access the PC keyboard functions. Exactly how the Macintosh keys transfer to their Windows equivalents can differ, depending on what form of Mac-based alternative you're using and whether you have a Macintosh regular or extended keyboard. In some systems, the Command key is the Windows Alt key. In others, the Mac Option key translates to the Alt key or the Shift key. Check your hardware or software manual to be sure!

The Mouse

Knowledgeable Mac user that you are, you might be tempted to skip this chapter. Don't. A Mac mouse and a PC mouse are quite different, and there are important PC things you can only do with a PC mouse.

The amazing two-headed mouse

NOTE!
If you are using Windows 98 and some of these mouse actions don't work, you're probably in the Internet Explorer interface. For now, turn to page 115 and follow the directions to change back to the Classic style (turn "Web View" off); then these directions will make sense. If you later decide you want the Internet Explorer interface, you can change it back.

Because you're a Mac user, you already know all the basic mousing methods. You can click and double-click, as well as press-and-drag, and you probably know how to use contextual menus (Control-click) and the click-and-a-half in Mac OS 8 and later. However, these Mac actions don't always produce the same reactions in Windows that you're used to, or there are different ways to do some of them.

Before we start mousing around, let's establish some conventions. There are two buttons on your Windows mouse, not just one, and the two buttons are not interchangeable. When we want you to use the left button, we'll just say "click," "double-click," or "drag," per usual. We'll say "right-click" or "right-drag" if you need to use the right button.

You can get through most Desktop functions, including working inside familiar applications, by using the left mouse button just like you're accustomed to. The trick, of course, is that there are some significant functions that require right-clicking.

This is the Microsoft IntelliMouse.

If yours is a new system, you might have a Microsoft IntelliMouse. It has two buttons at the top, with a small, gray, raised button in the center. The mouse curves to the left, which makes it very comfortable if you're right-handed, but very awkward if you're a southpaw. If your mouse only has two buttons, don't worry. You've heard the phrase "third wheel" before? Right now, that's what the third button (or wheel) is. Until more software programs support it, the wheel button is still just a minor enhancement, not a crucial element in using a Windows mouse.

Selecting and deselecting

An icon retains its selection border even after it's deselected.

Try this: Click once on a Desktop icon to select it. Now click anywhere on the Desktop to deselect that icon. Notice there is still an outline around the icon even after you deselect it. This feature can be useful: if you click somewhere else in the window inadvertently, you can still find the last icon you used. (It's also not bad if you're absent-minded and can't remember what you were doing before the phone rang.)

To get rid of the selection outline, click in an open window or in the Taskbar (the gray bar at the bottom of the screen) if the selected icon is on the Desktop. If the selected icon is in a window, click anywhere outside the window the icon is in or in another window to get rid of the outline.

Selecting more than one file

Just like on your Mac, you can select more than one file at a time. To do this, use the same two basic techniques you would on your Mac:

- With the pointer, drag around the objects you want to select. **Or:**
- Hold down the Control key (instead of the Shift key, as on a Mac) and click each file you want to select.

  That's called **Control-click** (on the Mac the key combination you use is called Shift-click).

Being a Mac user, you might Shift-click instead of Control-click to select more than one file. Unfortunately, Shift-click on a PC does something that looks similar to but is actually quite different from Control-click, and it can make you crazy.

The Shift-click combination selects files *in a sequence*, as long as you select files from *one* column or row. Try this:

1. Click (you don't need the Shift key held down) to select the first item of the sequence. In the example to the right, that would be the folder "Robin's email."

2. Shift-click on the last file (in the example, that would be "06.wmu"). Everything between the click and the Shift-click is selected.

   What will make you crazy is trying to select *other* files in *other* columns or rows with the Shift key down—try it and see. You'll quickly learn to use Control-click to select individual files that are separated throughout the window, and Shift-click to select a number of files that are in a contiguous list or row.

You can use a **combination** of Shift-click and Control-click. Let's say you want to select all the icons in a row, *except* for one in the middle: Click the icon on the left end of the row, Shift-click the icon on the right end of the row, then Control-click the one you want to **deselect.** Try it.

Invert the selection

Here's a selection feature you'll find useful. How many times have you wanted to select everything in a window *except* one or two files? On the Mac, you Select All, then Shift-click to deselect the files you don't want in the selection. In Windows, there's a faster method:

1. Control-click on two different files in a window.

2. From the Edit menu, choose "Invert Selection" (Alt E, then I). Everything is selected *except* those two files, quickly and easily.

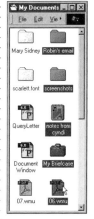

The selected files in the right-hand column are in sequence; they're contiguous.

See—when we find something in Windows that we wish we had on the Mac, we're willing to admit it. It just doesn't happen very often.

The right mouse button

Until Windows 95, the right mouse button was simply decorative. Now it's not only functional, it's an integral part of the Windows environ-
right-click: Click using the right-hand mouse button.
ment. You can do many things with a *right-click*, and what you can do depends on what you click on. Different applications utilize this feature in different ways. Experiment with right-clicking in your applications, dialog boxes, and games. Below are some examples of the menus that appear when you *right-click* on Desktop icons and what happens when you *drag* with the *right* button down.

A document.

The icon for "My Computer."

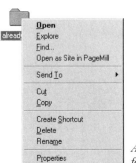

An ordinary folder.

A folder inside "My Computer."

The Taskbar (gray bar at bottom of screen).

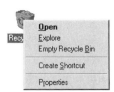

The Recycle Bin (trash can).

Blank area in an open window.

The Desktop itself.

The window's menu bar.

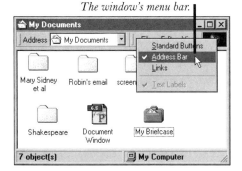

*If you hold down the right button as you drag a file, you have different options than if you left-drag! This is an easy way to **copy a file** to another folder or to make a **shortcut** (alias) to a file.*

Right-clicking and property sheets

One of the most important things a right-click does is give you access to the *property sheet* for a file. A property sheet is where you change defaults, settings, and preferences for a file. A property sheet is a bit like a Mac's *Get Info* window on steroids. Property sheets tend to be fairly complex on the PC.

Right-click anything, including the Taskbar (the bar across the bottom of the screen), the Desktop, or even menu bars to bring up a menu; if that item has a property sheet, the last choice in the right-click menu will be "Properties" (shown below).

To view a typical property sheet

1. Right-click on a file.

2. Choose "Properties." (If "Properties" is not in the pop-up menu, right-click on a different file or on the Desktop.)

3. Most property sheets have more than one labeled *tab* (circled below). Click the various tabs to view the various settings.

4. **To close the property sheet *without saving any changes*,** click on the X in the upper-right corner of the title bar, or press Alt F4.

    To close the property sheet and *save the changes you made*, click OK.

Get Info: Every file on the Mac has a Get Info window that supplies information about the file, such as when it was created or last modified, what kind it is, where it's stored, etc. To get the Get Info window, select a file on the Desktop, then from the File menu choose "Get Info," or press Command I.

This is "Cancel" in property sheets!

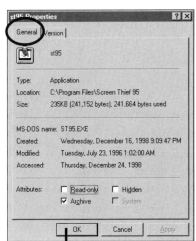

Right-click a file on the Desktop to get the pop-up menu. Click on a tab to view or change settings.

Click the OK button to save your changes.

The IntelliMouse wheel button

This is Microsoft's IntelliMouse. The wheel button is that little round thing in the middle.

As we mentioned on page 84, Microsoft made a new mouse called the IntelliMouse, and it has a third button. There aren't many applications that use the third button (shown to the left), called a wheel. Versions of Microsoft software released since the IntelliMouse have, of course, implemented it to some extent. For example, Excel uses it to scroll around cells in a spreadsheet. Some applications that come with Windows also recognize it. If you have an IntelliMouse, try it out in the Notepad:

1. Click the Start Menu, and slide up to "Programs," then out to "Accessories," then out again until you find "Notepad." Click once on "Notepad" to select it.

2. Drag the lower-right corner of the Notepad window (exactly as you would on a Mac) to resize it very short and narrow.

3. Check the Edit menu to make sure "WordWrap" is on—if it is on, there will be a checkmark next to it; if it isn't on, select it. (WordWrap fits your text to the size of the window. If you don't have WordWrap on, Notepad will just keep typing all your text on one line, never returning to the left margin.)

4. Type any brilliant thoughts that come to mind until you have enough text to make the window's scroll bars appear. Click anywhere on the scroll bar to move the contents of the window.

5. **Now** you can see the mouse wheel in action! Position the cursor anywhere inside the Notepad window, and roll the mouse wheel button towards you with one finger. Your screen should scroll down toward the bottom as you do this.

Make sure "WordWrap" has a checkmark next to it. Can you believe WordWrap is off by default?

In some applications, you can combine the wheel button with the Control key to zoom in or out of a view.

The wheel button is a nice concept, even though it's kind of limited. In fact, it's still so limited even Microsoft seems to forget it exists. For example, Notepad recognizes the wheel button, but Windows Help, which sometimes creates long scrolling windows where the wheel could be very useful, does not.

Customizing the mouse

Now that you know how the mouse works and what property sheets are, let's customize the mouse to your needs. If you're left-handed, you can switch the "left" and "right" programming so you can use your index finger on the button you need most. You can also optimize many other ways in which you use the mouse.

To open the mouse property sheet

1. Click the Start Menu, slide up to "Settings" and over to "Control Panel." **Or** open "My Computer" and double-click on the "Control Panel" folder.

2. In the Control Panel folder, find the Mouse icon (shown to the right). Double-click it to open Mouse Properties.

3. The options in Mouse Properties will vary depending on which mouse driver is loaded. Below is what you'll see in Windows 98 with a standard two-button mouse. Click on the labeled tabs at the top to peruse or alter different sets of settings.

Mouse

This is the icon that represents the Mouse Control Panel, which is actually called Mouse Properties.

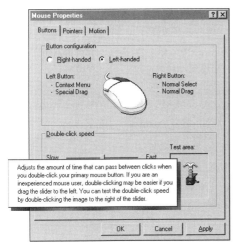

Right-click on various settings to get a tiny menu that says, "What's this?" Click on that menu and you will get lots of useful information about all the settings, as shown in the box to the left.

Buttons settings

Use the Buttons settings to adjust your double-click speed, and to swap the left for the right button if you're left-handed. If you do switch to left-handed, remember to swap the directions in this book (and every other book) left-for-right too! That is, when we say "click," use the *right* button; when we say "right-click," use the *left* button.

Pointers settings

The Mouse property sheet has settings for the pointer. As you know, on your Mac the mouse pointer looks different depending on what it can do at that particular moment; its icon is a visual clue. The Mac has an arrow, I-beam, watch, crosshairs, and dozens of other pointers specific to different applications. Windows has a similar set of mouse personalities, which it displays in the Pointers settings.

You can choose your mouse pointer icons from among a group of pre-set "themes" (each one sillier than the other). A theme is a coordinated collection of Desktop icons, *wallpaper*, and sounds. Windows has a mania for customization, and Desktop themes are downloadable at shareware sites everywhere.

wallpaper: a repeating pattern, picture, or design that replaces the solid color of your Desktop.

Themes and schemes

One of the subsets of a Desktop *theme* is a mouse pointer *scheme*, several of which ship with Windows 98.

To install the scheme mouse pointers

1. Open "My Computer," double-click the Control Panel folder, then double-click "Desktop Themes."

2. From the "Theme" menu, choose one of the themes in the list.

3. On the right side of this dialog box, choose the settings you want to install. To install only the mouse pointers, uncheck all the other boxes.

4. Click "Apply" to see a preview; click OK to install the new pointers.

For more about themes, see Chapter 12, *Display Settings*.

Motion settings

In the Motion section you can change the "speed" of the mouse. This doesn't really change how "fast" the mouse moves—it changes how far you have to move the mouse with your hand to move the pointer across the screen. For instance, set the control to the slowest speed and watch how far you have to move the mouse to get the pointer across the screen. Then change it to the fastest setting and try again.

Use the slow setting in graphics programs where you need to move details in small increments; use the fast setting if you have a small work area or if you just like to keep your hand movements to a minimum.

Tip: Pointer trails are a useful feature for instructors—the trail helps students follow the mouse on overhead projections.

If you click "Show pointer trails," the cursor will leave a trail of cursors fading behind it every time you move the mouse. Microsoft doesn't offer this feature for the IntelliMouse.

Other settings

Some mice, especially trackballs, offer considerably more choices. The Microsoft IntelliMouse, for example, deals with the standard options somewhat differently. This is an example of what you'll see with Microsoft's IntelliMouse installed:

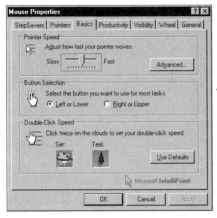

These are the Mouse Properties if you have installed an IntelliMouse.

Click on the "Visibility" tab for options that make it easier to locate your mouse onscreen: set it up so when you press the Control key without touching the mouse, concentric circles will zero in on your mouse pointer.

Many of the options that come with Windows mouse s(like Smart Speed in the StepSavers settings, which slows down the mouse as you roll over icons and buttons) seem like overkill. Others are nice features you might wish you had on your Mac mouse.

Before you decide to make any changes in these properties, click the "Apply" button to see how they look or work. The "Apply" button implements changes without closing the Properties box. When you're done, just click OK to close the box and save the changes (don't click the X button in the upper-right corner or you will lose any of the changes you made!).

If you've got a specialized mouse but you don't see any special settings in the Mouse Properties, check your documentation. Some mouse manufacturers, like Kensington, include a completely different set of property sheets which do not install in the Control Panel or as part of Mouse Properties (although changes in Mouse Properties will affect how these mice work). You'll need to install any software that came with your mouse to take advantage of any extra options it offers. Once you've done so, look for a new mouse icon in the Taskbar tray (see Chapter 8 for details), or check your Start Menu to find your mouse software.

Mouse emulation on a Mac

If you want to use a software emulation of Windows or an add-on board like the OrangePC, you need a way to access those right-hand mouse button functions.

Add-on boards sometimes come with a PS/2 port (see Chapter 3) which will allow you to use a standard Windows two- or three-button mouse as long as you load the required driver in Windows. Boards that don't, like Apple's PC Compatibility Card, will recognize a Mac's two-button mouse or touch pad. There are several varieties of two-button Mac mouse devices on the market, and they work perfectly well on both platforms.

On the other hand, some of us are on budgets or hope to use the Windows side of our Mac as little as possible—we don't necessarily want proof of its existence staring us in the face every morning. If you fall into this category, you can use the keyboard to emulate the right click. How you do this depends on which software or hardware solution you've chosen.

The PC Compatibility Card maps the right-click to the equal sign (=) on the numeric keypad (not the equal sign that's in the row of numbers across the top of the keyboard). This means you can press the equal sign and the right-click menu will appear. Frankly, this is a bit of a pain, especially if you're left-handed or use some alternative form of input like a tablet or touchpad. Many of the newer emulation and hardware alternatives use the Command-click combination instead, which is fairly intuitive and easy to remember and find.

Part Two

Controlling the Desktop

Things are seldom what they seem;
Skim milk masquerades as cream.

—Gilbert and Sullivan

Anatomy of a Window

Desktop windows are the fundamental building blocks of both the Mac and Windows. They help us visualize collections of code as real, tangible objects. How we look at and arrange our windows affects the way we work and how we organize and catalog our files. Fortunately for Mac users, the way Windows now displays and organizes digital documents is similar enough to a Mac that we needn't learn a whole new system. This chapter is a comparative anatomy lesson where we dissect window elements on Windows and measure them against the Mac versions.

Windows in Windows

Macs have two slightly different kinds of windows. There are **folder windows** on the Desktop that show you the contents of a disk or folder. And inside of applications there are **document windows** that often have extra elements, like rulers at the top or buttons in the lower-left corner. Other than these application-specific extras in the document windows, the two window types are basically the same. You can arrange and work with them as you'd like without having to remember which one is which.

But there are three different types of Windows on a PC—folder windows, application windows, and document windows—and they operate in distinctly different ways.

Desktop folder windows

Folder windows act a lot like Mac folder windows, although they have menu bars as well as title bars. The windows for hard disks, floppies, CDs, and removable disks are also called "folder" windows.

Application windows

When you launch an application, the application opens into its own window. Most of the time application windows open to cover the entire Desktop and hide everything else on the screen.

Although it has a title bar, close buttons, and other window elements, an application window is more like another Desktop. It has its own menu bar and its own Desktop area where document windows open. In most applications you have to close or minimize the window before you can use the regular Desktop—you can't just move the application window to the side.

Document windows

So you open an application window, and then your document opens in a document window *inside* the application window. A document window has a title bar, but no menu bar.

The most confusing thing about this document window inside an application window is that you can end up with two sets of scroll bars. And the application window can cover up the scroll bars of the document window. So just be aware that this can happen, and when it does, resize the application window so you can see your document window edges.

A typical Desktop folder window

The window below is typical of just about any *folder* window you might find on the Desktop. (*Document* windows, the ones that are inside *application* windows, have a title bar but not a menu.)

As on a Mac, the **title bar** displays the name of the folder, disk, or file. In Windows, the title bar also displays several resizing buttons that let you determine how to display the window. To Mac users, these Windows buttons are just different enough from our familiar Mac boxes, such as the zoom box, close box, or resize box, to confuse us.

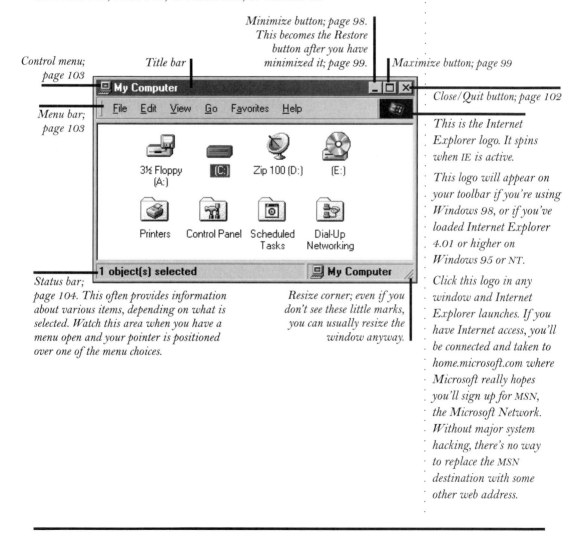

*Minimize button; page 98.
This becomes the Restore
button after you have
minimized it; page 99.*

*Control menu;
page 103*

Title bar

Maximize button; page 99

Close/Quit button; page 102

*Menu bar;
page 103*

*This is the Internet
Explorer logo. It spins
when IE is active.*

*This logo will appear on
your toolbar if you're using
Windows 98, or if you've
loaded Internet Explorer
4.01 or higher on
Windows 95 or NT.*

*Status bar;
page 104. This often provides information
about various items, depending on what is
selected. Watch this area when you have a
menu open and your pointer is positioned
over one of the menu choices.*

*Resize corner; even if you
don't see these little marks,
you can usually resize the
window anyway.*

*Click this logo in any
window and Internet
Explorer launches. If you
have Internet access, you'll
be connected and taken to
home.microsoft.com where
Microsoft really hopes
you'll sign up for MSN,
the Microsoft Network.
Without major system
hacking, there's no way
to replace the MSN
destination with some
other web address.*

Minimize button

This is the Minimize button, found on the right end of the title bar.

The **Minimize button** doesn't have an exact duplicate on the Mac. In Windows, it helps you keep the Desktop uncluttered while keeping the windows readily available. Click the Minimize button to *hide* the window, but not *close* it; a button for the minimized window appears in the Taskbar at the bottom of the screen. If you want the window open again, click its button.

1. If it isn't already open, open the window for "My Computer."

2. Look at the Taskbar (the bar across the bottom of the screen). When you open a window, a button representing it appears on the Taskbar, as shown below.

active: An active window is the one in front; if there's a bunch of windows, the active one is the one on top.

This is the Taskbar at the bottom of the screen (your Taskbar probably looks a little different). Notice the "depressed" button for the window "My Computer." That's a visual clue telling you that particular window is open and active *on the Desktop.*

3. Now click once on the Minimize button in the title bar; the window disappears from the Desktop. Look at the Taskbar; "My Computer" is now a raised button, as shown below. This indicates that the window for "My Computer" is *live* (not actually closed), but it's not active; it might not even be visible.

This is what "raised" buttons look like. This particular Taskbar indicates there are two "live" windows on this computer, but neither of them is the active window.

4. In the Taskbar, **click once** on the "My Computer" button. Its window is restored to the Desktop, and its button on the Taskbar is again depressed.

The more windows you keep open on the Desktop, the more buttons you'll get in the Taskbar. When the Taskbar runs out of room, it makes each button shorter so they'll all fit, even if the names won't fit on the buttons. Although many windows can be open, only one window can be *active* at a time, on the Mac or in Windows.

Maximize and Restore buttons

The **Maximize button** is just like the Mac "zoom" box that toggles
between two different sizes. Maximize enlarges the window to fill the
entire screen. If you have maximized the window, click the **Restore
button** to resize the large window back to the size it was previously. You
will generally see only one of these buttons at a time in the title bar
(except for document windows; see pages 100–101).

*The Maximize button
(left) and the Restore
button (right) act like
the Macintosh zoom box.*

To experiment with maximizing and restoring a window

1. If you don't already have a window open on the Desktop,
   open one now.

2. Click once on the active window's Maximize button. The
   window expands to fill the entire Desktop. Notice the Maximize
   button changes to its alternate version, called Restore (shown
   above, right).

3. Click the Restore button to restore the window to its smaller size
   and former position. The button changes back to the Maximize
   button. When you're in one window size, the button shows you
   the alternative size.

A maximized window might cover the Taskbar. You can customize
whether or not the Taskbar displays in front of the maximized window
or sits behind it; see Chapter 8.

Minimizing and Restore shortcuts

If you have lots of open windows and want to clear your Desktop
quickly, hold down the Windows key (the one with the Windows logo
on it) and tap the letter M. This minimizes all your windows at once. It
does not *close* them! Each window will have a button in the Taskbar.

To put the windows back the way they were, hold down the Windows
key and the Shift key, and tap the letter M. All of the minimized
windows will appear again.

Minimizing and maximizing *document* windows

When you launch an application, it opens in a window which is usually in full-screen, maximized view. It isn't always possible to have more than one application *visible* on the screen at one time, although several applications might be *live* in the background. Whether you can put two **application windows** side by side depends on the way each of the applications has been programmed—some applications let you resize their windows so you can view other application windows, but many do not. For instance, if you open Microsoft Works, you can't see anything else but Works; if you open PageMaker and Photoshop, you can see both applications side by side.

How a window resizes is determined by the individual applications, not by Windows itself. Thus the Maximize button in an *application* window can act differently than it does on a Desktop *folder* window. You'll just have to experiment and discover how your favorite applications handle resizing their windows.

Every **document** is in its own **window,** and that window is inside the *application's* window. You can open a number of documents in each of your applications in Windows, just as you can on your Mac. And you can minimize each document window in the application, just as you can "roll up" each window on the Mac. You'll notice, as shown on the opposite page, that in Windows a minimized document window displays both the Maximize and Restore buttons at the same time. Click Maximize to open the window to a full screen; click Restore to open the window to the size it was before you minimized it.

Keep in mind that a document is in a window, and that *document window* is inside of an *application window.* You can usually resize the *application window* independently of the *document window.* For instance, if the scroll bars on a *document window* disappear, they might just be covered up by the *application window.* Resize the *application window* so you can see all of the *document window.*

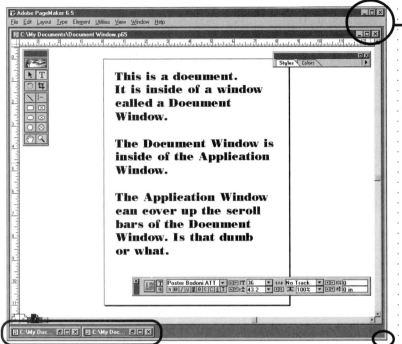

Notice the document *window has a title bar, and the* application *window has a title bar. If you click the Close button in the* document *window, it will close that document, but if you click the Close button in the* application *window, it will* **quit** *the application without even asking you. Sheesh.*

These are the minimized windows for other documents. Notice they are not in the regular Taskbar, but in the applications' own "docking" area. You might have to resize the active document window to see these minimized buttons. (Too bad you can't see the names of the files in the buttons, hmm? Not all applications treat the buttons like this—most you can actually read.)

Important: *You can resize most application windows (not Microsoft Works), even if you don't see any visual clue. Try it—position your pointer on the bottom-right corner of an application window; if the pointer turns into a two-headed diagonal arrow, you can press-and-drag to resize the window. For instance, even though there is no visual clue in the window shown above, you really can resize both the application window and the document window by dragging their corners.*

Close button

This is the Close button. It's also the Quit button if you happen to click on it in the last open window in an application.

In a Windows title bar, the **Close button** is on the right, the button with the X on it. This position is different from the Macintosh close box and is one of the hardest things for a long-time Macophile to get used to. The Close button functions differently in Windows, also, which adds to the frustration.

When you have an open *folder window* on the Desktop, such as the Control Panel folder or "My Computer," Windows acts the way you expect it to:

- Click the Close button and the window is gone. It works just like the close box on a Mac. All references to the window have disappeared from the Taskbar. **OR:**

- You can use a keyboard shortcut at the Windows Desktop to close *folder windows:* press Alt F4. (This is similar to pressing Command W on a Mac to close active windows.)

Close vs. Quit

Warning: **At the Desktop, you can close *folder* windows with the shortcut Alt F4.**

BUT if you try to close *document windows* with Alt F4, you will instead QUIT the application! So:

Close *folder windows* with Alt F4.

Close *document windows* with Control F4.

Close *application windows* (QUIT) with Alt F4.

Now this is one of those things about Windows that will make you crazy: if you click on a *document's* Close button, the *document* will close. But if you click on the *application's* Close button (which of course looks **exactly the same**), the *application* will **QUIT** without even asking you (if you have unsaved documents, you will be asked if you want to save them). Or if you're in a program like a World Wide Web browser and you have several different browsing windows open—you can close them up, but if you happen to close the last one, ooops—it quits. No warning. Windows doesn't know the difference between close and quit.

It takes a long time to get used to this. Mac users, particularly those who move from one platform to the other, are always re-launching programs they never meant to quit.

If you have enough memory to keep lots of files open, the easiest way to avoid this time-wasting behavior is to *minimize* documents rather than *close* them. When you're finished working in the application and intentionally hit the Close/Quit button, all the open documents will close with the application.

The Control menu

If you click the icon in the left corner of the title bar, you'll see the Control menu, which is another way to open, close, and resize a window. The Control menu is left over from the days of Windows 3.x when you couldn't just pick up and move a window, resize it from the corner, or even close it with a mouse click. (Isn't it always interesting to see how much of the Mac interface Windows has "borrowed," yet Windows users will tell you the Mac is "so far behind Windows." Sheesh.) As a Mac user, we don't think you'll have much use for this Control menu—you can ignore it.

This is the Control menu.

The Desktop folder window menu bar

Probably the first thing you missed when you turned on the PC was the familiar Macintosh **menu bar** across the top of the screen. On a PC, there is no menu bar across the top of the Desktop; instead *every folder and application window has its own menu bar.* Use a Windows window menu bar exactly as you would a Mac Desktop menu bar, either with the mouse to pull down the menus or with keyboard shortcuts.

In Windows, the menu options in every window can be different, even though some very familiar labels (File, Edit, View, Help) appear.

Although most of the menu options are so much like the Mac's you'll feel comfortable with them immediately, the File menu needs some explanation. On the Mac, the Desktop File menu is always the same; in Windows, there is a variety of commands in the File menu, and they change according to the type of folder that's open. Sometimes the same File menu will change its contents depending on which icon you have selected in the folder window. Eventually you will have a sense of what to expect, but don't ever expect it to be consistent.

In Windows 98, the menu bar includes two additional options to accommodate the integration of Internet Explorer, a browser application, into the Windows interface: "Go" (a list of recent Desktop and Internet destinations) and "Favorites" (a bookmark list of local or Internet addresses). These additional options allow you to keep track of your web activity from every folder window. You can use "Go" like a shortcut menu to bring you to a recently closed folder even if you aren't connected to the Internet. "Favorites," however, is only useful if you're using Internet Explorer (as opposed to a Netscape browser) to browse the Internet or an intranet.

The status bar

The bottom strip of an open window is called the **status bar.** It displays a variety of information, depending on what is selected in the window or highlighted in a menu.

Open the window for "My Computer," then click once on the C: drive icon. The status bar will display information about the disk's size and available space.

Note: If you don't see the disk size, it's because your window is too narrow—drag the bottom-right corner to the right to enlarge the window.

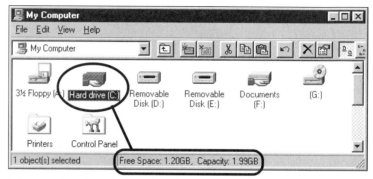

The status bar shows information about the selected file.

When you slide the pointer over a menu command, the information in the status bar is replaced with a line of copy explaining the command. This status bar feature is somewhat like the Mac's Balloon Help, but less wordy. As with Balloons, it's a nice feature if you're new to the PC. If you want to turn off these messages so they never appear:

- From the Views menu, choose "Status Bar" to uncheck it. Just click once to toggle it on or off.

Remember, by turning off the status bar you'll turn off any and all information displayed on it, including the disk space available.

If you resize a window to make it narrow, you'll notice the status bar information disappears. This is very annoying.

Note: You won't see any status information for a *removable* disk in "My Computer" status bar even if the disk is inserted into its drive because Windows doesn't mount removable disks until you force it to. To see the status information, double-click the removable disk icon to open its own window; you'll find the information in the disk window status bar.

Arranging files in a Desktop folder window

No two people like their window information displayed the same way. Some people swear by lists of files; others refuse to work with anything except large icons. As a Mac user, you're accustomed to changing views to suit your needs, and you have as many options in Windows as you do on a Mac. Every window has a View menu:

Windows 95 View menu.

Windows 98 View menu.

Windows 98 browser interface menu.

If you choose "List" from the View menu, the result looks like a Mac list, but there are no details at all, such as date or size—just a tiny icon and the name. If you have a very busy folder, the List view can be nice because it arranges files in multiple columns, as shown below, so you don't have to scroll down:

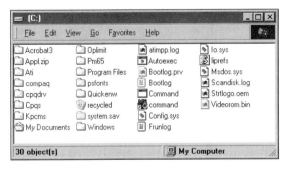

This is the List view.

Sorting and arranging columns

On the previous page, you arranged the files in the List view and noticed that you don't have information about any of the items. If you want a list of files with information about each file, choose "Details" from the View menu. You will get various information in columns, depending on the window you're in and what files it holds. Experiment with opening different folders and viewing by Details to see how different the details can be—try the Control Panel folder, the C: drive folder, and the "My Computer" folder. This will help you learn not to expect consistency.

Once you are viewing by Details, you can sort (organize) the information in different ways by clicking on the different column headings. For instance, if you want your files alphabetized by name, click the "Name" heading. If you want them alphabetized by name backwards, click "Name" again. Unlike a Mac, there is no visual clue in the heading that tells you how the files are currently sorted.

Sort the list: Click a column heading to sort by that feature.

Click the same heading again to sort by the same feature, but in the opposite direction (such as by size, largest to smallest or smallest to largest, as shown in these examples).

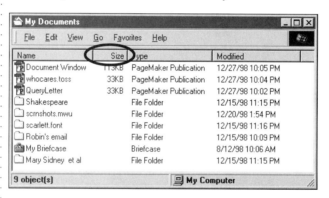

Resize the columns: When your pointer is positioned over the dividing bar between two columns, it will change to a two-headed arrow, as shown. Press-and-drag the dividing bar to resize.

Change the order of the columns: Press in any column heading and drag to the left or right.

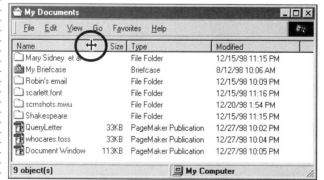

Sorting and arranging icons

Both Mac and Windows allow you to arrange your window icons in a number of different ways. In Windows, use the View menu and slide down to "Arrange Icons."

If you have a group of icons loose in a window and want them neatly aligned in rows, you'd choose "Clean Up" on a Mac. In Windows, "Line up Icons" does the same thing.

Once you have the icons neatly arranged, it's a pain to have to rearrange them when you change the window shape. On the Mac, to make the icons reorganize themselves whenever you change the size of the window, you probably know you can open the window, go to the View menu, choose "View Options...," then choose "Keep arranged." You can do a similar trick on the PC.

To make the the icons arrange themselves automatically

1. First make sure you are viewing the window by icons, either large or small (use the View menu).

2. From the View menu, slide down to "Arrange Icons," then click on the sorting method you want (by name, type, size, or date).

3. Go back to the View menu, slide down to "Arrange Icons," and click "Auto Arrange."

Windows cannot calculate folder sizes inside of an open window. That limits the usefulness of sorting based on size, whether you choose icons or a detailed list. The other ways you can sort on a Mac, such as label, comments, or the creation date as opposed to the modification date, are unavailable on the PC because Windows doesn't have those features.

Windows "Arrange Icons" options.

Arrange icons on the Desktop

If the icons on your Desktop rearrange themselves every time you move one (which makes you crazy), you can stop that awful behavior by using a technique similar to the one above.

To make the the icons STOP arranging themselves automatically on the Desktop

1. Right-click on the Desktop.

2. From the menu that pops up, choose "Arrange icons," then uncheck "Auto Arrange."

Options for opening windows

On a Mac, when you open a folder that's inside a window, the previous window stays open (unless you hold down the Option key when you double-click the folder icon). If you want to go back to a previous window, it's still sitting there. In Windows, you can choose to have windows open in this same manner, or you can choose to have the new window *replace* the previous one. (The default on a new PC might be to *replace* the previous window when you open a new one, which can really make you crazy if you don't know how to work with it.)

When you opt to replace open windows with new ones, the contents of the new folder you choose replace the previous contents of the old folder. The window itself remains a fixed size, no matter how the contents of the new window compare to what was in the window before. Using this method keeps your Desktop uncluttered and minimizes the number of windows you need to close when you're ready to shut down.

Navigating replaced windows

If you choose to browse your windows using a single window, you can use the File menu to go back to a previous window, as shown below.

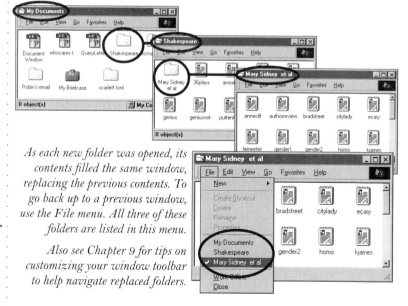

Macintosh tip: To view the hierarchy of folders on the Mac like you see in the File menu here, hold down the Command key and press on the name in the title bar of any Desktop window.

As each new folder was opened, its contents filled the same window, replacing the previous contents. To go back up to a previous window, use the File menu. All three of these folders are listed in this menu.

Also see Chapter 9 for tips on customizing your window toolbar to help navigate replaced folders.

To choose to use a single open window or many separate windows in Windows 98 (see the following page for Windows 95 and NT):

1. In the window menu bar, click "View," then click "Folder Options" to get the dialog box.

2. The General settings should be showing (click the General tab if not). Click the "Custom" option, and then click the "Settings…" button (the "Settings…" button is only active after you select the "Custom" option). This will bring up the Custom Settings dialog box.

3. In the section called "Browse folders as follows," choose the method you prefer. Click OK to close the box (if you click the X in the Close box, your settings will not be saved!).

   Whatever you choose will apply to every Desktop window on your computer, not just to the window you had open when you changed the option!

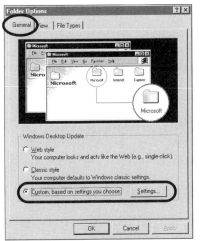 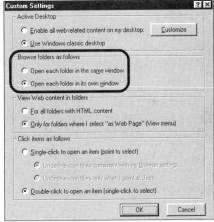

Check "Custom, based on settings you choose" then click the "Settings…" button to access the settings, shown to the right.

At any time you can open any folder window and go back to the Folder Options to change how the Desktop windows are displayed. The File menu, as you saw, changes depending on the contents inside the window, but you can always choose "Folder Options" from the View menu in any Desktop window.

To choose to use a single open window or many separate windows in Windows 95 or NT

1. In the window menu bar, click "View," then click "Options." This gives you the Options property sheet for Desktop windows.

2. Click the "Folder" tab if it isn't already in front.

3. Choose your option to browse folders with separate windows for each folder, or one single window that gets replaced with the contents of another folder.

4. If you want to save your settings, click the OK button. If you click the Close box with the X in it, none of your settings will be saved!

Whatever you choose will apply to every Desktop window on your computer, not just to the window you had open when you changed the option!

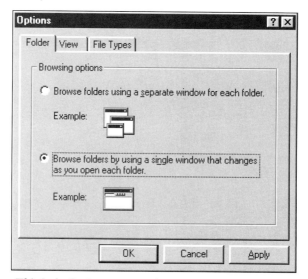

This is the Options property sheet.

This Options property sheet has several other tabs with more settings, but they don't really have a lot to do with arranging windows. We'll explore other aspects of the "View" settings later in the book.

Closing many windows

Of course, there are lots of good reasons to have many windows open at once. But having lots of windows open means having lots of windows to close. Clicking each Close button takes time.

There are two ways to deal with Desktop window clutter quickly. You probably know that on your Mac, you can press Command Option W and all the windows on the Desktop will close, or you can hold down the Option key and click in any window close box to close all the windows.

To close lots of windows with keyboard shortcuts

1. Open a number of folders.
2. Hold down the Shift key, and click once on a Close button (the X). **Or** press Shift Alt F4.

This Windows shortcut is not as smart as the Mac shortcut: it will close only windows that are nested inside of each other, and of those it will only close the windows that are higher in the hierarchy. For instance, let's say you open Window 1, then double-click a folder inside that one called Window 2, and keep opening folder windows until you have 5 windows on the screen that all nest into Window 1. If you Shift-click the Close button on Window 5, all 5 windows will close. *But* if you Shift-click the Close button on Window 3, only Windows 1, 2, and 3 will close; all other windows will be left open. Also, if you open nested folders from one of Window's special folders, such as My Documents or Control Panel, the special window will always stay open until you manually close it. Sheesh.

Windows offers you another Mac-like alternative. You might have used the shortcut on the Mac where you hold down the Option key as you double-click a window, and the previous window closes up. In Windows:

1. Open the window for "My Computer."
2. Hold down the Control key, and double click on the C: drive to open it. The contents of the C: drive will replace the contents of "My Computer" in the open window.

Closing many property sheets

Even though dialog boxes (sometimes called "property sheets" in Windows) also have a title bar, you can't use these keyboard shortcuts to close them all at once. If you open a series of property sheets, you'll have to go back and close each and every one of them. Do use the Alt F4 shortcut, though.

Moving a window

Move a window in exactly the same way you do on the Mac: drag the title bar. Be careful not to double-click it by mistake: On the Mac, a double-click on the title bar usually "rolls up" the window. In Windows, a double-click on the title bar zooms the window to full screen. If you do accidentally double-click on the title bar, just double-click again to restore the window to its previous size.

Locked windows

If you try to drag or copy a file into a folder window and you see this symbol, it's a visual clue that the folder is locked.

Some folder windows, such as the one for "My Computer," are locked. How can you tell if a window is locked? There is no thoughtful lock icon that you're used to on the Mac; no, in Windows you just have to figure it out manually.

Try this: Open the window for "My Computer," and open the window for the C: drive. Try to drag any document from the C: drive window into the window for "My Computer." The ghost copy image of the file you drag will be covered by the "forbidden" symbol, shown to the left, to indicate you can't do that because the folder window is locked.

The only way to add items to locked folder windows is to install them. In some ways this is nice, in a kind of protect-me-from-myself way. Other times this restriction just feels frustrating, like when you really would like to put an alias of something in a locked folder window to make it easy to get someplace specific. (Yes, Windows does have aliases, called "shortcuts." See Chapter 17.)

Applying a view to all windows (Windows 98)

Most of us use a variety of views because no one method serves all needs. Lists are nice when you need something specific in a very full folder. Icons are friendlier and better for recognizing categories and types of files. Many times, however, you need to look through several windows in a row for the same purpose. Windows 98 gives you the option to apply one type of view to all windows. *This is a **global change**, which means it will apply to every single folder window on your computer.*

To change every folder window on your Desktop to a particular setting:

1. Arrange a window's settings to suit your needs.

2. From the menu bar of this perfect window, choose "View," then click "Folder Options...."

3. In the Folder Options property sheet, click the "View" tab.

4. In the top section of the View settings, click the button "Like Current Folder" to switch every folder on your hard drive to the same view options as the folder you're currently in.

Windows isn't as smart as the Mac when it comes to updating the screen with new information, so any windows you already have open when you change views will retain their old views. The only way to update their look is to close them, then open them again. Choosing "Refresh" from the View menu doesn't work, even though updating views is exactly why the Refresh button exists. Sheesh.

Folder Options includes a new property sheet in Windows 98. It still has the "View" and "File Types" settings that are in the Options property sheet in Windows 95 and NT, but the "General" settings has taken the place of the one called "Folder." Among other things, "General" is where you can choose between the Internet Explorer browser interface (see pages 115–119) and the "classic" interface.

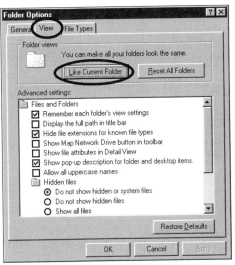

Warning: *There's no way to undo this global change after you click OK! The other button at the top, "Reset All Folders," is terribly misleading—it will change all your folders back to the **Windows default setting,** which is large icons, **not** to the individual arrangements you might have set up in different folders as you worked.*

Keeping the views you choose (Windows 98)

Here's another feature of Windows that can drive you completely mad. On your Mac, you're accustomed to setting your window preferences and trusting they will stay that way. But in Windows, one day you're going to open a folder you had customized to your liking and find that everything has changed. A window arranged by "Type" in "Detail" view will be in large icons again, unsorted. This doesn't mean your system crashed. It means the place where Windows stored that information has been written over by something else. There's no way to get the settings back—you just have to redo them.

Unless you're using Windows 98, that is. Take a look at the "Folder Options" property sheet, below. In the scrolling list called "Advanced settings," you see various options for "Files and Folders." If you check the first option, "Remember each folder's view settings," Windows will remember your settings instead of deleting them. This box is checked by default when Windows 98 is installed so you shouldn't have to worry about an infestation of large icons if you don't want them.

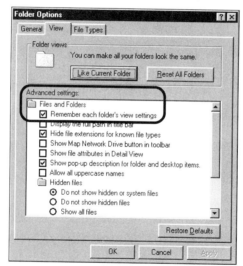

The browser interface (Windows 98)

One of the most controversial aspects of Windows 98 is its new "browser" interface. If you use this interface, your computing experience will not only look and feel quite different from classic Windows, it will be quite a change from the Macintosh OS. If you've ever used browser software, like Microsoft Internet Explorer, Netscape Navigator, or Netscape Communicator, the major features of this new Desktop interface will feel less foreign to you.

Although this browser interface is not the default on a new Windows 98 computer, someone might have chosen it for your machine or you may run across it on someone else's system. We'll explain what the browser interface offers so you can decide if you'd like to try it for yourself.

The two portions of Windows 98 that make up the new browser interface are called **Web style** and **Active Desktop.** Web style makes every folder window you open look and act like a web page; Active Desktop does the same thing to the whole Desktop, making it possible to incorporate pictures, animations, links, and other web elements into the space that usually just holds Desktop elements and icons. Although Active Desktop is turned on by default when you choose Web style, the two are independent—you can turn one off without affecting the other.

To turn Web style on

1. Open "My Computer" (or any other folder). From its View menu, choose "Folder Options...."

2. In the "Folder Options" dialog box, click the tab labeled "General" (it's probably already in front, waiting for you).

3. Click "Web style." Click OK.

   (continued on next page)

   Click the Apply button and the preview will display a "Web style" version of a Desktop window.

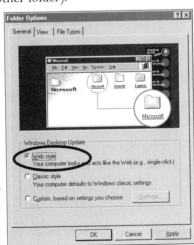

Why is this portion of Windows 98 controversial? Because the browser interface uses Microsoft Internet Explorer. Thus Microsoft's browser is now completely integrated into Windows 98 and is literally impossible to remove. There is no easy way for someone who doesn't like or want to use Internet Explorer as their browser to use a Netscape product instead. The Internet Explorer interface was the major focus of the U.S. government's law suit against Microsoft.

To turn Web style off

Follow the same steps for turning it on, but choose the "Classic style" button instead.

4. Windows recognizes that switching to the "Web style" is a serious decision since it's about to make a major change in how you use your mouse. It gives you a dialog box asking if you really want to use the "single-click" option. If you choose "Yes," your Desktop will change in the ways described below.

What Web style does

We mentioned above that Web style makes your computer act like a browser program. Browser interaction is different from regular Windows (or Mac) actions in these ways:

- **Mousing.** This is the most important change. Instead of single-clicking to select an item, you merely point to an icon to select it. Instead of double-clicking to open or launch an item, you single-click it. This change takes place for all mousing:

To do this	Classic style	Web style
Select	Single-click	Point (hover over)
Open	Double-click	Single-click
Select multiple icons	Ctrl-click	Press Ctrl while pointing
Select groups of icons	Shift-click	Press Shift while pointing

- **Icon names.** The names of icons are underlined, like text links on a web page.

- **Window appearance.** On the opposite page you see the new look that Web style bestows on your folders. If you resize the window smaller, you will see scroll bars between the left and right "frames," or sections of the windows.

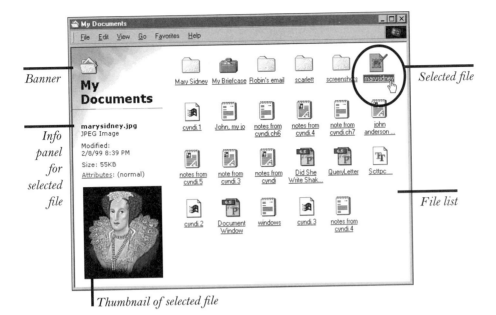

Banner

Selected file

Info panel for selected file

File list

Thumbnail of selected file

Web style *separates a folder into two "frames." On the right side, the* **file list** *frame displays icons. The icons look the same as they do in the Classic style, but their names are underlined.*

In the top of the left frame is the **banner** *that identifies the folder. Notice the banner is actually the name of the folder.*

If you click on an icon in the file list, information about it appears in the **info panel,** *which is in the bottom portion of the left frame.*

If the selected icon is a file type that web pages can read (like .htm and .jpg) you'll also see a **thumbnail preview** *of that selected file, as shown above.*

Customizing your folder window appearance

Web style allows you to customize this new folder window appearance. You can replace the plain white background with a picture. If you know how to edit a web page with HTML code, you can make sweeping changes in how a folder looks.

- **Open folders.** Any nested folders you open after changing to Web style will display in single-window format (see page 109). If you have the standard folder toolbar open (see Chapter 9 for more about toolbars), you'll be able to move back and forth through these nested folders using the Back and Forward toolbar buttons.

- **Active Desktop.** Choosing Web style turns Active Desktop on. Whatever background you may have set previously in your Desktop Settings (see Chapter 12 for more on customizing your Desktop) is replaced by the basic Active Desktop. This is a brilliant, deep blue background with (of course) a Microsoft Windows 98 logo in the upper right.

Active Desktop

JPEG file: Typically a digital photograph.

Java applets: "Java" is a programming language often used to program web applications. "Applets" are little applications that are relatively easy to write and are activated on a web server.

Although Active Desktop turns on as part of the Web style setting, it's a completely separate function. It allows you to create a web page to take the place of the simple Desktop background. The Desktop web page can hold any elements that you could put on a web page on the Internet, from simple *JPEG files* to complicated *Java applets*. You can also add Active Desktop components, like a clock, ticker tape, and a weather map; download these things at www.microsoft.com (follow the links at the site to Internet Explorer 4.0 or 5.0).

Browser interface pros and cons

Does it make sense to use the browser interface? Many Windows users, particularly those who are already very familiar with the Internet Explorer browser, like these changes in the Desktop environment. But what about Mac users?

Good things about the browser interface

- Single-click mousing is easier on the hands.
- If you love Internet Explorer and mostly use a computer for the Internet, the learning curve on Windows will be fairly easy.
- The info frame in the Web style window is almost like having a Get Info box right in your folder window.
- If you love your relatives, friends and pets, you can have pictures of them in every window you open.

Irritating things about the Web style browser interface

- On the Internet, when you accidentally double-click a link or icon, the second click is just ignored. On the Windows Desktop, though, a double-click can result in unwanted open windows and applications. If you plan on moving back and forth between the Mac and Windows, you'll have a much harder time retraining yourself to work in Windows.
- It's not Netscape. Long-time Internet Explorer foes may find this interface makes it even harder to accept working on a PC.
- The web page look for folders can be useful, but it's a terrible Desktop real estate hog. All of your windows need to be wider to accommodate the new layout. If you don't have a large monitor (or two), you'll feel cramped.
- The one-window browsing set-up will drive you slightly nuts, especially if you like to organize work by dragging files between open windows.
- Active Desktop sounds like an interesting idea, but ends up making it hard to separate the disk icons from the hectic Desktop activity. The most interesting downloadable functions (like the stock ticker tape and weather map) require that you be connected to the Internet; otherwise they're just flashing wallpaper. And it takes so long to refresh the screen that you'll have time to make a fresh pot of coffee.

Mix and match Desktops

Cyndi admits that she really doesn't like most of these Internet Explorer functions, particularly the Web style mouse actions. Sometimes, though, she finds the web page folder arrangement useful—she likes being able to select a file and immediately see its size, date, and a decent-sized thumbnail. Fortunately, you can select portions of the browser interface without swallowing the entire menu.

To pick and choose Desktop features

1. Follow the instructions on page 115 to turn on "Web style." When you get to the "Folder Options" dialog box, choose the button for "Custom, based on settings you choose."

2. Then click the "Settings..." button. Here, each of the separate elements that comprise the browser interface can be turned on or off.

   - **To turn off Active Desktop,** choose "Use Windows classic desktop" button.

   - **To turn off the web page look in folders,** choose "Only for folders where I select 'as Web Page.'" This allows you to pick those folders where the added information can be useful.

   - **To return to double-clicking,** choose "Double-click to open an item." Notice that when you return to double-clicking, your icon names are no longer underlined, even if you still have "View Web content in folders" set to "For all folders with HTML content."

The Taskbar and Start Menu

The **Taskbar,** the gray bar at the bottom of your desktop, is one of the most versatile items on the Windows Desktop. Think of it as a multi-function organizer that keeps track of your windows and applications. As we discussed in Chapter 7, the Taskbar acts as a holding shelf and launching pad for all of your open, but minimized, windows. It also provides tools so you can arrange your Desktop to suit the way you work.

But the Taskbar is more than a Desktop cleaning service. Just as the Macintosh menu bar holds the Apple menu, the Windows Taskbar holds the **Start Menu,** which is an all-important Windows element. This chapter introduces you to the Taskbar roles.

Arranging windows on the Windows Desktop

Windows provides several methods to help you tidy up the windows and icons on your Desktop. As you know from Chapter 7, you can always minimize windows and let them sit on the Taskbar. But often you need several windows open at the same time, like when you want to drag a file from one open window to another, or compare the contents of two or more folders. The Taskbar gives you access to several Desktop configurations that make multiple windows accessible and tidy.

The illustration below shows a disorganized Desktop. Open windows are all over the screen, and many of them overlap each other. What can you do?

Use the Taskbar menu to create order out of chaos. There are several options for arranging the windows.

To use the Taskbar menu to tile windows

1. Position the pointer on a blank spot on the Taskbar (where there aren't any buttons), and right-click:

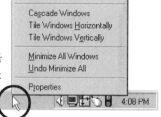

To get the Taskbar properties, right-click on an empty part of the Taskbar.

2. From the pop-up menu (shown above), choose either "Tile Windows Horizontally" or "Tile Windows Vertically."

Now the open windows are sitting in a neat grid:

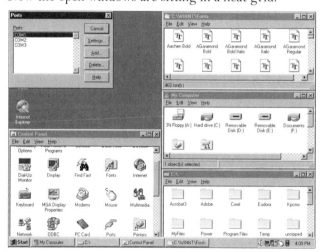

Experiment with horizontal and vertical tiling to see how they differ. You'll get a sense of which layout is best for different windows; for instance, you might want your email window horizontal so you can see all the data across the row, but you might want a vertical arrangement for windows that display lists.

Or try a cascading arrangement

- Right-click on a blank place on the Taskbar. From the menu, choose "Cascade Windows."

Cascading the open windows makes each window title bar visible so you can quickly choose the one you want.

Revert to the previous arrangement

Naturally, the more open windows, the less screen real estate per window. Tiling the windows can hide the Desktop, but that's no big deal—once you've completed whatever task you needed to accomplish, you can return your windows to their previous positions.

- Right-click on a blank place on the Taskbar. From the menu, choose "Undo Tile" or "Undo Cascade" (the menu option changes depending on how the windows are currently arranged). The Desktop will return to its *prior** state.

    * You can only undo the *most recent* Desktop rearrangement. For example, if you tile horizontally and *then* cascade, "Undo Cascade" will only return the windows to the horizontal tile arrangement, not to the original, chaotic screen.

You can undo the most recent arrangement.

Clear the Desktop

The Taskbar offers another really nice clean-up feature. Sometimes you have a lot of windows open and you want to clear the Desktop quickly. In Chapter 7, we showed you several methods for *closing* windows. But sometimes you just want to *minimize* all of them so you still have their buttons on the Taskbar. Try this:

- Right-click on the Taskbar. From the pop-up menu, choose "Minimize All Windows."

  (This command won't minimize property sheets because the Windows operating system doesn't consider them to be windows.)

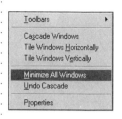

Minimize all the windows at once!

Taskbar icons: Tray interesting

There's a little "tray" on the far right of the Taskbar. Sometimes all it displays is a digital clock; other times it displays a number of tiny icons.

This Taskbar tray is similar to the Macintosh Control Strip that pops out on your Desktop. The icons represent changeable Desktop settings and background utilities. When you position your pointer over one of the icons and wait a second or two, a label pops up to tell you what that icon represents. Click, double-click, or right-click these icons; they will display menus or panels of the settings you can change. There's no standard format for the tray panels, as you can see below:

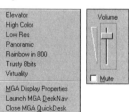

These are panels for Norton Software, the monitor display, and sound.

If nothing appears when you click or double-click one of these icons, don't worry—think of them like the extensions that display when a Mac boots up. They're a reminder that Windows has some process running behind the scenes.

Customizing the Taskbar tray

The icons that display in the Taskbar tray are determined by what startup utilities you have installed. You can only add more icons permanently by installing more software.

Sometimes you can remove an icon from the tray by "closing" it or prevent it from displaying on startup. Whether or not you can do these things depends on the software—since every Windows software developer can do whatever they like without standardizing, it's impossible to predict which icons you can close and which you can't. To find out, double-click on a tray icon and look at its menu, or look for a "View" or "Options" tab in a panel.

If the software will let you customize its icon display, one of its menus or panels will offer a choice like you see here, "Close MGA QuickDesk."

We recommend that you look, but don't touch. Although "closed" icons will just reappear the next time you restart your system, icons you've told the software not to display at all will disappear. Finding the panel again that let you turn them off can be terribly frustrating. When she was just learning Windows, Cyndi turned off her "Volume" icon and later played a CD too loud. She suddenly realized how useful the tray icon was, but couldn't find the panel she'd used to turn it off. After half an hour of cursing, she stumbled upon it in one of the settings in the Multimedia control panel.

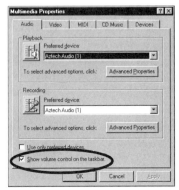

Taskbar Options

Take a look at the options in the Taskbar property sheet.

1. Right-click the Taskbar and choose "Properties" from the menu.

2. There are four checkbox options in the "Taskbar Options" section. Click each option and the little window inside the property sheet shows you what to expect. Try it.

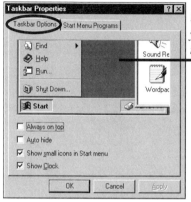

Watch this space when you check or uncheck the various options.

Always on top doesn't mean the Taskbar will appear at the top of the screen—it means it will stay on top of any open windows. If you *uncheck* this box, a maximized window will expand to cover the Taskbar, providing more usable space for the window. But then you can't get to the Taskbar. A flexible arrangement is to *uncheck* "Always on top," and when you need to get to the Taskbar, use the keyboard shortcut Ctrl Esc (Escape key) to bring the Taskbar to the front and open the Start Menu.

Auto hide makes the Taskbar slide gracefully south, leaving only a tiny sliver showing at the screen's edge. Touch the gray Taskbar border, and it floats back up; click on the window and the Taskbar floats back down. Combine "Auto hide" with "Always on top" to get a flexible working environment: application windows expand to fill the screen, but you can always get to the Taskbar.

Show small icons in Start Menu should always be checked because otherwise you get a big, fat Start Menu with a big, fat, blue Windows logo border.

Show Clock will display the clock in the Taskbar.

Resizing the Taskbar

The Taskbar fills up with buttons very quickly. You can easily create a second row (or more) for buttons.

1. Position your pointer on the edge of the Taskbar. The pointer will change to a double-headed resizing tool, as shown below.

2. Press-and-drag upwards, and the Taskbar will grow in thickness one row at a time. Do this in reverse to bring the Taskbar back to the size it was before.

Drag upwards to make the Taskbar thicker.

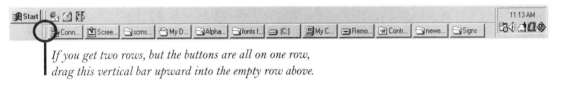

If you get two rows, but the buttons are all on one row,
drag this vertical bar upward into the empty row above.

With two rows of buttons, you can actually read the names on each button.

Tip: If you're in the process of setting up your Desktop work area, experiment with resizing the Taskbar before you add lots of shortcuts (aliases) to the Desktop because when the Taskbar expands, it pushes all aliases into the remaining Desktop space. This usually causes the icons to reposition themselves all over the screen instead of just moving closer together. There's no automatic way to put the icons back where you had them, so if you change your mind about resizing you'll have to move them all back by hand.

Moving the Taskbar and the Start Menu

Want to move the Taskbar to the left margin, or (gasp!) to the top of the screen? Yes, it's really possible to work from the top if you want.

- Press in a blank area on the Taskbar and drag it to one of the other edges of the screen. It may not look like anything is happening while you're dragging, but don't let go! When your pointer gets near an edge of the screen, the Taskbar pops into that position. When it's stuck to the edge you want, let go.

Below are examples of two ways to position your Taskbar. On the left you see a Taskbar that was moved and resized wider. In the right example, the Taskbar is in a Mac-like position at the top of the screen.

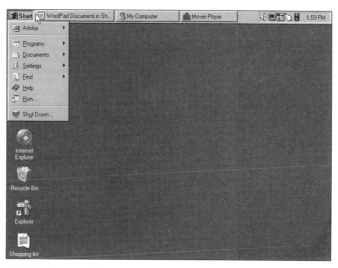

*The Taskbar on the
left of the screen.*

*The Taskbar at the
top of the screen.*

Unfortunately you'll run into a bit of a problem if you put your Taskbar at the top of your screen. Many Windows applications refuse to move their windows down below the Taskbar, which means you won't see the application's menu bar! Most of the time you can drag the window down below the Taskbar manually, but sometimes it's just impossible to grab an active piece of it. Fortunately, there's a very stable, well-behaved shareware product called Shove-It (www.phord.com) that will "shove" windows below the Taskbar for you, and it works well on all versions of Windows.

One of Shove-It's side effects, however, is a little irritating: a default is set so it won't let you drag a window partially off the screen to make room for other windows. If this happens:

1. Right-click the Shove-It icon in the Taskbar tray, and from the pop-up menu, choose Properties.

2. Make sure the "General" tab is selected.

3. In the section labeled "Shove-It from the," uncheck all the boxes except the one labeled "Top," as shown below.

4. Click Apply, then OK to close the property sheet.

Now you'll be able to drag windows off three edges of the screen.

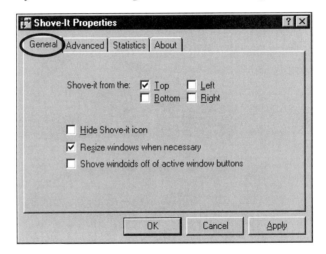

The Start Menu: the Apple menu incognito

On the Mac, everything of importance drops down from the top of the screen. Doesn't it just figure that, in Windows, important things are on the bottom? The Start Menu is the most valuable item on the Taskbar. Despite its funny position in the bottom-left corner, it's the Windows version of the Apple menu. Click once on the Start Menu button, and you'll get something like this:

This is the Start Menu. If the Start Menu button isn't visible, you can open the menu by pressing Ctrl Esc or hitting the Windows key.

You don't have to hold the button down while scrolling up the menu. The Start Menu will stay where it is unless you click somewhere else on the Desktop.

All Windows menus are "sticky"—that is, they don't roll up and disappear when you release the mouse button. In fact, unlike the Mac, they don't ever close without some action from you. The stickier a Windows menu is, the better. Windows is so menu-intensive and the menus can have so many different levels that it would be difficult to navigate the Desktop if they closed up quickly.

You'll notice the Start Menu looks similar to a Macintosh menu, with the little triangles indicating submenus. Once you see your choice of item, just click once on it.

The Start Menu: Programs

Click on Start and slide up to "Programs." In the submenu that pops out is a list of applications and utilities. Windows created some default categories in this Programs menu list, such as "Accessories" (which we'll look at in Chapter 14).

Adding to the Programs menu

When you install new software, the installation process generally puts the name of the program in this list. If you watch carefully during the installation process, you'll notice it usually asks if you want the software name in the Start Menu, and exactly where in the menu do you want the name. Use this opportunity to arrange the Start Menu to suit the way you like to work.

If you always accept the default position for a Start Menu item, or if the installer doesn't give you the chance to make your own choice, the program you want to launch could be four submenus down from the Start button itself. For example, if you have Adobe Illustrator on your machine, your path through the Start Menu to the application itself can look like this:

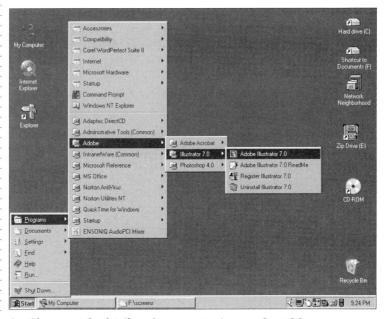

See Chapter 15 for details on how to customize your Start Menu.

The Start Menu: Documents

The "Documents" option in the Start Menu is exactly the same as the Apple menu item on your Mac called "Recent Documents." It contains a list of the files you have been working on. The next time you want to open a file you used recently, you can use this menu rather than dig through your folders to find that document. If you haven't created or opened any files in Windows since you bought the computer, you won't see anything listed in the Documents menu.

This is an example of the Documents list in the Start Menu.

If you or anyone else has been using the computer, you'll find a list of the fifteen most recent documents that have been opened. You might want to clear this list, especially if you're working on a shared computer and you'd rather not broadcast to whoever uses the computer next what you've been doing lately.

To clear the Documents list

1. Right-click on the Taskbar to get the pop-up menu, then click "Properties."

2. Click the "Start Menu Programs" tab. At the bottom of the property sheet, under the section "Documents menu," click "Clear" and your secrets are safe.

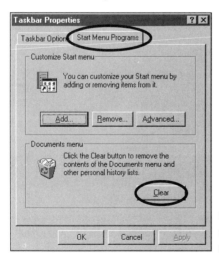

Click the "Clear" button to delete any document names in the Documents menu.

The Start Menu: Settings

The "Settings" option on the Start Menu provides access to the folders for Control Panels and Printers, which are the same folders that are in the window for "My Computer." The Start Menu can be a more convenient way to access these items instead of having to open the window for "My Computer," especially if your Desktop is already full of windows.

There's also a menu option called "Taskbar" in the Settings list, which brings up the same property sheet you get when you right-click on the Taskbar itself.

This redundancy is very typical of the way Windows is organized— there are always multiple roads to the same end. Some people like this because they can use whatever method feels right to them at that particular moment. Don't be intimidated, though—you don't need to memorize *all* the different ways to get to a folder window or a menu, just the one that works best for you.

The Start Menu: Help

It wouldn't hurt to poke around in the Help files. Just choose "Help" from the Start Menu, and the rest is pretty self-explanatory. Choose topics, enter a word to search for information, or go through the tutorials.

The Start Menu: Find

Use the Find command as you would on the Mac. For details about how to use it, see Chapter 20.

The Start Menu: Favorites (Windows 98)

The Favorites item is an example of how the Microsoft Internet Explorer web browser has been integrated into the operating system— Favorites is just a shortcut to the Favorites list in Internet Explorer. Choose an item from this menu, and Windows will dial your modem and attempt to connect you to the web address you've chosen from the Favorites list. If you prefer to use Netscape as your browser, this new feature won't be useful at all since there's no way to replace the Internet Explorer Favorites with Netscape Bookmarks.

The
Toolbars

9

Because operating systems and applications offer so many options, menus have become extensive and complex. Some menu choices are more important than others, though, and it's hard on your hand and patience to drag and click to get at them. Windows uses **toolbars** the way the Mac uses keyboard shortcuts — to provide instant access to frequent actions.

Toolbars are bars of button icons at the top of a window, just below the menu bar. If you use Microsoft Office or any of its components on the Mac, you've at least seen them even if you haven't used them. They're found on all programs and utilities written for Windows, although programs originally designed for the Mac tend to stick with keyboard shortcuts. They're in Desktop folder windows, as well as Open and Save As dialog boxes.

Some Mac users don't care for these button shortcuts. Toolbars on the Mac do take up a lot of the screen, and their non-intuitive pictures make pop-up labels necessary. But in Windows, toolbars can be very useful. They offer an alternative to the ugly, impossible-to-memorize Windows "keyboard shortcuts" that we showed you in Chapter 5.

Displaying Desktop folder window toolbars

Desktop folder windows share a common group of toolbar buttons. In Windows 98, the default is to have the toolbars turned *on* in every window, so if you don't want them you'll have to turn them off. In Windows 95 and NT, the default is to have the toolbars turned *off,* so if you want them you need to turn them on.

There are numerous ways to display the toolbars and menu in each window. Below are examples of some of the possibilities in **Windows 98.** Experiment with the "Toolbars" options in the View menu to see what sort of arrangement you like best. (The View *menu* is different from the "Views" *button* on the toolbar; see page 141 for the button information.)

These are the options in the View menu in Windows 98:

Standard Buttons displays the big buttons in addition to the basic menu.

Address Bar displays the box that looks like the location box in a web browser.

Links adds a toolbar of icons you can click to get to web pages. The contents of the web page open directly in the folder window. See pages 145–146 for details.

Text Labels displays labels for the buttons.

*Just the basic Desktop window **menu**; no toolbars at all.*

*This displays the **Address Bar** and the basic Desktop menu.*

If you don't like the Address Bar and menu on one line, press on the dividing line (as shown below) and drag it downward.

*This window displays the **Standard Buttons** and **Text Labels.** If you don't see all the buttons, open the window wider. Notice the pointer turns into a double-headed arrow on the dividing line between sections—press on a dividing line and drag up or down to rearrange the sections into rows, as shown below.*

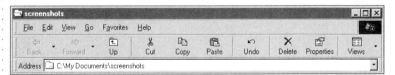

Back and Forward for browsing; see opposite page.

The toolbar options you choose in Windows 98 will apply to every Desktop window. You might *think* you are customizing the toolbars in individual windows because you *can* make three different arrangements in three different open Desktop windows, but if you close all three (close them, don't just minimize them), and then open them again, every window has the same arrangement, which is the last arrangement you chose. Is that annoying or what. (In Windows 95 and NT, when you open a new folder you'll have to turn its toolbar on or off manually. There's no global switch to change the toolbar setting for all windows.)

Back and Forward buttons

The Back and Forward buttons are enabled if you add the Links toolbar to a Desktop window and click on a link (yes, even in the "Classic style" of Desktop folders). As you browse web pages, the Back button will take you back through any web pages you've been to, and back to your files in that folder. The Forward button takes you to pages you've previously backed away from, just like in a browser.

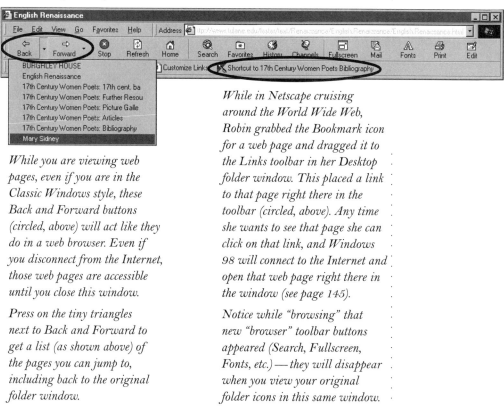

While you are viewing web pages, even if you are in the Classic Windows style, these Back and Forward buttons (circled, above) will act like they do in a web browser. Even if you disconnect from the Internet, those web pages are accessible until you close this window.

Press on the tiny triangles next to Back and Forward to get a list (as shown above) of the pages you can jump to, including back to the original folder window.

While in Netscape cruising around the World Wide Web, Robin grabbed the Bookmark icon for a web page and dragged it to the Links toolbar in her Desktop folder window. This placed a link to that page right there in the toolbar (circled, above). Any time she wants to see that page she can click on that link, and Windows 98 will connect to the Internet and open that web page right there in the window (see page 145).

Notice while "browsing" that new "browser" toolbar buttons appeared (Search, Fullscreen, Fonts, etc.) — they will disappear when you view your original folder icons in this same window.

The toolbars in **Windows 95** and **NT** are quite different from those in Windows 98, although they do use many of the same buttons and icons.

Windows 95 or NT standard toolbar.

"Address" (Windows 98) or "Go to a different folder" (Windows 95/NT)

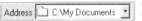

Windows 98 Address field

Windows 95 or NT "Go to a different folder" field

In Windows, the term "folder" is a much broader term than it is on the Mac in that hard disks, floppy disks, CDs, or any removable drives are also considered "folders." The "Address" or "Go to" toolbar element displays the name of the "folder" whose contents are displayed in the window. If you click the downward arrow at the end of the box, you'll see a list of other "folders" you can access. If you are browsing the web in Windows 98 through your Desktop windows, you'll see website addresses here as well.

Even though you might see the *names* of removable drives in the Address list, you'll only be able to choose one if there's actually a disk or cartridge already in the drive.

When you choose one of the disks or folders from the list, the current contents of the window changes to the contents of the chosen disk or folder, although the window itself stays the same. Using this toolbar feature drastically cuts down on the number of windows you have to open and close.

Up one level

This button is called "Up one level."

This toolbar button is an alternative to using the "Address" or "Go to" box. Instead of *replacing* the contents of one window with another's, it opens a *new* window. In the new window are the contents of the folder one level above the one you're working in. This button is useful for transferring files up to a higher, more accessible folder on the same disk or for doubling back to compare folder contents.

The "Up one level" button works nicely when you combine it with the Taskbar cascade option (see pages 123–124) so you can see all the window title bars you've opened.

"Map network drive" and "Disconnect network drive" (Windows 95/NT only)

These buttons are only useful if you have a network in the first place. "Mapping" is what gives a network drive its letter name (such as F: or Z:) and puts its icon inside "My Computer." The "Map network drive" button is a shortcut to the dialog box of the same name. "Disconnect network drive" eliminates the icon and disconnects the network drive. Mapping is better left to a system administrator; apparently Microsoft finally realized this because in Windows 98 you have to use the "Folder Options" under the View menu to put them in your toolbar.

The left button is "Map network drive," and the right button is "Disconnect network drive."

Cut, Copy, Paste, and Undo

Most Mac users would much prefer to use the keyboard shortcuts for the cut, copy, paste, and undo functions than keep the Toolbar open for them. Since Windows has no "Duplicate" command as on a Mac, you can use the "Copy" command to duplicate a file or a folder.

The Cut, Copy, Paste, and Undo buttons.

Delete

Clicking the "Delete" button is the same as dragging something to the Trash. As usual, you need to select an icon before you can delete it. Read Chapter 10 to understand how deleting in Windows is a little different from deleting on a Mac.

The Delete button.

Properties

The "Properties" button brings up the property sheet for a *selected* file. This button can be especially useful if you're running Windows on a Mac and don't have a two-button mouse because you can usually only get property sheets by right-clicking. This Properties button doesn't give you access to the *window's* own properties (to do that, right-click on a blank area inside the window).

The Properties buttons in Windows 98 (left) and Windows 95 (right).

Views (large icons, small icons, list, and details)

Here's where the toolbar actually comes in handy as an alternative to the menus. In Windows 98, click on the Views *button* (which is different, remember, from the View *menu* item) to cycle through the various views available. Or press the downward arrow to get the list of views to choose from.

Windows 98 Views button.

In Windows 95 and NT, click any of the four buttons to change the window display. This is much more efficient than using the View menu.

Windows 95 View buttons.

Application toolbars

On the Mac, the basic keyboard shortcuts are consistent in all applications. To emulate this consistency, Windows uses buttons for cut, copy, paste, and undo in *application* toolbars, as well as in the Desktop window toolbars you were just reading about.

But unlike the Desktop folder window toolbars, many application toolbars can be customized. You can add buttons for functions that you use frequently, delete any default buttons for actions you don't use, and even add additional toolbar rows to hold more button shortcuts. There is no standard way to make or change an application toolbar, so you'll have to consult your application's user manual for instructions.

Many application toolbars can be moved to any edge of the application window or pulled into the middle as floating palettes, as shown above.

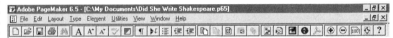

This is a toolbar for the application PageMaker. You can choose to hide it.

Dialog box toolbars

Dialog boxes such as Open, Save As, or Import also have toolbars, and learning to use them can keep you from going crazy. In the example shown below left, all of the files in the dialog box are displayed in a jumbled order. It's very difficult to find the file you want.

To display the files in one detailed list that can be sorted:

1. Click the "Details" list icon on the far right (circled, below left). That will display a detailed list like you get in a folder window on the Desktop.

2. Then click the "Name" column heading to sort the files by name (in the example below, by number). Click "Name" again if you want to sort them in the opposite order. Now you can find the file.

You might think that next time you open this dialog box, all of these files will still be sorted, right? Wrong. You're using Windows.

Click this button to:

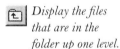 *Display the files that are in the folder up one level.*

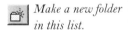 *Go straight to the Desktop level.*

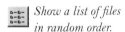 *Make a new folder in this list.*

 *Show a list of files in random order.*

Show a detailed list of files that you can sort by any column heading.

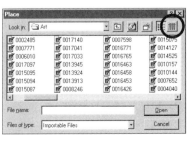
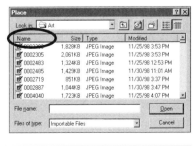

Make your own toolbars in the Taskbar

Mac users tend to prefer covering the Desktop with aliases of frequently used programs and folders instead of using the Windows Start Menu to access programs. If you have Windows 98 (or the version of Windows 95 with Internet Explorer integrated into the system) you can use toolbars that sit right on the Taskbar as a nice compromise between aliases and the Start Menu. These toolbars might remind you of the Mac's Launcher, although they take up less space and can be more efficient.

There are two kinds of Taskbar toolbars—Quick Launch and custom toolbars. Quick Launch displays only icons to represent your programs or documents; a custom toolbar displays both icons and text labels. Both of these formats can be useful. Quick Launch is very space-efficient, but can be confusing if you aren't familiar with a program's icon, or if you want more than one document or folder in the launch pad—they aren't labeled so you can't tell one document or folder from another without mousing over it. For those types of shortcuts, you'll probably prefer to create a custom toolbar.

This is an example of a customized Quick Launch bar with icons only.

This is an example of a customized toolbar. Notice it has labels as well as icons.

If you combine one of these toolbars with the Taskbar's "Auto hide" option (as discussed on page 127), you have a great combination: you can use your Desktop aliases, but you don't have to interrupt work in an application to start new work, print, or connect to the Internet.

Any item in the Taskbar, whether it is in QuickLaunch or a custom toolbar, requires only a single click to open the file.

To access and customize the Quick Launch toolbar

1. Right-click on a blank spot on the Taskbar. From the menu that appears, slide up to "Toolbars," and choose "Quick Launch" from the submenu. The Quick Launch toolbar will appear just to the right of the Start Menu button. Before you customize it, it displays four icons representing Internet Explorer (the globe with the "e"), Mail (the globe with an envelope), Show Desktop (the blotter and pencil), and View Channels (the satellite dish).

2. **To add an item to Quick Launch,** just drag the item to the Quick Launch portion of the Taskbar. This puts a shortcut of the item into Quick Launch.

3. **To delete an item from Quick Launch,** just right-click on the icon and choose "Delete" from the menu that pops up, or drag the icon from Quick Launch and drop it in the Recycle Bin. Since everything in Quick Launch is a shortcut (alias), deleting the item will not delete the original file or folder.

   If you don't use Channels in the Internet Explorer Web style interface (see Chapter 7) or Microsoft's Outlook Express, delete their icons from the Quick Launch toolbar. You can always put them back later.

3. **To hide Quick Launch,** right-click on the Taskbar to get the pop-up menu. From the "Toolbars" submenu, choose "Quick Launch" to deselect it. The Quick Launch toolbar will vanish from the Taskbar.

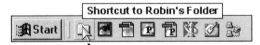

If you position the pointer over an icon in Quick Launch, a note appears telling you exactly what the item is, as shown above.

In this Quick Launch you see icons for Photoshop, a Photoshop document, PageMaker, a PageMaker document, Netscape, the Desktop, and an icon to connect to the Internet.

To make a custom toolbar in the Taskbar

1. Open the window for your hard drive (C:).

2. In the hard drive window, go to the File menu, choose "New," then choose "Folder."

3. Give the new folder a really short but descriptive name. This name will become the toolbar label, so you want to be sure the name isn't so long that it overwhelms the Taskbar, which is where the folder will sit when it's closed. A name about ten characters or less usually works well.

4. Fill this folder with shortcuts (aliases) of things you want quick access to. To make a shortcut, right-click on a file and choose "Create Shortcut."

PageMaker

These are shortcuts. The file on the right is the same shortcut as on the left, but it has been renamed.

The name of your folder will become the name of your custom toolbar when it's displayed in the Taskbar.

This window is filled with shortcuts. The icons for shortcuts have tiny arrows, very similar to the alias icons on the Mac OS 8.5. Feel free to rename your shortcuts.

Tip: It's best to delete the words "Shortcut to" at the beginning of each alias, or follow the instructions in Chapter 17 for preventing them from being added to your shortcuts when they're created. Otherwise, when your toolbar displays all the names will be truncated (cropped) to the first few characters, and everything will look alike!

5. Right-click on the Taskbar. From the menu that pops up, choose "Toolbars," then click "New Toolbar...." The "New Toolbar" dialog box appears:

The folder you chose is shown here.

This dialog box displays your files in a "tree" format.

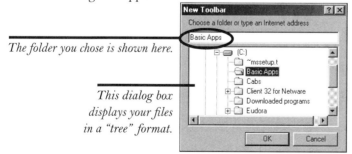

6. To find your folder, click on the + symbol next to the drive you made your shortcuts folder in. If you followed these directions, it should be right on the C: drive. If your shortcut folder is deeper inside the drive, keep clicking on the plus signs until you find the right one. Click once on your folder to select it.

7. Click OK, and your new toolbar label (the name of the folder) will appear on the Taskbar. The example is called "Basic Apps," and you can see it on this Toolbar in its closed form:

8. Double-click the name of your toolbar to open it. Everything on the Taskbar will slide over to make room for your toolbar shortcuts, as shown below. Double-click the name again to collapse the list.

Use the navigation arrows to slide to the left or right to find your other shortcuts.

You can **add to this custom toolbar** simply by making a new shortcut and placing it in the folder with the rest of the shortcuts. The new item will be immediately available on the custom toolbar.

Use the Taskbar's pop-up menu to hide the custom toolbar.

When you right-click the Taskbar, the names of any custom toolbars you create join the list in the "Toolbars" submenu. **To hide a custom toolbar,** simply uncheck its name from that submenu. When you want it back, you would think you could just choose its name again from the Toolbars submenu, right? Wrong. As soon as you hide the custom toolbar, its name disappears from the list. You have to choose "New Toolbar…," navigate to the folder you created, and select it again.

If you like this way of working, you might want to make more than one custom toolbar so you can group different kinds of things together. If you don't group them, your list of aliases will get very long and you'll have to click through several entries in the toolbar to get to the ones at the end of the list.

The Links toolbar

One of the options in the menu bar of every window is the "Links" toolbar. This special toolbar holds shortcuts to web addresses; click once on the link icon and Windows will log on to the Internet (if you're not connected already) and display that web page directly in the window.

The Links toolbar only works with Internet Explorer. Even if you have Netscape as your default browser and you drag your URLs (web addresses) and links from web pages that you opened in Netscape, when you activate them in the Links toolbar they'll launch Internet Explorer.

To add icon links into the Links toolbar by dragging and dropping

Choose to display the Links toolbar first. Then while you are browsing the Internet, drag any of the items below from a web page and drop it onto the Links toolbar in any open window.

- URLs from Internet Explorer's address line

- Individual URLs from Internet Explorer's "Favorites" list (but if you drag a *folder* of URLs from the Favorites list, the link in the toolbar loses all the URLs inside)

- Web links from open web pages

To delete icon links from the Links toolbar

Right-click on the icon in the toolbar, and choose "Delete" from the pop-up menu.

Open your links in Netscape

There's a nice work-around that lets you use the Links toolbar as a shortcut to your Netscape bookmarks: Save your entire list of Netscape bookmarks as an HTML file and put that list in your Links toolbar. Choosing a link from that list will actually launch Netscape.

1. Launch your version of Netscape.

2. Press Ctrl B to open the bookmark editing window.

3. While the bookmark window is in front of you, press Ctrl S so you can save the list. When the "Save As" dialog box appears, navigate to the "Links" folder (look in your C: drive, open the "Windows" folder, then open the "Favorites" folder, then open the "Links" folder). Save the file here. You can leave "bookmarks.htm" as the file name, or change it to something more descriptive.

4. Open a Desktop window. Your Netscape bookmarks shortcut will appear in the Links toolbar, as shown below. Don't worry about the Internet Explorer icon you see there. When you click the bookmark link, Netscape will launch and display your bookmarks as clickable links, also shown below.

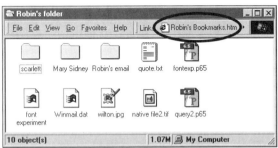

Putting the link in the toolbar is simply a shortcut —you can now launch Netscape from any open window.

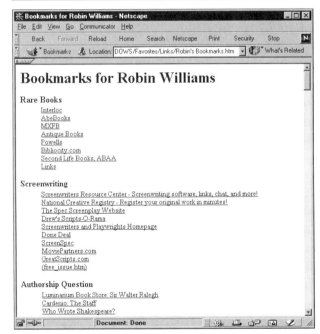

This is just a list of your bookmarks exactly as you have them organized in your browser.

Trashing: the Recycle Bin

Windows calls its trash can the Recycle Bin. (Cyndi guesses that "shredder" had bad connotations and "compost heap" would have given rise to too many jokes.) As a Mac user, you already know what the trash can is for and how important it is to your everyday work. This short chapter shows you how to transfer your existing knowledge to Windows without tripping over the messy little differences between the two systems.

Putting files in the Recycle Bin

Empty Recycle Bin.

Just like on your Mac, when you put files in the Recycle Bin, its icon changes to show the virtual trash in it (shown to the left). A full Recycle Bin icon means the files are still on the hard disk—they'll wait in the bin until you empty it.

There are several ways to dump things into the Recycle Bin. Two methods just **move** the files to the bin; they'll stay on the hard disk until you physically choose to empty the Recycle Bin. Other methods don't move the file to the bin—they instantly **delete** the file from the disk.

Recycle Bin with files in it.

To move files into the Recyle Bin

- Drag files to the Recycle Bin and drop them in. **OR:**

- Select the file you want to get rid of, then press the Delete key. *Note: In Windows, the Delete key and the Backspace key are not the same key! You need to press the key that's actually labeled "Delete"— it's in the small group of edit keys above the arrow keys.*

When you use either of those two methods, you'll get the following message. Notice it's just checking to make sure you want to send the file to the bin; Windows is not actually deleting it from the hard disk yet.

Tip: If your View Option is set to "Show all files," you may find a Recycle icon in your hard drive window. This is a shortcut that appears if you have files from this drive on hold in the Recycle Bin. You can drag things to this local icon as you would to the original, which can be very useful if your Desktop is covered with a multitude of windows and your Desktop Recycle Bin is buried.

To permanently remove files from your hard disk

- Select the file you want to delete. Press Shift Delete (use the Delete key in the edit keys, above the arrows). **Or** in Windows 98, press Ctrl D.

  You'll get the following message. Notice Windows is actually *deleting* the file, not just moving it!

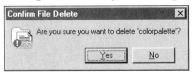

Putting files from removable disks into the bin

When you drag any file from a removable disk to the Recycle Bin, Windows doesn't store it in the bin for you—it's deleted from the disk immediately. You will get a confirmation request, as shown above.

Deleting automatically

Files in the Recycle Bin, like in the Mac's trash can, are actually just sitting on the hard disk in another container, similar to being in a folder; they're taking up hard disk space. You can use the Recycle Bin property sheet to arrange to delete files without storing them in the Recycle Bin first. Be warned, however! Bypassing the Recycle Bin means you'll never be able to recover a file you accidentally dragged and dumped.

To skip the Recycle Bin and immediately delete the files

1. Right-click on the Recycle Bin to get the pop-up menu, and choose "Properties." Click the "Global" tab.

2. Check "Do not move files to the Recycle Bin. Remove files immediately on delete," then click OK.

   Everything currently in the Recycle Bin is history, as well as everything you drag into it in the future.

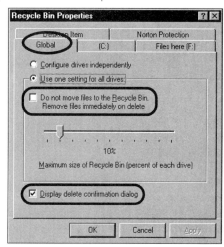

You can also **delete individual files immediately.** Instead of changing the global setting as described above, you can use this technique to instantly delete selected files from the hard disk:

- Hold down the Shift key while you drag the file to the Recycle Bin. In Windows 95 and NT, you won't get any warning message, so be careful!

Use the property sheet to control the Recycle Bin.

Get rid of the warning

Just like on the Mac, you can turn off the warning that yells at you every time you put a file in the trash. Use the Recycle Bin's property sheet.

To turn off the warning messages

1. Right-click on the Recycle Bin to get the pop-up menu, and choose "Properties." Click the "Global" tab.

2. Uncheck the box "Display delete confirmation dialog." Click OK.

   Files will still be stored in the Recycle Bin until you choose to delete them, but you won't be annoyed with the warning.

Emptying the Recycle Bin

The files stay in the bin (and thus on your hard disk) until you choose to empty it. It's easy to empty.

- Right-click on the Recycle Bin to get the pop-up menu, and choose "Empty Recycle Bin." You'll get a message asking if you really want to do that. If so, click "Yes."

Emptying files selectively

You can delete individual files from the bin.

1. Double-click the Recycle Bin to open its window.

2. Select a file. From the File menu, click "Delete."
   You'll be asked if you really want to delete the selected item.

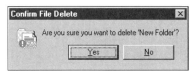

3. Click "Yes," and the selected item will be permanently deleted.

Restoring files

Sometimes you throw things away, then realize that you need them after all. Just like the Mac's "Put Away" feature, Windows has "Restore." When you choose to restore an item, Windows puts it back in the window it came from.

1. Double-click to open the bin's window.

2. Select a file. From the File menu, click "Restore."

The Recycle Bin is just a window like any other. You can change its arrangement in the View menu to see Details. When you do this, you can see where a file was located before you put it in the bin. This can sometimes be very useful, especially if you have two files with the same name that were thrown out from different folders, and you want to restore a particular one. (No, we didn't make a mistake here. Windows can tolerate several files with the same name in the Recycle Bin, even if they are two copies of the exact same file.)

If you actually deleted files from your hard disk, it is sometimes possible to recover them. See Chapter 28.

Limiting the size of the Recycle Bin

Anything you don't consciously delete or restore could stay in the Recycle Bin indefinitely, were it not for the Recycle Bin's size limitations. Windows assigns a default chunk of megabytes to the Recycle Bin; that chunk is equal to a fixed percentage of the hard disk. If your disk is small, you'll be surprised at how quickly the Recycle Bin can fill up with large graphic files. Use the same good sense you've always used on the Mac, and empty the trash . . . um, recycle the bin . . . on a regular basis. If you think your bin is too small (or too big), change the size setting.

To resize the Recycle Bin on your main hard disk

1. Right-click the Recycle Bin, then choose "Properties." Click the "Global" tab.

2. The size of the Recycle Bin is set as a percentage of your hard disk. If you have a 1 gigabyte hard disk, your Recycle Bin is probably set to the default of 10 percent, which would be 100 megabytes of hard disk space. **To change this percentage,** drag the slider bar to the left or right.

To resize the Recycle Bin for different disk drives

- Click "Configure drives independently," then move the slider.

  Setting differently sized Recycle Bins will only work, however, if you have more than one *physical* hard disk. That is, a *partitioned* drive (one hard disk that is divided into sections, each with its own drive letter) uses the one allotment for all the partitions. You can't set a size limitation at all for removable drives because their files don't go into the Recyle Bin—they're immediately deleted.

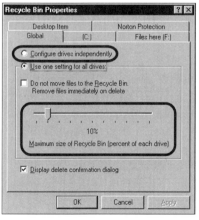

Use the Recycle Bin property sheet to resize the hard disk allotment for trashed files.

The optimum size for your Recycle Bin

With a little math, you can figure out the best size for your Recycle Bin. After you've had your computer for a while and you've gotten into a rhythm of saving and deleting, open up your Recycle Bin. Change the View to Details if it isn't already set that way, and make sure that your status bar at the bottom of the window is enabled (from the View menu, choose "Status Bar").

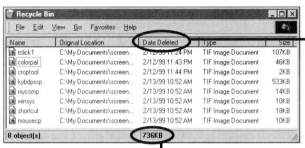

Click the heading "Date Deleted" to sort the files by date, newest first. Click it again to sort the files by date, oldest first.

The status bar information tells you how much hard disk space the trashed files are using.

Now ask yourself how long you think a file ought to stay in the bin. Is a week enough? A month? Once you've decided on your time frame, delete any files in the Recycle Bin that are older than your cutoff date. (If you need to keep any of those files, then your cutoff date is too optimistic!) Now look at your status bar. The disk space amount that you see there should be a pretty good indication of how much space you really need for your Recycle Bin.

So add a few megabytes to round this number up to one that ends in a zero. This will give you a little wiggle room and also make the math very simple.

1. Take the size of your hard disk in gigabytes; let's say it's 6.

2. Divide it into the Recycle Bin number; let's say you decided 30 megabytes was plenty.

3. Divide 6 into 30 and the result is 5; thus the percentage of your drive that you need to assign to the Recycle Bin would be 5 percent.

Moving and Copying

Copying and moving files on a Macintosh is practically effortless and just about foolproof. That's not really true in Windows, particularly for a Mac user who comes to the PC with expectations that familiar actions will bring familiar results. In this chapter, we'll first interpret the Windows mouse icons, which are your keys to understanding what Windows is actually doing when you drag Desktop objects. The rest of the chapter is devoted to the process of moving and duplicating files, applications, and disks.

Selected files stay selected

Okay, we admit this is a neat Windows feature: As you know, on the Mac when you select a bunch of files in one window and then have to click elsewhere for some reason, like to open or move a window, all of the files you so carefully selected in the first window are deselected. Well, Windows remembers which files you had selected in the first window. When you switch back to that original window, it might *look* like your files were deselected, but click once on a blank space in the original window and you'll see that your selected files are still selected.

Standard cursor icons and what they mean

Before you move things from folder to disk to window, you should be familiar with the visual clues that the mouse pointer icon is giving you. This is what the icons indicate:

Mouse pointer icon	What it stands for
	Selecting or about to move
	About to copy
	About to make an alias
	Busy working
	Unavailable, can't do it

The ambiguous plus sign

When you see a plus sign (+) added to the pointer, as shown above, it indicates you're about to make a copy of the file. It also indicates:

- The drive the pointer is hovering over is not the one your file is currently on, which is why dragging the file to that drive will make a copy of the file.

- Making a copy onto this drive *may* be possible (Windows doesn't check to see if a disk or cartridge is in a removable drive until you let go of the mouse button, so you might not *really* be able to copy).

Moving and copying files on the same disk

On a Mac, you press-and-drag to move files and copy them. In Windows, moving things around is a tad more complex; it actually matters what *kind* of thing you're trying to put *where*. Remember, when you **copy** an object, the computer makes a **duplicate;** when you **move** an object, the computer **does not make a duplicate**—it moves the original file to a new place.

To move or copy a FILE from one place to another ON THE SAME DISK

- **MOVE a file or folder:** Press-and-drag a file to its new location.

- **COPY a file or folder:** Hold down the Ctrl key, and press-and-drag the file or folder from one place to another.

  You'll get a "copy progress" dialog box that shows papers flying from one folder to the next.

To move or copy an APPLICATION (an .EXE file) from one place to another ON THE SAME DISK

- **MOVE an application:** Hold down the Shift key and press-and-drag the application icon to its new location.

  Windows makes you hold down the Shift key because it really doesn't like the idea of you moving applications hither and yon and wants to make absolutely sure you mean it.

  If you drag an application file *without* the Shift key down, the mouse pointer changes to a curved arrow. That's the shortcut symbol that tells you the computer is about to make a shortcut (an alias) of the file. The application itself won't move. This method of making a shortcut/alias only works with applications. See Chapter 17, *Creating Folders, Files, and Aliases,* for details on making shortcuts for other files.

  The weird thing is you can press-and-drag to **move a folder** that has an **application** inside of it because Windows can't see the contents of a folder until you open it.

- **COPY an application:** Hold down the Ctrl key, and press-and-drag the application icon from one place to another.

License.pdf   Help

On the left is a document file icon, and on the right is a folder icon.

AcroRd32.exe

This is an application icon.

Copying files from one disk to another disk

- To copy anything from one disk to another, press-and-drag the file. Yes, this is exactly the same as moving a file from one place to another on the same disk.

Moving files from one disk to another disk

Remember, *copying* leaves the original in its place; *moving* physically moves the file from one place to another, and there is no original one left in the original location.

To convince Windows that you know what you're doing and you really do want to **move** the file, **click-Shift** and drag. Read that carefully! First click once to select the file, *then* press the Shift key and drag the file. (If you do the opposite—first hold down the Shift key and then click on the file—you might very likely end up selecting multiple objects. Then you could be moving everything in the window to the other drive.)

Using "Send To"

The "Send To" feature is nice if you have to transfer lots of files from one place to another on your PC. It saves you the trouble of opening and closing multiple folders when all you want to do is move a file to a specific destination on your disk or copy it to another disk.

To use the "Send To" feature

1. **Right-click** on a file or folder to get the pop-up menu, then click "Send To." You'll get a submenu like the one shown to the right.

2. Then just click on the destination disk or folder to select it.

To add a destination to the "Send To" list

If you have a disk or folder that you copy files into regularly but it isn't listed in the "Send To" menu, you can add it to the list.

1. Use the Find dialog box (see Chapter 20 if you're not sure how to use it) to locate the "SendTo" folder (it's usually in the Windows folder in Windows 95/98 and in the Profiles folder in Windows NT). When you find the "SendTo" folder, double-click to open it.

2. Open "My Computer" if you want to add a removable drive to the list, or open the window that holds the folder you want as a destination.

3. **Right-click** on the drive or folder icon, hold the mouse button down, drag it to the "SendTo" folder, and drop it.

4. From the pop-up menu that appears, choose "Create Shortcut(s) Here."

   Delete the words "Shortcut to" at the beginning of the icon's label so the "Send To" menu will be as easy to read as possible. (See Chapter 17, *Creating Folders, Files, and Aliases*, on how to prevent the "Shortcut to" prefix from appearing.)

5. Close up the windows, and your new destination is available in the "Send To" list.

To remove a destination from the "Send To" list

1. Follow the directions in Step 1 above to find and open the "SendTo" folder.

2. Drag the destination shortcut from the "SendTo" folder to the Recycle Bin.

If your destination is listed in this menu, just click on it, and let the transfer begin!

My Briefcase

This is the My Briefcase icon. It's probably on your hard disk.

Look carefully for the Briefcase option.

My Briefcase

If you need to move files back and forth between computers, "My Briefcase" can be a great time-saver. Like its real namesake, you can put files into the Briefcase, take it with you, work on the files on the airplane or at home, and bring the Briefcase back to the original computer. The Briefcase keeps track of files that have been updated and automates the process of replacing old versions of files with new ones. You probably have an icon called "My Briefcase" sitting on your Desktop already.

Making a Briefcase if you don't have one

If you don't see an icon for "My Briefcase," that doesn't mean you can never use one. To see if you have the feature installed in your version of Windows, right-click on the Desktop to get the pop-up menu, click "New," and see if "Briefcase" appears as a choice. If it doesn't, you'll have to install it from your Windows CD; look in the "Portable" option. If "Briefcase" does appear, follow the steps below to make a new one.

To create a new Briefcase if you have no icon for it on the Desktop

1. **Right-click** on the Desktop. From the pop-up menu, choose "New," then "Briefcase."

2. A generic icon named "New Briefcase" will appear on the Desktop.

Naming the Briefcase

You can change the name of the new file to "My Briefcase" if you're the only person using the computer. But if your Desktop is shared with other people who might also like to use this feature, give the new briefcase a personalized name before you start to put things in it!

Even if you rename "My Briefcase," Windows still knows it's a special folder. It will search around the disk, find your personalized briefcase, and ask if you want it to be recognized as "My Briefcase." Click "Yes," and you can use the "My Briefcase" option whenever you find it in a menu. If you click "No," you'll need to follow the procedure outlined on the previous page to make a shortcut in the "SendTo" folder.

Making multiple Briefcases

You can create multiple briefcases. You might want to keep certain files together that are related to one client or job, or you might have some files that need special treatment. Just remember to give each Briefcase a unique, easy-to-remember name.

Putting files into the Briefcase

Files that go into a Briefcase folder should always be **copies,** not the originals. Use either of these methods to put files in the folder.

- Use the "Send To" option (described on page 157) to copy files or folders to your Briefcase.

- You can add copies to and delete from "My Briefcase" as you would any other folder, but don't change the name you've given "My Briefcase" once you start using it or Windows won't be able to synchronize the folders.

Taking Briefcase files to another computer

The point of using a Briefcase is to move files back and forth between different computers easily and automatically update any files that were changed. When you're ready to take your Briefcase with you, **move** it to your removable drive (which is like picking up a real briefcase and taking it home):

- Select the Briefcase, hold down the Shift key, and drag the Briefcase icon to the removable drive.

  This will **delete** the Briefcase from the Desktop so when you bring the Briefcase back later, you can move the updated folder back onto the hard disk without having to replace an old one. Remember, Windows doesn't always update the screen very quickly, so even though it might look like your Briefcase is still on the Desktop, it isn't. That leftover icon will soon disappear.

Editing Briefcase files on the Mac

You can use the Briefcase files on the Mac, but to make sure the Windows Briefcase will recognize the folder and its contents when you take it back to the PC, you have to *edit your files directly on the removable disk that the Briefcase is on.* That is, don't copy the files onto your Mac's hard disk first, because if you copy them over, make changes to them, and copy the files back to the portable Briefcase, you'll get a message when you bring the disk back to the PC and try to update the files; the message tells you the files in the Briefcase are "orphans" and will not be updated.

Orphans are files that the Briefcase database can't match up with the original Windows files. Of course you could copy and move each file by hand, but this defeats the purpose of using Briefcase at all.

Taking Briefcase files back to the PC and updating them

When you return to the original computer, **move** your Briefcase (click-Shift-drag) back to the Desktop. Then "synchronize" the updated files in the Briefcase with the original files on the hard disk (or vice versa).

A time-ly warning: Sometimes we get sloppy and don't update our computers for daylight savings time. Other times we lose our Mac clock because the battery dies and some of our file dates get strange. Or maybe we're sharing files with people in an earlier time zone than ours. Whatever the reason, DON'T USE A BRIEFCASE TO KEEP FILES SYNCHRONIZED UNLESS BOTH COMPUTER CLOCKS ARE SYNCHRONIZED.

Although you can override Briefcase's plans before they're acted on, if you have lots of misdated files you're just creating additional work for yourself.

To transfer file changes from the Briefcase to the original computer

1. After you move the Briefcase from the removable drive back onto the Desktop, right-click on its icon. Scroll down the menu and choose "Update All." If Briefcase sees differences between the Briefcase and its former database, you'll get this dialog box:

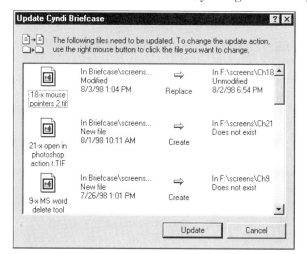

This dialog box gives you a preview of every file Briefcase recognizes as having changed and explains what it plans to do about each file. Take the time to look through and verify that you're not about to lose something critical because of a naming or date error.

2. If you need to make a change, right-click on the file, and choose from the following menu options:

You can thus override Briefcase's decisions on any or all of these files, but once you've accepted this list by clicking the "Update" button, you're stuck with the changes.

Refreshing after moving or copying

On your Mac, when you move or copy files to another window, the new
file takes its place in the window based on how you've arranged the view.
Not in Windows—the new file shows up at the bottom of the list no
matter how you've sorted the window.

*A folder before adding
a file to it.*

*The same folder after adding
a file to it.*

As you can see in the example above, the new file appears in the window
at the bottom of the list, no matter what type of file or folder it is or how
the window is sorted. It will stay in this position even if you switch
views or minimize the folder, until you close the window and reopen it.

To force a window to re-sort without having to close the window

- From the window's View menu, choose "Refresh."

- If you're using the Details view, click on one of the heading
  buttons to sort and Windows will refresh the folder.

Spring-loaded folders

You may be wondering if you really need to open and close all those windows each time you want to copy a file. Mac OS 8.0 and later provides "spring-loaded action" when you drag and drop files. Whether you have "automatic expanding folders" (which is what Microsoft calls the closest thing to spring-loaded folders that Windows offers) depends on which version of Windows you're using.

This ability to open folders automatically is limited in Windows and is not as intuitive as it is on the Mac. It only exists on Windows 98 or a Windows 95 version that's integrated with Microsoft Internet Explorer, the web browser. And you'll have to use the feature called Windows Explorer to have the spring-loaded effect—you can't just do it on the Desktop.

To use automatic expanding folders

1. Launch Windows Explorer: **right-click** the "Start" button and choose "Explore" from the menu.

2. Navigate through the folders in the *left* panel until the item you'd like to move appears in the *right* panel of the Explorer window.

3. Drag the file from the *right* panel over to the *left* one. Hold that file over a folder that has sub-folders, and the view will expand to display the sub-folders. Hold that file over a sub-folder with sub-sub-folders, and the process will repeat until you find the folder to drop the file into. Let go of the mouse button.

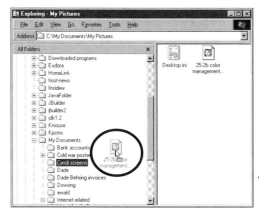

This file is being dragged from the right side over to the left side to drop into a folder.

Running out of disk space while copying

When you try to copy files to a disk on the Mac, you know immediately whether or not there's enough space available. The Mac does a quick calculation; if there's not enough space on the disk, it tells you exactly how much more space you need to make a successful copy.

Windows approaches the copying process in a completely different way. This is probably not such a surprise if you've already tried to copy a large group of files in Windows 95 or NT. You get an info box with animated documents gracefully flying from one folder to the next and the name of the file involved. You also get a cute little dashed line that looks like the Mac's status bar, but in fact is pretty lame since it doesn't give you any information—you never know whether the copy will take five seconds or fifteen minutes. (In Windows 98 you get a real status bar, not a fake one.)

You don't get this information because *Windows* doesn't even know it. Windows sees every file as an individual item; it doesn't look at the entire group of files as part of one process.

Since it can't think ahead, if there isn't enough room on the disk eventually Windows reaches a file that would overfill the receiving disk. When this happens, Windows asks you to find a new disk to replace the existing one. If all goes well, you swap the disks and the system picks up where it left off, and you'll end up with your files divided between the two disks.

Duplicating an entire disk

You can copy an entire disk in two ways: you can drag the contents of one disk to another, or use the Windows "Copy Disk" utility.

Remember: You can't copy hidden files. To make hidden files visible, go to any window and from the "View" menu choose "Options." In the property sheet, click "Show all files."

Drag-and-drop the disk contents

The easiest and most foolproof method to copy a disk is to select all the contents and drag it into a folder onto another disk, such as your hard disk. You need to make the folder first, of course.

Use the "Copy Disk" utility

Windows has a "Copy Disk" utility that does the same thing as the Mac's "Disk Copy." *It won't work unless both disks have exactly the same capacity, and it erases all information from the target disk before it puts the new information on it.*

To duplicate a floppy disk or cartridge

1. First put the source disk in the drive. Open "My Computer," and right-click on the icon representing the source disk in the drive.

2. Choose "Copy Disk," and the Copy Disk dialog box will appear:

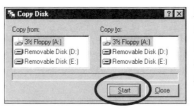

Notice the A: drive is selected in both the left and right panels. Copy Disk is indicating there is only one available drive of this type so you'll need to switch disks to make your copy.

3. Click the Start button, and you'll get a reminder to put the disk in. Don't panic and think there's something wrong with the disk you've already inserted. Remember, this isn't a Mac where the system recognizes and mounts disks immediately—Windows hasn't even checked the drive yet.

4. Click OK, and Windows will begin copying. You'll be prompted to switch disks periodically until the process is complete.

If you need to copy an entire hard drive, you can either use the modified drag-and-drop method mentioned above, or, more efficiently you can use a backup program. Many external removable drives come with backup utilities which allow you to make selective or global copies of hard disk contents and restore them later.

Part Three

Accessories and Control Panels

It is better to fail in originality
than to succeed in imitation.

— *Herman Melville*

Display Settings

If you spend a lot of time on your computer, you know how much you value being able to change the way your Desktop looks. It won't take long in Windows before you feel this overpowering urge for change—whether it's for a functional reason like increasing resolution or just because you're sick of all that teal and royal blue.

Fortunately, the Windows Desktop is much more flexible than it may initially appear. This chapter covers the basics of adapting the Desktop to your needs and desires, from color depth and resolution to background pictures.

Important note

All of the information in this chapter revolves around using the Display Properties to make changes to your monitor settings. The different Windows operating systems apply these changes very differently. Be sure to read pages 180–181 about testing and applying new options!

Desktop property sheets

Display

Note: This property sheet has suffered numerous changes in the different versions of Windows. In most cases, we're showing the basic Windows NT and Windows 95 versions for the illustrations and how-tos because it's a little harder to do things in these versions than in Windows 98, and people working with them need more help. When something has changed radically enough in Windows 98 so that the NT and 95 guidelines would mislead you, we've explained the differences.

The Mac divides different functions of the Desktop into different control panels (such as Appearance, Desktop Pictures, and Monitors and Sound) and menu items (such as Label, Preferences, and View Options). Windows gathers all these sorts of functions into a big property sheet bundle called "Display Properties." There are two ways to open the Display Properties:

- Right-click anywhere on the Desktop. From the pop-up menu that appears, choose "Properties." **Or:**

- From either the Start Menu or "My Computer," open the Control Panel folder. Double-click on the "Display" icon.

Changing the background pattern or picture

Open the Display Properties as described above. The Background setting is the Windows equivalent of Macintosh Desktop Pictures.

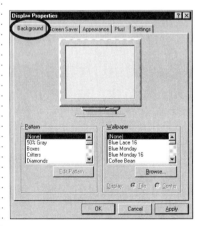

This is the Display Properties in Windows 95 and NT. The monitor in the middle displays a preview of your choices.

This is the Display Properties in Windows 98. Notice it doesn't have the "Pattern" option you see in Windows 95.

Applying and editing patterns (Windows 95/NT)

Patterns on the Mac are not the same as patterns in Windows. On the Mac, patterns are textures or illustrations that repeat, or tile, on the screen until they fill it. In Windows, such things are called "wallpaper," and *patterns* are simple bitmap grids that overlay the color background like lace.

In the Background section of your Display Properties, you'll see two scrolling menus side by side. In the "Patterns" list, "None" is probably highlighted, which means just the solid background color will display.

To overlay a pattern on this colored background

- Scroll down the "Pattern" list and single-click any option except "None." A preview of the pattern appears. Click the Apply button to see that pattern painted on your whole screen. When you find the one you want to keep, click OK.

To create your own bitmap pattern, which is really kind of fun

1. Scroll down the "Pattern" list and single-click any option except "None." A preview of the pattern appears.

2. Click the "Edit Pattern" button. The "Pattern Editor" dialog box appears. To edit the pattern, click on the image inside the box, as shown below.

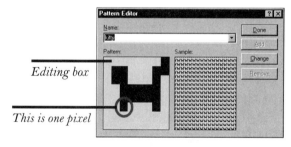

Editing box

This is one pixel

Click on a black pixel to delete it. Click on a background pixel to change it to black. By clicking pixels on and off this way, you draw a simple, tiny pattern. The computer repeats the pattern all over the screen. What's nice about this function is that it doesn't require a graphics program or any graphics knowledge, and it doesn't take up much system memory.

3. When you've finished editing your pattern, click "Done." The dialog box will give you a choice between replacing the original pattern or saving this one with a new name.

This is the Wallpaper section of the Display Properties in Windows 95.

Wallpaper

In the Background settings of the Display Properties, the list on the right (it's the *only* list in Windows 98) is "Wallpaper," which is a repeating pattern that covers the screen. Click an option in the list and that wallpaper pattern will display in the little preview monitor. (Don't worry if it looks like the tiles don't match up properly at the edges— that's just the result of displaying the patterns so small.)

Windows only supplies a few patterns and pictures to get you started. If you don't like any of the images that come with Windows, you can make or install your own. Any .BMP file (a bitmapped paint file) can become your Desktop picture. Windows' accessory called Paint can create .BMP files, as can most commercial painting or image editing programs, including Photoshop.

To add a new picture or pattern to the Wallpaper list

1. Make sure the .BMP picture file you want to use is on your PC hard disk.

2. In the Wallpaper section, click "Browse" and find your .BMP file.

3. Double-click the .BMP file name. A miniature version of the new Desktop picture will appear in the preview.

4. As you probably know from using the Mac's Desktop Pictures, there are a couple of different ways to display a Desktop image.

   - To create a repeating pattern that covers the background color, click the "Tile" radio button.

   - To center one large image on the screen, click "Center." The background color will appear around the outside of the centered image, as shown below.

In Windows 98, you can enlarge the image to fill the entire screen, as shown below: use the "Display" menu option to "stretch" the image.

Windows 95 or NT: **Older versions of Windows 95 or NT cannot enlarge an image to fill the Desktop screen. But you can buy software from Microsoft called Plus! that adds a new set of options to your Desktop Properties, which includes the ability to resize a Desktop picture.**

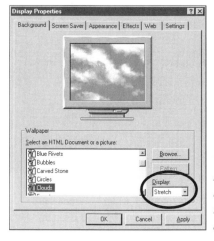

The menu labeled "Display" has three choices: Tile, Center, and Stretch. "Stretch" resizes the picture or pattern to fill the entire screen.

Once you've made your background changes, click "Apply" to see how they look on the big screen. Click OK if you're finished, or go back and make further changes.

Changing the background color

No matter what pattern or picture you choose to display on your monitor, that pattern or picture will sit on *top* of the background color, even if you don't see it. The background color of the monitor is part of a total Desktop color "scheme."

To change the color of the background

1. If the Display Properties are not open, right-click anywhere on the Desktop to get the pop-up menu and choose "Properties."

2. Click the "Appearance" tab to get the settings (shown below).

   The Appearance settings in Windows are arranged very differently from the Mac Appearance control panel, but if you look closely you'll find most of the same options.

3. Look at the section called "Item," circled below. The word "Desktop" is probably displayed. To the right of "Desktop" is the "Color" menu. Unless someone has already changed it, the color in this box is probably the Windows teal blue.

Make sure "Desktop" is chosen in this box, or you'll change the color of something other than the background!

4. Click the downward arrow in the "Color" box. You'll get a small palette of twenty colors, as shown to the right. Click a color spot to replace the current background.

5. **To mix your own color:** Click "Other..." in the little color palette. This will bring up the Desktop color picker, shown on the next page.

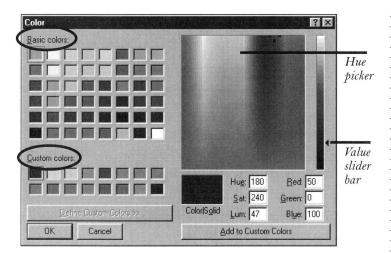

Hue picker

Value slider bar

6. **First** click one of the empty boxes in the "Custom colors" section. This tells Windows where to save the new color you're going to make. (If you forget this step and try to select a blank box later, any color you click on from the "Basic colors" section will replace the new color you made. You'll have to start all over.)

   You can *make* as many colors as you like, but you can only *save* a **maximum of 64 colors.** That's the total number of color boxes available if you combine the Custom and the Basic colors.

   The **hue picker** (shown above) is arranged by *saturation*, with the most brilliant, colorful shades at the top and the most neutral ones at the bottom.

   The **value slider** (shown above) takes any hue you choose and shows different values of light and dark, called the **luminescence.**

   The color you create is displayed in the **Color|Solid** box you see below the hue picker.

   You can also define a color by changing the values for Red, Green, and Blue, or for Hue, Sat (saturation), and Lum (luminescence).

   Once you create a color you like, click "Add to Custom Colors" to make it available as a Desktop color choice.

7. **To apply the background color,** click inside its color box (either click on a custom color you just made, or on any basic color), then click the OK button.

hue: Basically refers to the name of a color, such as red, purple, or orange.

saturation: Refers to how strong or pure a color (hue) is.

luminescence: Refers to the relative lightness and darkness of a color. Also called brightness.

Changing accent color and text settings

If you've been following along in this chapter and have gone to all this trouble to customize your background, you probably would like to customize other Desktop elements as well. On a Mac, you can set an accent color for scroll boxes and the like and specify the highlight color for selected text or icons. In Windows, you can change the color of title bars, the highlight color, and a host of other things.

Windows ships with several pre-set color combinations called "Schemes."

To see the existing Schemes

1. If the Display Properties are not open, right-click anywhere on the Desktop to get the pop-up menu and choose "Properties."

2. Click the "Appearance" tab.

3. Click the "Scheme" arrow to get the list.

4. Click the name of a Scheme. An example will preview in the display, as shown below. Choose a scheme you like, then click OK.

Notice in these examples that when the scheme changed from one to another, the type sizes, buttons, etc., all changed in addition to the colors. A pre-made scheme includes pre-selected fonts, sizes, etc.

Notice in the right-hand example that the pointer is pointing to the "Inactive Title Bar," as identified in the "Item" box. The other settings indicate the current type size, color, font, etc., for that item.

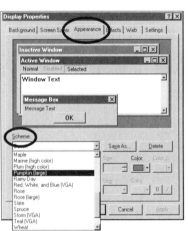 

You might think the preview is just a static picture. Surprise: it's a live, clickable window. Every Desktop element, from typeface to title bar to window border, can be selected in the preview and customized. Instead of settling for one of the pre-set combination schemes, you can change your Desktop piece by piece, either to make a minor change in a chosen scheme or to create a brand new one. If you just want to identify an element, click on it in the preview, then look at the "Item" box for its identifying name.

To change a Desktop element and apply that change on your Desktop

1. Click on the element in the picture, then check its name to make sure you've selected the item you want. If the element you want to change isn't in the preview (like the background color in Help windows), you can choose it from the "Item" menu.

2. Change the color of a Desktop element the same way you changed the background color (see page 172–173): click the "Color" arrow and use the color picker.

   The **Size box** indicates how wide the selected element is, horizontally or vertically, in pixels. Use the up and down arrows to resize title bars and scroll bars. For instance, you might want the title bars thicker so you can see the little minimize and close boxes better.

   If the element you're changing has **text** on it, you can change the typeface, weight, point size, and color.

   Any **changes** you make are displayed immediately in the preview window. Click the Apply button to see how your choices look on the whole screen, but **be careful!** As a Mac user, you are accustomed to clicking the Apply button and if you don't like it, you click Cancel and any changes you "Applied" are canceled. Well, you're in Windows now. If you click Apply, hate the look, and click Cancel, the property sheet closes and all those changes you hated are now on your screen.

   Windows 98: Notice that the active and inactive title bars have two colors choices, not just one. If you choose two different colors, you'll get a title bar that's a color blend between the two. Try it.

Save your own scheme!

Once you've made all the individual changes you'd like, save the combination of changes as your own personal scheme.

To save your own personal scheme

- Click the "Save As" button (it's in the middle of the property sheet, not at the bottom). In the Save As dialog box, give your scheme a name and click OK. Your personalized scheme will then appear as an option in the menu.

Changing color depth and resolution

If you're using a computer with a tiny monitor and only 256 colors, this section won't mean much to you. More likely, though, you've got a 17-inch monitor, a video card that can display 16 million colors at some resolution, or both. If you do, there'll be times when you need to switch down to 256 colors for a game or up to a higher pixel resolution to fit more on the display screen.

To change monitor settings

1. If the Display Properties are not open, right-click anywhere on the Desktop to get the pop-up menu and choose "Properties."

2. Click the "Settings" tab to get this window:

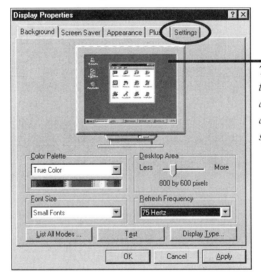

This preview changes to display your screen at different resolutions as you change the specifications.

The list of possible settings can be a little overwhelming. Macs support a more limited number of options than do Windows machines, which is actually a good thing because it makes it easier to figure out what your own computer setup can support. There are too many possibilities in Windows 95 and many of them won't even work, so you have to experiment to find a workable combination.

See pages 180–181 before you try to apply any color depth or resolution changes in Windows 95 or NT.

About resolution, colors, and refresh

There's a relationship between the **screen pixel resolution** and the **number of colors** you can display: the more pixels on the monitor (the resolution), the more **memory** it takes to send lots of color to every single pixel.

So the more colors you want to see, the lower the pixel resolution range your monitor card will be able to support. For instance, an inexpensive card that doesn't have much video memory might be able to show you 16 million colors if you have only 800 pixels x 600 pixels, but if you change the resolution to 1024 pixels x 768 pixels, the card might only have enough memory to send 16,000 colors to that many pixels, instead of millions of colors. A really inexpensive or older card (because it has less video memory) might only be able to show 256 colors (or fewer!) on a 17-inch monitor.

The **refresh rate** (the speed at which the monitor completely redraws what you see on the screen) is also dependent on the number of colors and the screen resolution you choose. Some monitors and video cards can support a range of refresh rates, but might need to refresh at a slower rate at 1152 x 864 (because there are so many pixels) than they would at 800 x 600 pixels. A slow refresh rate can result in a flickering monitor that tires your eyes.

To change the number of colors the screen displays (called the color depth)

- Click the downward arrow in the "Color Palette" box (in Windows 98 it's the "Colors" box) to see the options. The options look a little different from the Mac. Here's a translation:

Mac choice	Equivalent PC	Bit values
256	256 Colors	(8-bit)
Thousands	65,536 Colors	High Color (16-bit)
Millions	16,777,216 Colors	True Color (24-bit)

In **Windows 95 or NT,** nothing on your monitor will appear to change as you make choices. See pages 180–181 before you try to apply any color depth or resolution changes in Windows 95 or NT.

In **Windows 98,** click Apply, then choose whether to keep the change. If you don't like what you see, change it to something else before you click OK or Cancel.

Important Note:
Images look *better* on your screen with more colors. Everything on your screen looks *smaller* with more pixels.

Monitor resolution is very different from printer resolution, where we are accustomed to thinking that more dots per inch means higher resolution (and thus better quality). How well images are "resolved" on a monitor depends not on pixels per inch, but on the number of colors creating the image. Experiment and you'll see what we mean.

Color Palette.

Change the resolution

This is the Windows 95 resolution slider.

In the Display Property "Settings," Windows is being precise when it refers to the resolution slider bar as "Desktop Area" ("Screen Area" in Windows 98), because that's what is really being changed, the Desktop area. Monitor resolution is a greatly misunderstood thing. The PC monitor's actual resolution can be anywhere between 72 to 100 pixels per inch, and it's most typically about 96. When you change the monitor resolution on a computer to what seems like a "higher resolution," like 1280 x 1024, everything looks smaller. When you change to a "lower resolution," like 800 x 600, everything looks bigger.

To adjust the display resolution

- Drag the "Desktop Area" slider one notch toward "Less" or "More." The resolution number below the slider will change. Let go of the slider, and look at the little monitor preview. You'll see a pretty good example of what your Desktop will look like if you make this change. Remember that the higher the resolution number, the harder it will be to see small things, including type.

Change the refresh rate (Windows 95/NT)

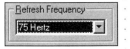

Change the refresh rate here in Windows 95.

In the Display Property "Settings," the "Refresh Frequency" refers to how many times per second the image on the screen is redrawn. If the number is too low, your screen will flicker. If this number is too high, your screen will look like a blocked cable station on TV: dizzy and fuzzy.

To change the refresh rate, click the downward arrow to get the menu of possible rates. You'll want to select the highest refresh rate your monitor can support. New monitors can usually handle refresh rates in the 70–75 Hertz range, but you don't take anything for granted—check the monitor's manual. If you've inherited an older monitor, you'll need to experiment with this setting.

Change the refresh rate (Windows 98)

If you dig around in your Advanced settings, you'll find the refresh rates. But you don't have to worry about them in Windows 98—the system has finally figured out how to choose the optimum rate and set it for you.

Change the font size

If you have problems reading text on the screen, you can change the default to "Large Fonts," which increases the size of on-screen type by 25 percent. You might appreciate this change if you've started to need glasses to read the screen or if you've changed the resolution so everything is smaller. This doesn't change the type size that *prints*.

To change the screen font size (Windows 95 and NT)

1. If the Display Properties are not open, right-click anywhere on the Desktop to get the pop-up menu and choose "Properties."

2. Click the "Settings" tab. In the "Font Size" box, click the downward arrow. You can toggle between the two options of "Large Fonts" and "Small Fonts."

Change the font size here in Windows 95.

3. Click OK to save the change and close the dialog box. You have to restart the computer before the changes will take effect.

To change the screen font size (Windows 98)

1. Follow the steps above to the "Settings" section, then click the "Advanced" button. You should see a dialog box with font specifications you can change.

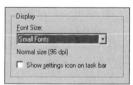

This is one example of what you might see in your Advanced section, depending on your monitor and card.

2. Click the "Font Size" downward arrow. You can choose between "Small Fonts" or "Large Fonts," or you can choose "Other…" and use the slider (shown below) to specify exactly how large you'd like your text to be. When you're done, just click OK on these windows. You have to restart to see the changes.

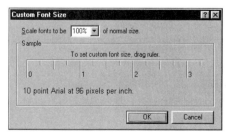

This font size doesn't apply to menu bars and buttons in toolbars, but it does apply to all other places where system fonts are used, as well as the text you type on screen (but it doesn't affect the size of the type you print).

Testing your monitor changes

Windows NT, 95

Test

Run a test on Windows 95 before you OK all the settings.

After you've played with monitor changes and are ready to apply them, click the "Test" button in the "Settings" section. You'll get a video test screen. If you can see everything on the screen clearly, your computer setup can support the settings you've chosen. If you can't, you'll have to lower one of your requirements and test again. If you can see things clearly but you don't like the quality of what you see—maybe you get posterized blends or dithered (spotty) colors—you might want to increase the number of colors.

If you need to make a change, start by decreasing the refresh rate. Anything above 65 Hertz should be acceptable unless you're very visually sensitive. If that doesn't work, decrease the resolution or the color depth (number of colors), depending on what you need to do: If you word process, email, or create web graphics, you need fewer colors than if you edit full-color photographs.

Windows 98

You don't have to test your changes! Windows 98 is much more Mac-like than Windows 95 in how it handles monitor displays. It won't allow you to choose a combination that your system can't support. If you've set your colors to millions and then you try to up your resolution to the stratosphere, the system will gently correct you by snapping the slider back to the highest resolution you can use at that color depth. And you don't have to worry about refresh rates any more than you do on your Mac—it's all done for you.

Applying the monitor changes

Once you've tested and you know that everything works, you need to make these changes happen on your screen. Windows versions do this in different ways. Up until very recently, a Windows user had to restart the entire computer to apply any color depth or resolution change!

On Windows 98

If you're using Windows 98, you are a lucky person! You can make changes without having to restart your system. Just click "Apply." You may see the "Compatibility Warning" dialog box:

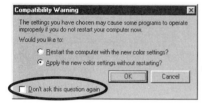

This warning primarily applies to older programs, particularly DOS ones. If you don't want to be warned in the future, check "Don't ask this question again" at the bottom of the screen.

On Windows 95

If you've changed your color depth or fonts, you'll probably be told that the system needs to restart to make your changes. This certainly is a pain. Fortunately, there is a perfectly acceptable work-around available.

To avoid restarting after making changes, first you'll need to visit www.microsoft.com and download and install "PowerToys for Windows 95." This is a collection of free utilities and enhancements that were meant for the original release of Windows 95, but Microsoft was too far behind schedule to incorporate them into the operating system. One of these enhancements is called "QuickRes." It alters your Display Properties "Settings" section to give you a menu of the only resolution options that match your hardware. After making your changes, it lets you apply the changes without a restart.

On Windows NT

Whether you need to restart or not will depend on your video hardware and what exactly you're trying to change. Sometimes when you click "Apply," you get a dialog box telling you that a restart is about to happen. Other times your system obediently makes your changes right then and there. NT is harder to set up initially, but it has a good grasp of its installed hardware. Except for font display changes, odds are very good that your screen will update without problems.

About dual monitors

Macs have supported dual monitors since the first component Macs in the late 1980s; there's a section of the Monitors control panel devoted to arranging two video displays. For the first time in PC history, Windows 98 tries to support two monitors. If you put two video cards into a Windows 98 system, whether you actually get a dual monitor display or not depends on the identity of the second card. Many video cards just aren't recognized as a *second* card, although they work fine as the *first* one.

If you have two monitors on your Windows 98 system, the Display Properties "Settings" will show two monitor icons, not just one. As on the Mac, you can move the icons around to determine whether they'll display side by side or top to bottom, and you can change resolution and color depth separately by clicking first on the monitor icon and then making your changes.

If you are using any other form of Windows, you can support two monitors with a hardware add-on. It requires that you install two video adapter cards capable of recognizing and supporting a dual-monitor system. On a system with this extra hardware, the video adapter software will provide specialized control panels or property sheets for arranging monitors and changing settings. This hardware solution is not as flexible as the Windows 98 or Macintosh options. You probably won't be able to set your two monitors to individual resolutions or color depths.

Control Panels

Control panels make your life easier by managing resources and setting preferences on your system. Many wonderful Mac control panels exist because the Mac is a neat little machine. It can be an unpleasant surprise to discover that a control you've taken for granted and relied on has no Windows equivalent. For example, in Windows there is no Extensions Manager because there's no way for a non-expert to manage extensions. If the stars are right, the moon is new, and you've backed up your Registry you can *sometimes* boot a troubled system from another drive, but there's no quick and easy way to set a different disk (like a Zip or a second hard disk) as the system startup drive.

This chapter dwells on the possible. We'll walk you through the functions usually handled by control panels on the Mac, looking at how you can do the same things on the PC. We ignore any Windows control panels that don't have a Macintosh match—the majority of those other control panels deal with hardware installations or offer complex technical information about the system. By the time you'll need them, you'll no longer be a Windows newbie.

Control Panels in Windows

Like the Mac, Windows groups its control panels all together in one folder. Unlike the Mac, which gives you direct access to each control panel individually from the Apple menu, you have to open the Control Panel folder first, then double-click the individual control panel icon. Also unlike the Mac, the Windows Control Panel folder is locked. You can't add to or delete items from the window by dragging and dropping, not even shortcut files. Control Panels can only be added by installing their applications.

Getting to the Windows Control Panel folder takes a few steps (like most Windows actions).

Open the Control Panel in either of two ways

- Click the Start button, slide up to "Settings…," then choose "Control Panel." **OR:**
- From the Desktop, open "My Computer," and double-click on the Control Panel icon.

This is a typical Windows Control Panel window. Different Windows types have slightly different collections of Control Panel icons. This collection came from a Windows NT system.

Control Panel

This is a shortcut to the Control Panels folder that you can keep on your Desktop for easy access.

Since having to use the Start menu or open Desktop windows is very tedious, you might want to make a shortcut of the Control Panel folder to keep on your Desktop.

To make a shortcut of the Control Panel folder

- **Right-click** on the Control Panel icon and drag it to the Desktop. From the menu, choose "Create Shortcuts Here."

General Controls

Windows and the Mac don't see eye to eye about what a general control is and where it ought to be located. Many of the items in the General Controls on the Mac simply aren't available as part of the Windows interface. Where appropriate, we tell you where in this book to find similar controls over the features you're accustomed to using.

"Show Desktop when in background"

Windows doesn't have an option to show or hide the Desktop while you're in an application, but you can get a similar effect by clicking the maximize button to enlarge a window to full screen, or clicking the minimize button to hide a window or application you aren't actively using. See Chapter 7, *Anatomy of a Window.*

"Show Launcher at system startup"

There isn't a Launcher in Windows, but you can customize the Taskbar in Windows 95/98 to act like the Launcher. See Chapter 8, *The Taskbar and Start Menu.*

"Folder Protection"

See Chapter 20, *Finding File Information*, to learn about locking and hiding files.

"Documents"—setting a default folder for saving files

See Chapter 16, *Installing and Using Applications.*

"Shut Down Warning," "Insertion Point Blinking," or "Menu Blinking"

Not applicable or customizable in Windows.

Date/Time and Map

Date/Time

Every system needs to keep track of the time and provide basic calendar information. There's a digital readout of the time on the Windows Desktop, in the bottom-right corner of the Taskbar. However, there isn't any way to change the clock's format or display the date. The only changes you can make in the Date/Time control panel are to set the time, month, day (select it in the monthly calendar), and year. To change the digital display to a 24-hour clock, use the Regional Settings control panel, as discussed below.

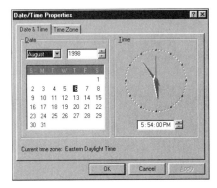

Time Zone

The Time Zone settings in the Date & Time control panel mimic the look of the Macintosh's Map control panel, but it's even more useless than the Macintosh Map. Change the time zone from the menu.

Regional Settings for foreign styles

Regional
Settings

To customize the style of the month, day, and year for various countries, use the Regional Settings control panel.

To set the date style

- Open the Control Panel folder, double-click on "Regional Settings," then click the "Date" tab. Use the menus.

To set the time style

- Open the Control Panel folder, double-click on "Regional Settings," then click the "Time" tab. Use the menus.

There's more about the Regional Settings control panel in the "Numbers" and "Text" sections on the next page.

Numbers

To adjust the number and currency settings for foreign countries, use the "Number" settings in the control panel called Regional Settings. It's more fully featured and complicated than the Mac Numbers control panel. Of course, the average person won't need or use half of these settings.

Regional Settings

If Windows was installed specifically for you by the PC vendor, the regional defaults you need are probably already set up for you. If you bought a generic PC, the default of English (U.S.) will appear in the dialog box of the control panel.

If you aren't in the U.S., you'll probably want to change the U.S. English default—have your install disk for Windows handy because you may need to grab new settings from the CD. If you install new settings, all of the information in the Numbers control panel will automatically update.

Text

The Mac's Text control panel adjusts things like language-based capitalization, the way numbers and currency are displayed, and the way certain items are sorted. Windows makes similar display and behavior changes in most applications when you assign a language and country in the Regional Settings control panel (discussed above, shown below).

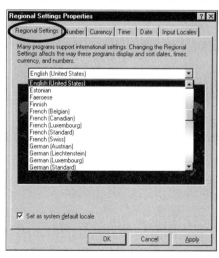

If you use your computer in different parts of the world, or if you create documents that need to be in the format for a particular country, change the settings here.

Modem, PPP, and TCP/IP

Modems

The Modems control panel in Windows includes the elements for setting up a *modem* on a computer and offers various connection settings that we usually see in other Mac control panels.

modem: The device that allows computers to communicate with other computers using the telephone lines.

To tell your computer what kind of modem you have

1. Open the Control Panel folder.

2. Double-click the "Modems" icon in the Control Panel folder. If your system came with a modem already installed, its name should appear in the Modem dialog box. If so, ignore the rest of this section and skip to "Set the modem sound preferences" on the opposite page. If not, click the "Add" button. You'll get a warning that your modem should be turned on and no programs that use a modem should be running.

3. Click "Next," and Windows will check its ports for new modems. If successful, the computer will recognize the modem and the connection; click "Finish" and you're done. If unsuccessful, you'll be asked to select the modem port. Select it from the list, click "Next," then click "Finish."

   Sometimes Windows recognizes there's a modem installed but can't figure out what kind of modem it is. You'll get a dialog box telling you it has found a "Standard Modem." That's not good enough. If you want your connections to work, you'll have to manually tell Windows exactly what kind of modem you have and where to find it.

4. In the "Install Modems" dialog box where Windows selected the "Standard Modem" for you, click the "Change" button. You'll see the "Install New Modem" dialog box, shown below.

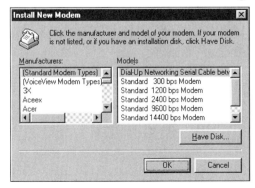

5. In the "Install New Modem" dialog box, there's a list of manufacturers on the left side. Scroll through and find the manufacturer of your modem, then click once on that name to select it. The list on the right will change to display all of the modems from that manufactuer that Windows has *drivers* for. If your modem is listed on the right, click its name to select it, then click OK, and skip to Step 8.

driver: **the software that tells the computer a device exists and what to do with it.**

6. If your modem is still not listed, hunt up the disk or CD that came with your modem, insert the disk into the computer, and click the "Have Disk" button.

7. Windows needs you to find the modem driver on your disk. If there is a choice, make sure you choose the driver for the correct version of Windows you're running or your modem won't work. Click your modem's model, click OK, and your driver will load.

8. Click "Next," then click "Finish." This process should set up your modem type, and also tell the computer what port your modem is on (the place where it's plugged in) and the connection speed that the modem can handle.

Set the modem sound preferences

Once your modem driver is loaded, you'll probably want to set the sound preferences as you would on a Mac. (To set the dialing preferences, see the next page.)

To set the modem sound preferences

1. If you're not already there, return to the Modems control panel and click the "Properties" button.

2. In the "Speaker volume" section, drag the slider all the way to the left and your modem will dial soundlessly. As you move the slider to the right, the sound will get progressively louder.

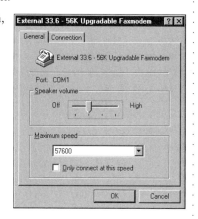

Set the modem dialing preferences

Use the Modems control panel to set up the phone numbers and other specifications for getting online. You can set up different sets of specifications for different dialing situations; for instance, if you connect to the Internet using a portable computer, you might need to use different phone numbers, a code to get an outside line, or a calling card number, depending on where you are calling from.

To set various modem dialing preferences

Modems

1. Open the Control Panel folder (it's in "My Computer").

2. Double-click on the "Modems" icon in the Control Panel folder.

3. If it's not already showing, click the "General" tab, then click "Dialing Properties" to get the dialog box.

4. You can now create a personal dialing profile. Begin by giving your new location a name, like Home, Office, On the Road, Paris, or Internet Cafe. Type in your area code, and choose a country.

   Now be really specific:

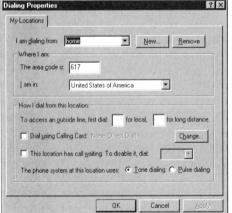

- If you need to dial a certain number to get an outside line, then enter that number. If your company requires that you dial a company code to make long distance phone calls, enter that number.

- If you want to connect from a hotel without paying outrageous long distance surcharges, check "Dial using Calling Card," then click "Change…" to enter your number.

- Enter a code to disable "call waiting" temporarily, otherwise your connection will be disconnected by an incoming call. The code to disable call waiting is *70.

- Specify tone or pulse dialing. Most modern urban phone systems use "tone" because that's what you need for touchtone phones. Only if you have a very old phone system (one that dials) would you choose "pulse," and it's lousy for data transfer.

Once you have your specifications set up, you can use the Modems control panel to choose the set you need to get online depending on the location or the situation. For instance, choose the "Office" set on your laptop when you're at the office, and the "Home" set at home.

Monitors

See Chapter 12, *Display Settings*, to find out how to change your screen colors and resolution.

ColorSync System Profile

Windows 98

ColorSync on the Mac uses something called *ICC* profiles to manage the colors on your monitor. Windows 98 incorporates compatibility with ColorSync in the "Advanced" section of Display Properties. See Chapter 25 on *Color* to find out how to add a color profile to your computer.

ICC profile: International Color Consortium profile, which is a description of the color range of a device such as a monitor or scanner.

Windows 95 and NT

There is no control panel in which to input monitor profiles. To calibrate your Windows monitor, you'll need to invest in color management software. Two inexpensive software packages, Pantone's Personal Color Calibrator and Sonnetech's Colorific, will allow you to match the functions of Apple's ColorSync 2.5.

QuickTime Settings

Although Windows does not ship with QuickTime, the QuickTime player for Windows is available as a download from www.apple.com. When the QuickTime Settings control panel is installed, its icon appears in the Windows Control Panel folder. This control panel in Windows bears absolutely no resemblance to the one you have on your Macintosh. It's very complicated and detailed for optimizing your system for recording audio and video clips. You won't need to do anything in the control panel to just use the QuickTime Player.

QuickTime 32

This control panel has one quite-wonderful section that has nothing to do with QuickTime but should be incorporated in every Windows control panel, utility, and application: "File." The File section shows a list of every file, system file, and extension that the QuickTime installer loaded onto your computer and where to find them. This is great because Windows installers put files everywhere, without documentation. If all Windows developers provided a list of their files like this, even basic users could start to understand their Windows systems.

If you're looking for QuickTime-like functions without having to load QuickTime, read about the Windows Media Player accessory in Chapter 14.

Sounds of actions

Sounds

If you have a sound card installed in your Windows computer, you'll hear alert sounds when things happen on your computer, just as you do on the Mac. Without a sound card, your PC is totally silent!

Windows has different sounds assigned to different actions, called "events," like mouse clicks and alerts. There's a default set of these sounds. You can replace the whole set, called a scheme, with a completely different scheme, or you can mix and match individual sounds for different events.

To replace one scheme with another

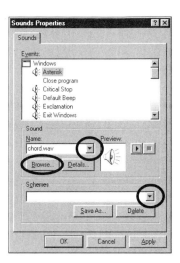

1. Open the Control Panel folder (it's in "My Computer").

2. Double-click on the "Sounds" icon in the Control Panel folder.

3. In the "Sounds Properties" dialog box, click the down arrow in the Schemes box to get a list of possible sources. Windows comes with a few schemes (besides the default) to get you started, and you can get hundreds of other schemes to install by down-loading them from shareware sites on the Internet.

4. To install a scheme that isn't part of the original group, click the "Browse" button and locate the new scheme on your hard disk. Schemes must be on the hard disk in your computer before you can use them—don't try to install a scheme that's stored on a floppy disk or removable cartridge.

To assign a new sound to an event

1. In the dialog box shown above, scroll through the list of "Events" until you find the one you'd like to change. Click on it.

2. In the "Sound" section, click the arrow next to the edit box for "Name" (circled, above), scroll through the options, and choose one. Click the "Preview" arrow button to hear it. When you've got what you want, click OK.

Audio settings, volume

The Mac provides a group of options for audio input and output in the
Monitors & Sound control panel. Windows has audio options too, but
they're buried within the Multimedia control panel.

Multimedia

To change the audio settings

1. Open the Control Panel folder (it's in "My Computer").

2. Double-click on the "Multimedia" icon in the Control Panel
   folder to get the property sheet.

3. Click the "Audio" tab.

   Exactly what you see in this section will depend on what kind
   of sound card is in your PC and what version of Windows
   you're running:

Windows 98

Windows NT/95

You can't make many changes in this audio section. You can change the
output volume, and you can assign the output sound quality level, but
the quality is limited to whatever your sound card can handle.

ODBC

ODBC (Open DataBase Connectivity) is available on both Macs and PCs. Among other things, it allows users to share and access information in a variety of different database formats. This is a very high-level and specialized panel. If you're already familiar with ODBC on the Mac, you don't need to be told how to use it here. If you don't use ODBC on the Mac, you probably won't use it in Windows, either.

Others

The following Mac control panels have no direct equivalents in Windows, but here's where to find comparable information.

Apple Menu Options
Obviously there is no Apple Menu in Windows, but if you want to customize your Start Menu, see Chapter 15.

Appearance and Desktop Pictures
See Chapter 12 on *Display Settings* for discussions of Desktop settings, backgrounds, and customizing the Desktop.

File Sharing and Users and Groups
See Chapter 27, *Multiple Users on One PC*, for file sharing in Windows.

Keyboard
See Chapter 5, *The Keyboard*.

Mac OS Easy Open, MacLinkPlus Settings, and PC Exchange
Although nothing like these compatibility control panels exist in Windows, we show you how to use these Mac tools to read PC media on your Mac in Chapter 21, *Mounting PC Media and Reading PC Files*.

Memory
To understand why there's no Memory control panel in Windows, read the "Application Memory" section in Chapter 16, *Installing and Using Applications*.

Mouse
See Chapter 6, *The Mouse*.

Mac Desk Accessories à la Windows

Desk accessories are the little Mac utilities we just can't do without. When Macophiles start working in Windows, we look frantically for their equivalents and are frequently disappointed. Not only are a lot of them missing, but the ones with similar names don't necessarily do what we might expect.

This chapter is organized to let you look for a Mac accessory and find its Windows equivalent. Rather than go through every Windows accessory, we've concentrated on those that do things that Mac users recognize. If there isn't an equivalent accessory, we'll tell you. Many of the things we do on the Mac using desk accessories Windows does in other ways, so if you don't find what you need in this chapter, be sure to check the index. And several Windows accessories offer options with no Mac equivalent; we discuss some of these in other appropriate chapters in the book.

Locating Windows accessories

You'll find all of the Windows accessories in the Start Menu, which is in the bottom-left corner of your screen. Click "Start," slide up to "Programs," then to Accessories. You'll have to scroll out one more level to get to some of the items you need; as Microsoft added more of these features, they grouped them into category folders, as you can see below.

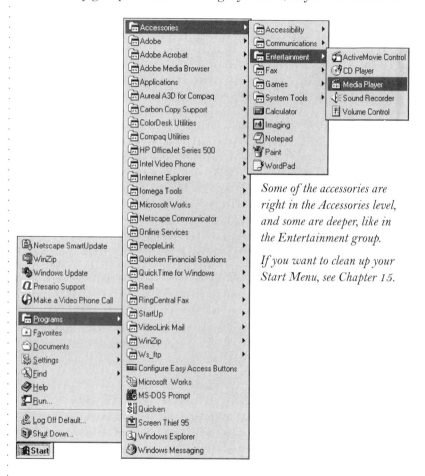

Some of the accessories are right in the Accessories level, and some are deeper, like in the Entertainment group.

If you want to clean up your Start Menu, see Chapter 15.

Mac: Calculator

The Macintosh calculator is a simple, basic-function accessory, good for quick figuring but extremely limited. Its best feature is that you can copy the results and paste them into your documents.

Windows Accessory: Windows Calculator

There are actually two versions of the Windows calculator: the Scientific (shown below, left) and the Standard (below, right). You can toggle between the two versions from the View menu. What are all those functions on the Scientific calculator? If we have to tell you, you don't need them.

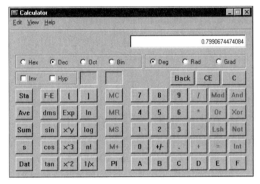

Like the Mac's version, you can copy and paste results into your documents.

This is a nice little accessory, even for the mathematically challenged, and it's much more like a real calculator than the Mac's. Have you ever noticed that you can't clear a mistake on the Mac calculator—you just have to start over? To correct an error in the Windows calculator, just hit the "Back" or "Backspace" button (or the Backspace key on your keyboard), delete to your mistake, and correct it. This calculator also has memory functions (the "M" buttons), just like a real calculator.

You can use the numerical keypad on your keyboard to input numbers, as well as the regular keyboard number keys, or you can use the mouse to click on the numbers on the calculator on the screen. If you use the numerical keypad and the numbers don't appear in the calculator, press the Num Lock key in the keypad (it's above the 7 key).

Right-click on any button, and you'll see a label that says, "What's this?" Click that label and you'll get a message telling you not only what the function is, but the keyboard equivalent for that function so you never have to take your hands off the keyboard to use the calculator.

Mac: Video Player

Macs are better video computers out of the box than Windows machines. There's nothing to match the Mac Video Player's real-time playback of video from MPEG files, video feed, or live TV (not to mention that the control panel itself is so elegant). But there is a player on the Windows side of things, known as Media Player.

Windows Accessory: Media Player

From the Start Menu, slide up to "Programs," up to "Accessories," find the "Entertainment" submenu (Windows 98) or the "Multimedia" submenu (Windows NT and 95), and choose "Media Player."

The Media Player is kind of a Swiss army knife. It lets you read sound and video files in several different formats. If you load QuickTime for Windows, you can play it here as well as in QuickTime's own player.

To see the options you already have available

1. If you already know what kind of file you want to play, just choose the type—sound, CD, video—from the "Device" menu. You'll get an "Open" dialog box to find the file on a drive.

2. Double-click the name of the file. While it loads, Media Player will read the length of the clip and change its duration scale to fit how long the file is. The file window will open up to exactly the dimensions of the video or animation you want to play.

3. Click the Play button (▶) to run the clip. To pause it, just click inside the window once with either mouse button.

This image is one frame of a really dumb twelve-second clock that Microsoft provides as a sample .avi file.

AVI is Microsoft's competitor video format to Apple's QuickTime.

Here are some of the things you can do with the Media Player.

Center the window in full-screen

Click the "Device" menu and choose "Properties." Use the radio buttons to toggle between window and full-screen views.

Set up your clip to loop (repeat)

From the Edit menu, choose "Options" You'll get a tiny little dialog box. Select "Auto Repeat" (another name for "loop"). You can also choose to have the clip rewind automatically so you can play it another time without looping.

Listen to a small piece of a sound clip you're thinking of sampling

From the Edit menu, choose "Selection…." You'll see another tiny dialog box that lets you set exactly how much of the file you want to play. You can really fine-tune things here since the display lets you set time lengths in hundredths of a second.

Copy any video or sound clip from Media Player into a document (if the document's application can support the format your clip is in)

1. Open your video or sound file in Media Player.
2. From the Edit menu, choose "Copy Object."
3. Minimize the Media Player (click the ▬ button in the upper left).
4. Open the document in which you want to place a clip.
5. Click your cursor in the place in the document where you want the clip to play. The "insertion point" should be flashing.
6. From the Edit menu, choose "Paste." The clip will appear where the insertion point was flashing.
7. Double-click the clip icon in the document to play it. Amazing.

The clip isn't really part of the document, it's just a reference the computer uses to find the media file on a disk or to play back a track from a CD. If you send this document somewhere, you must send the original clip along with it. If the original audio source can't be found on the computer, the sound or video won't play in the document.

Play multiple devices at the same time

If you are playing a CD audio track, you can return to the Device menu, choose "Sound…," and overlay the sound of Star Trek phasers onto Bach's *Toccata and Fugue* while you play a video clip. Or maybe not—but it does keep young computer users occupied while you do other things.

Tip: Would you like a box around the video clip? Before you use "Copy Object" in Media Player, go to the Edit menu and choose "Options." Click the checkbox "Border around object." Close the window. Now when you "Copy Object," you'll have a black border setting the clip off from the rest of page.

Mac: AppleCD Audio Player

The CD players are pretty straightforward. There's very little difference between the Mac's player and the one in Windows, although once again, the Mac's window actually looks like the front panel of a CD player, while the Windows player looks like every other Windows dialog box.

Windows Accessory: CD Player

Although you can play CDs through the Media Player, you'll have more precise control over them if you use the CD Audio Player instead.

From the Start Menu, slide up to "Programs," to "Accessories," find the "Entertainment" submenu (Windows 98) or the "Multimedia" submenu (Windows NT and 95), and choose "CD Player."

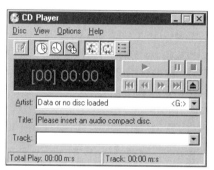

The Windows CD player is just as easy to use as the Mac version, although it's not quite as pretty.

To use the CD player

1. Put an audio CD in your CD-ROM drive.

2. From the Options menu in the CD player accessory, choose between "Random Order" (shuffle), "Continuous play," or "Intro Play," which is a neat little browsing feature that will play short clips from the beginning of each track.

3. To set the length of clip you'll hear when you browse with "Intro Play," go to "Options," choose "Preferences," then use the buttons to set your choice between 5 and 15 seconds.

Set a "play list" (on the Mac it's called a "program") to play your cuts in a specific order

1. From the Disc menu, choose "Edit Play List...."
   The "Disc Settings" dialog box appears:

2. If you have a multi-changer CD, you might want to input the artist and title information. We like to do this even with one CD player because it feels less anonymous, although we wish the CD player could read the information itself.

3. From the "Available Tracks" list on the right, click the track you'd like to hear, then click the "Add" button to insert it into the "Play List" on the left. You can play any track as many times as you'd like simply by choosing it from the "Available Tracks" multiple times.

4. When you've chosen your music tracks, click OK, and the music begins. You can go back and change the Play List anytime.

Mac: Key Caps

The Mac's Key Caps feature is a great accessory because it show you how to type the special characters such as ©, ™, or ¢.

Windows Accessory: Character Map

This Windows keyboard map shows you all of the characters in a select font. You can find the character you need, then copy it from Character Map and paste it into your document, or you can see the keyboard sequence you need to type to make that character appear on your page.

To use Character Map

1. From the Start Menu, slide up to "Programs," to "Accessories," find the "System Tools" submenu, and choose "Character Map." (In Windows 95 and NT, Character Map is in "Accessories.")

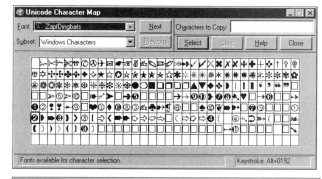

Character Map in Windows 95 and NT.

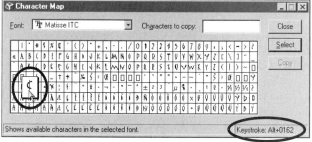

Character Map in Windows 98.

2. In Windows 95 or NT, make sure the choice under "Subset" is "Windows Characters."

3. In all versions: Scroll through the Font menu and choose the font you need. The typeface in the grid will change to your chosen font, and every character in that font will be displayed.

4. Look for the character you need. To enlarge a character so you can actually see it (as shown, circled), press the mouse button down on a key. With the mouse button down, drag across the other characters to see them enlarged as well, or press the arrow keys to move the enlarged selection around.

5. Choose one or more characters to copy into your document: Double-click on a character to select it. It will appear in the "Characters to Copy" box. Click the "Copy" button.

6. Now you can close the Character Map, open your application, and paste the character or characters into your document.

7. If the characters in your document are not what you expected, they're probably just in the wrong font. Select them, then choose the same font you used in Character Map.

Typing special characters in your documents

You can hit the Control or Alt keys in Windows from now until the next millennium and you'll never type even one of those special characters you're accustomed to using on the Mac, such as Option G to get the © symbol. To type any of those characters directly into your application (instead of having to copy and paste from Character Map constantly), you have to find the "Alt code," then type that code on your page.

Tip: Some applications, such as PageMaker, have a number of special characters built into keyboard shortcuts. Check the shortcuts list in PageMaker's Help menu.

To find and type the Alt code for a character

1. In the Character Map, choose the font and click on the character you want to type in your document, such as ¢.

2. Look in the lower-right corner of the Character Map to find the "Keystroke," as shown on the previous page. Write down those four numbers (in the lower example, 0162).

3. Go to your document. Hold down the Alt key. Using the numbers on the numeric keypad (not the regular keyboard!), type those four numbers, then let go of the Alt key and the character will appear.

Just for fun in Windows 95 and NT

Next time you're in Character Map, choose a font like Arial and quickly hit the "Next" button several times. This will change the Subset keyboard listing to display alternate characters and languages. Most of the keyboard displays will be those boring square placeholders where no character has been assigned. But a few surprise characters and dingbats will appear, and you'll be treated to an interesting list of languages.

Mac: Chooser

Oh, we wish Windows had a Chooser equivalent, even though Apple itself seems determined to get rid of it. If Windows had a Chooser, the printing setup would be a whole lot easier.

Windows Accessory: not

Alas, there is nothing comparable to the Chooser in Windows. Anyway, there's no point in telling you how to set up a printer on your Desktop in this section because Chapter 26 on Printing covers everything.

Mac: Note Pad

The Macintosh Note Pad is a kind of automatic placeholder for ideas and information, and it saves what you write automatically. You can store web addresses in there, then pull them directly from the Notepad onto a browser to open that web page; you can make "text clippings" that you can drag into just about any application; you can use Note Pad just to store little reminders to yourself. There are only eight pages, but each page can scroll longer.

The Mac Note Pad.

Windows Accessory: Notepad

In Windows, there's nothing quite like the Mac's Note Pad. That's a shame, because Windows cries out for places to leave short, intimate messages and reminders. It's much too structured for that, alas.

There *is* an accessory with almost exactly the same name, Notepad, but with a different mission. The Windows Notepad is more like the old Apple TeachText, but it's geared toward programmers and system administrators. They often need to do programmer things like write quick batch files and keep logs, so Notepad gives them two tools with which to do that. Notepad is a "text editor" where you can write infinitely long lines without word wrapping, which is useful for some people (not for us). It can also automatically time-stamp and date-stamp anything.

The Windows Notepad.

Like TeachText, Notepad only makes and reads limited-size files—Notepad's limit is 56K.

Mac: SimpleText

SimpleText is an uncomplicated word processor that lets you do simple font formatting and is flexible enough to open a wide variety of files. Even though it's not technically a desk accessory, SimpleText is just as important a Desktop tool as any of the other accessories.

Windows Accessories: WordPad

Word processing is the universal desktop application, so of course there's a word processor in Windows. In fact, there are two. If Notepad is equivalent to TeachText, WordPad is more like the original Mac-Write. It offers more formatting and word power than SimpleText, although it isn't a file "lock pick" the way SimpleText can be.

WordPad will look familiar to anyone who's done even simple word processing. It will look particularly familiar if you use some version of Microsoft Word since it looks and feels like a simplified Word, even down to the same keyboard shortcuts. In fact, if you happen to be a person who doesn't need sophisticated word processing functions because you do page layouts in other programs, WordPad is a great way to avoid Office 97's bloat. It also saves files as Word 6 and RTF (Rich Text Format) files.

Let's just look at what WordPad's features are. You can:

- Change typefaces, sizes, font colors, alignment, and basic styles. You'll find these options under the Format menu.

- Set tabs: click inside the ruler wherever you want a tab stop to appear. If you want to specify right indents as well, you can set those definitions from within "Format" by choosing "Paragraph" and filling in the dialog box.

- Find and replace text with WordPad's simple "Find and Replace" function, which you can find in the Edit menu.

- Insert just about any type of file into a WordPad document. It takes everything from *.pdf* files and bitmapped images to movie clips and sounds. To insert a file onto an existing page:

    From the Insert menu, choose "Object…" for a list of formats supported by WordPad. Choose your object type from the list; click OK. Locate the file you want to insert.

    If you load new software on your computer that creates a special kind of file format, that new format will be added to this list.

RTF: A file format for bringing formatted file information from one program (usually a word processor or spread-sheet) to another.

PDF: Portable Document Format, a file created by Adobe Acrobat. PDF files can be read on any computer with the Acrobat Reader or plug-in. They display fonts, graphics, and layout of complex documents, but can't be edited without Acrobat Exchange.

Windows Accessories: Quick View

WordPad does a good job of opening and creating text files, but it's not the universal file wrench that SimpleText has become, useful for opening just about any kind of file, even graphic files. Windows doesn't have such an accessory anywhere—what it does offer is Quick View.

If you're familiar with Adobe Acrobat Viewer, you already know how Quick View works. It doesn't allow you to edit or annotate files, but it sometimes at least lets you view them. If Quick View recognizes the file extension, even if the program that created it isn't installed, you'll actually see the image of the file on your desktop. You can open a file to read its contents, increase or decrease the font size, or even rotate it.

To view a file in Quick View

1. Make sure the file is inside a folder on the hard disk. Select the file's icon in the window.

2. In that folder window, go to the File menu. If the file is a type Quick View might recognize, you'll see "Quick View" listed in the menu, as shown to the right.

3. Click "Quick View," and the selected file will open in view-only mode.

Windows 98 users:

Quick View isn't loaded as part of the basic installation process. It's easy to find, though:

1. Insert your Windows installer disk.

2. Click the Start button, go to "Settings," and choose "Control Panel."

3. Click "Add/Remove Software."

4. Click the "Windows Setup" tab.

5. Double-click "Accessories."

6. Check the box for "Quick View." (You don't have to uncheck anything else.) Click OK.

7. Click OK to install Quick View on your computer.

8. You do not need to restart.

If Quick View doesn't appear in the File menu (which means the selected file isn't in a format Quick View recognizes), you can still use Quick View to figure out the document's file type. The following technique will open the file as text. This can be a little scary because you'll see pages of PostScript code instead of a beautifully composed newsletter. But even in such a seemingly difficult situation, being able to read the text portion of the file may help you figure out who owns the file and what application created it.

Double-click the file you want to view to get the "Open With" dialog box with a list of programs. Choose Quick View from the list, uncheck the box, "Always use this program to open this file," and click OK. You'll get the dialog box shown below. Click "Yes," and you see the text file.

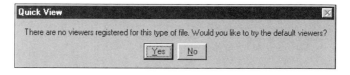

Mac: Clipboard and Scrapbook

The Clipboard is where any copied or cut item, such as text, graphics, sound, or an animation, is stored temporarily. If you want to keep the item on hand permanently, you move it to the Scrapbook where it's saved to your hard disk, and the file stays there until you decide to delete it. Scrapbook files can be pasted into documents or dragged to the Desktop to become clipping files.

Windows Accessory: Clipboard Viewer or Local ClipBook

Windows has a Clipboard that acts much the same as the Mac's, which means that most of the time you use it without having to think about it. But if you want to move information between different applications or to archive items for future use, you may need Clipboard Viewer.

In Windows 95 and NT, Clipboard Viewer has two windows: the Clipboard and the Local ClipBook. Local ClipBook is a sadly anemic shadow of the Mac Scrapbook. It's more complicated to put things into it, and it's less useful because you can't make clipping files like you might be used to on the Mac. Windows 98 doesn't even have a Local ClipBook, so there's no special place to archive small bits of text and graphics.

Put something in the Clipboard

- Select your text or image, then Cut or Copy it. Just as on the Mac, this puts the file into the Clipboard.

- If you quit out of the application you've cut or copied your text or image from, you might get this dialog box in Windows 95 or NT:

Be sure to answer "Yes" to this question, or Windows will empty the picture from the Clipboard.

Tip: If you go to the Accessories menu and you don't find "Clipboard Viewer," it may not be installed! Use Find File (see Chapter 20) to search for CLIPBRD.EXE. If you find it, follow instructions in Chapter 15, *Customizing the Start Menu*, to put the Clipboard Viewer in the Accessories section of the Start Menu where it belongs.

If you don't find the CLIPBRD.EXE file, insert your Windows installer CD. Just like the Mac's folder of Apple Extras, Microsoft has additional goodies in other folders on the CD. Use the "Windows Setup" settings in the control panel called "Add/Remove Programs" to load it.

Using Clipboard files

Tip: Don't be surprised if a Clipboard picture looks distorted. The window doesn't "see" the dimensions of a picture, so it might stretch the display strangely. This won't affect the actual information, but if it bothers you just resize the window.

On the Mac, the "Paste" or "Paste Special" command places whatever was in the Clipboard into a document, and it always works. In Windows, however, sometimes it doesn't work right when you're cutting and pasting between applications. You might get nothing when you paste or you might get strangely garbled stuff because Windows doesn't always recognize the type of information you're trying to move.

It's possible to solve this problem by using the Clipboard Viewer to change what's in the Clipboard into a different format.

To use Clipboard Viewer to change formats

1. From the Start Menu, choose "Programs," then "Accessories," then "System Tools," then "Clipboard Viewer" (in Windows 95 or NT, the Viewer is in the "Accessories list"). The information you previously cut or copied will appear in the window.

2. In the Viewer menu bar, click "Display" (in Windows 95 or 98, click "View"). The choices in the menu vary depending on what kind of information is in the Clipboard.

3. Choose a file type from this list that can be used by the application you want to paste the Clipboard information into. Then you can paste the file into the other document.

Transfer Clipboard items to the Local ClipBook
(Windows 95 or NT only)

Unlike the Mac's Scrapbook, there's no way to paste information directly to Windows' Local ClipBook. If you want to save small files in the ClipBook, you need to do it in two stages: cut or copy something to the Clipboard Viewer, then paste it to the Local ClipBook.

To transfer items to the Local ClipBook for permanent storage

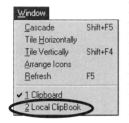

While in the Viewer, choose "Local ClipBook" to switch to the ClipBook.

1. While you're in the Clipboard Viewer, you need to switch to the Local ClipBook. To do this, from the Window menu, choose "Local ClipBook" (shown to the left).

   Notice the title bar of the window changes to tell you which part of the Clipboard you're looking at. This is a very useful clue because there is very little visual difference between the Clipboard Viewer window and the Local ClipBook window. The Local ClipBook window will be blank if no one has ever used the ClipBook on your computer before. If it has been used, the last clipping item to be added will be displayed.

2. From the Edit menu, choose "Paste."

In the dialog box that appears, you'll be asked to give the file a name. Name it carefully because you can't edit the name later! If the name you type is already in use, you'll be prompted to choose another.

To view Local ClipBook contents

Check to make sure your file has been archived:

- From the View menu, choose "Table of Contents." You should see your file's name in the window.

To arrange Local ClipBook files in two other ways

- From the View menu, choose "Thumbnails." A black and white bitmap image of the picture will show up. Because there isn't any way to make these into color previews, thumbnails are more useful for text than for pictures.

- You can cycle through your clipping items one by one: In the window you'll see arrow buttons just below the vertical scroll bar. The top button scrolls backward, the bottom one forward. The status bar displays the page number of the image in the ClipBook.

 Press these arrows to scroll through the ClipBook files.

Using a Local ClipBook item

To use an item you've previously archived, you need to put it back on the Clipboard. Follow the instructions above, "To view Local ClipBook contents." When you find the file you want to use, go to the Edit menu and choose "Copy." Then go to your document and paste it in.

Deleting a Local ClipBook item

Unlike the Mac Scrapbook, the Local ClipBook doesn't use disk space efficiently. On the Mac, Scrapbook pictures are in the file format called PICT, which are small files. In Windows, Local ClipBook pictures are gargantuan because they're saved in several different formats at once. If you don't edit periodically, the Local ClipBook will devour your hard drive. Fortunately, deleting items is easy: View the picture you don't want, then hit the Delete key; or go to the "Table of Contents," select the file name, and then Delete.

Mac: Stickies

Stickies on the Mac are virtual Post-it® notes that you can strew all over the Desktop. People who use them swear by them. Cyndi really loves Stickies and was upset to find out they don't exist on the PC.

Windows Accessory: WordPad scrap

kludge (pronounced "kloodge"; it does not rhyme with "fudge"): A dorky fix for a problem, usually meant to be temporary but often ending up to be permanent.

This is really a kludge. Windows has a totally lame version of clipping files called "scraps." You can make pseudo-stickies in WordPad by using these scraps.

To make a scrap

1. From the Start Menu, slide up to "Programs," to "Accessories," and open "WordPad."

2. In WordPad, go to the "View" menu and turn off all the bars and rulers so all you have is a nice, simple window with a menu.

3. Type the text you want on your pseudo-stickie.

4. When you're done, choose "Select All" from the Edit menu, or press Ctrl A. All of the text should be highlighted.

5. Press and drag this selected text from the WordPad window to the Desktop. When you let go, look at the Desktop. There's now a little file there with this selected icon:

 This is called a WordPad "scrap."

6. This file is automatically saved, so you can just quit WordPad.

7. As you can see, the file name is too long. Click on the name, and delete everything except the words in quotes, which will be the first few characters of the message you typed in WordPad. If those words (like in the example) are not terribly useful, you can rename the file to be something more generic, like this:

Shopping list

8. When you need to edit or look at the scrap, double-click on this icon. WordPad will launch and display your text.

Mac: About This Computer

Don't we take this little Apple menu window for granted? It gives us a lot of very useful information in a tiny little space. It not only tells us how much memory we have and how much we're using, but exactly what's using that memory. Not to mention the fact that it's an ever-flowing source of *Easter eggs*.

Mac: System Profiler

This is a handy Mac OS 8 addition that goes well beyond "About This Computer." It tells you everything that's stored in your System Folder, including what extensions and control panels are loaded and whether they're Apple items or third-party additions. It also gives a concise readout of your SCSI devices and their addresses.

Windows Accessories (Windows 98)

- Resource Meter
- System Monitor
- System Information

Cyndi has a good friend who is a very technically savvy Windows 95 user. He recently upgraded to Window 98 and sent her an excited email, praising its system monitoring and profiling tools. So she went and investigated all of them. Not a single one tells the average person anything useful, although they're probably a terrific stimulant for Windows techies. We're showing them to you because when something goes wrong with your Windows 98 computer, you'll probably call technical support. The tech support people will ask for some of this information, and you'll be less frustrated if you know how to find it.

- Click the Start Menu, slide up to "Programs," then over to "Accessories." From Accessories, find "System Tools." There are lots of individual accessories in this collection. On the next few pages we show you the ones that provide information about your computer system, hardware, and software.

Easter egg: A surprise built into the software by the programmers. For instance, this is an Easter egg: On the Mac, hold down the Option key and go to the Apple menu. What used to say "About This Computer" now says "About the Finder." Choose it. That's an Easter egg.

Wait about ten seconds for the second part of the Easter egg to appear.

Windows Resource Meter

In Windows, the Resource Meter is the closest thing to the Mac's informational box, "About This Computer." It's not very close. Here's what the Resource Meter information looks like:

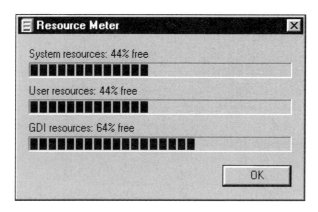

Tip: On the Mac, to see exactly how much memory an open application is using, go to the Apple menu and choose "About This Computer." Then go to the Help menu and choose "Show Balloons." Position your pointer over one of the bars that indicates the memory allocation for an application. The balloon that pops up will tell you exactly how much of the available memory that application is using.

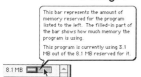

On the Mac, use "Show Balloons" to see the memory allocations of open programs.

The term "Resources" is Windows' reference to "accessible memory." The bars for "System resources" and "User resources" track memory available to the operating system and applications. In the computer whose performance is displayed above, 44 percent of the system memory is available. But how much memory *is* that? And *what's* using it? The Resource Meter doesn't give us the kind of application-specific information we can see on a Mac in the "About This Computer" dialog box. In Windows, we don't know what programs are loaded and how they've divided up the available memory.

The bar called "GDI resources" refers to the memory that the Graphic Device Interface (GDI) uses. This indicates what percentage of your video memory is being used for graphic purposes, like printing or on-screen rendering. If the free percentage number is very low, your video board is probably too slow for the work you're trying to do with it.

Windows System Monitor

The Windows System Monitor is a real-time readout of everything that's going on in your computer. Once you add a few graphs to the display (as explained below), you can see a constantly updated window of your system's memory use and potential conflicts.

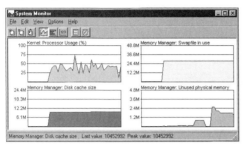

The System Monitor displays real-time graphs of your computer's activity. "Kernel Processor Usage" tells you what percentage of the time your CPU is active. The "Memory Manager" keeps track of your RAM usage and how much of your disk is being used for virtual memory.

Non-tip: For most users, System Monitor's data is so technically-oriented that it gives you little troubleshooting help. Like a screen saver, System Monitor is best used as a focusing device when you need to stare into space and think of nothing at all.

To add graphs to the monitor

1. From the Edit menu, choose "Add Item."

2. In the "Add Item" dialog box, choose a system process from the "Category" list. When you choose one, the "Item" scrolling box to the right will display several options of processes to graph. The more options you choose, the more active and full of primary-color graphs your screen will become.

To print system information from Windows 95 and NT

Windows 95 and NT do not have any system *accessories*. But you can access system *information* and print summaries of it.

Windows 95

1. Right-click on "My Computer" and choose "Properties."

2. Click the "Device Manager" tab, and then click "Print."

3. Choose "All devices and system summary," then click OK.

Windows NT

1. To find the System Overview information, begin at the Start Button, slide up to "Programs," over to "Administrative Tools," and click on "Windows NT Diagnostics."

2. Click a different tab for each piece of information: To see the version of Windows you're running, click the "Version" tab. For the type and speed of the computer processor, click the "System" tab. To see how much RAM, click the "Physical Memory" tab.

Windows System Information

This accessory, like the Mac OS 8 "System Profiler," is designed to give you useful information about what's on your computer. The problem is, you won't understand it. Don't feel bad. Almost no one else understands it, either.

This is what the Microsoft System Information window looks like:

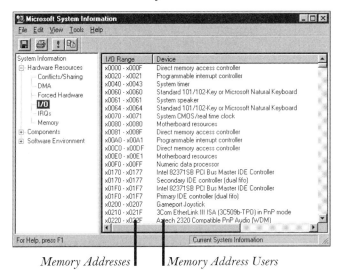

Memory Addresses ┃ ┃ *Memory Address Users*

This "System Information" dialog box also includes a set of diagnostic and repair utilities, which you can access from the Tools menu. If something goes wrong, a tech support person may ask you to run one of these utilities and print out the result.

Customizing the Start Menu

The Start Menu is the key to getting around in Windows. Unlike the Mac aliases that can get covered up by windows, the Start Menu is always accessible, wherever you are and whatever you're doing. Such an important tool should be lean, intelligently organized, and easy to use—but this is Windows.

Windows begins by placing a mountain of accessories in the Start Menu, regardless of whether or not you need them. Every program you load installs a link to itself in the Start Menu as well. If you have a lot of applications and then add a few utilities, the menu can take forever to navigate. It's hard to remember where things are and even when you do remember, some of the most important items are buried four levels deep. In this chapter, we look at ways to control the Start Menu and make it more useful for you.

Using the keyboard to navigate the Start Menu

We've mentioned that Windows doesn't support as many keyboard shortcuts as the Mac does and that it's very menu-heavy. Fortunately the Start Menu—the most complex menu of them all—does respond to the keyboard. You may find the following tips really useful when you're typing or using a drawing tablet and don't want to have to pick up the mouse:

1. There are two ways to open the Start Menu from the keyboard.

   This is the Windows key, found only on recent models of PCs.

   - If you have a recent model of computer, press the Windows key (it's near the Spacebar and has a Windows logo on it, as shown to the left).
   - If you don't have a new computer with the Windows key, press Ctrl Esc (Control and Escape keys together).

2. Once the Start Menu is open, press the first letter of any program or category in the list to jump to it. If there's more than one item starting with the same letter, press the same letter again to jump to the next item that starts with that letter.

3. To open the next level of menus to the right of a triangle, tap the right arrow key on your keyboard.

   If you go too far over to the right in the menus, retrace your steps using the left arrow key.

   Windows 98: If you select a category that has a submenu, that next menu level opens automatically. For example, if Norton Antivirus is the only program in the Start Menu that begins with "N," Windows will select Norton Antivirus and open its submenu when you press the "N" key.

   If there is more than one item in the list that starts with "N," such as Norton Antivirus and Netscape Navigator, Windows will not open either submenu; it will wait for you to choose between the two options that both start with "N."

4. Press the Enter key to launch any selected item.

Putting new things in the Start Menu

Although many programs add their names to the Start Menu whether they're invited to or not, other items hide in ignored corners of the hard disk. If you have an application or a utility that you want easy access to through the Start Menu, you can add it.

There are two ways to add the name of an application or other Desktop item to the Start Menu: a quick way and a longer, more useful way.

Here's the quick method to add items to your Start Menu

1. On the hard disk, find a file, folder, or application you use a lot.
2. Drag the item over to the Start button.

   Windows 98: Don't let go of the item! The Start Menu will open and you can drag the item above the dividing lines and drop it right there, or you can drag out to any submenu and drop it.

   If you would be happy to have the item right on the first level of the Start Menu, don't bother to open the menu—just drop the item on the Start Menu button and it will appear in the list.

   Windows 95 or NT: When you drag the item over the Start button, you'll see the shortcut arrow. Let go. This will put a shortcut of the item right in the Start Menu, in the top portion, alphabetically. The shortcut will be named exactly the same as the item you dragged, including its extension, if it has one.

That's so simple, but if you do it the longer way you can do a couple of extra things:

- You can create folder categories to organize your Start Menu instead of searching through the long Start or Programs list. (Windows 98 will not organize your folders alphabetically for you; if you wanted them sorted in a certain way, you'll have to drag them around yourself.)
- You can rename an item on the Start Menu.
- You can spend some time reorganizing, moving, renaming, deleting, etc., all from one dialog box.

The best way to reorganize your Start Menu is to use both the quick and the more complete methods, but for different purposes. Save the quick method for folders and documents which you'll probably move in and out of the Start Menu as you need them, but use the longer method (described on the next page) for overall, long-term reorganization.

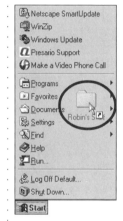

You can see the icon being dragged into the Start Menu now has the little arrow attached, which means it is now an alias, or shortcut (see Chapter 17 about shortcuts). The shortcut is on its way to the upper section of the menu.

You can't put anything in the section with "Programs," "Favorites," etc.—Windows keeps that for itself.

Here's the longer method to add items to your Start Menu

1. Right-click the Taskbar to get the menu, then choose "Properties."

2. In the property sheet, click the "Start Menu Programs" tab.

3. Click the "Add" button, and you'll get a dialog box asking you to type the location and name of the file (shown to the left).

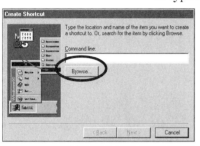

Don't type anything in this unless you're comfortable with Windows paths (see Chapter 19 on paths and file names)—it's too easy to type something incorrectly. Instead, click the "Browse" button. This leads to the same kind of dialog box you get when you save or open a file, as shown to the left.

4. If you don't see what you're looking for on the C: drive, go to the "Look in" box and click the down arrow (as shown to the left). This gives you access to other drives.

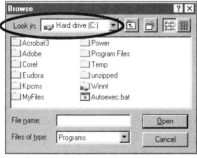

If you're looking for an application that you know is on the C: drive but you don't see its name on a folder in the window, double-click on the folder "Program Files"; Windows stores most of your applications in this folder.

5. When you find an individual *file* you want to add, double-click its name and skip to Step **6.**

By default, the Browse dialog box opens at the C: drive because that's where Windows expects all applications to be.

When you see the *folder* for an *application* you want to add, double-click to open it. There are probably lots of files in this folder, but the actually application usually has an .EXE extension at the end of its name. In Windows 98, however, it might not show the .EXE in this window! To see which file is actually the application, click the "Detailed List" button on the right end of the menu bar (shown to the left, circled). Then click the column heading "Type" to organize the files by type. Find the one that says it's an application. Double-click this icon.

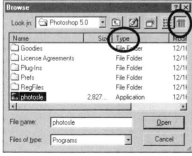

If you want access to a whole folder, go back to the first dialog box (shown at the top, left) and carefully type the whole path to the folder. Then go to Step 6. (Remember, in Windows 98 you can use the quick method to add a folder to the Start Menu.)

6. After you double-click the file, you'll be back at the "Create Shortcut" dialog box, and the path to your folder or application will be displayed, as shown to the right. Click the "Next" button to continue.

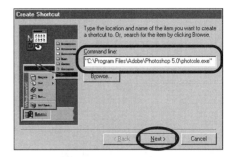

7. This is the good part. You get to choose where in the Start Menu to put the application. The "Programs" folder will be selected by default, but you can choose any folder you want.

8. Click once on a file to select it, then click the "Next" button. Windows will ask you to name this file. The application file or folder name will already appear in the box, but you can replace it with a different name and the system will still find the original. You can delete the .EXE, if there is one, lengthen the name and make it more descriptive, or even name it after your favorite pet.

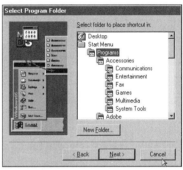

9. Click the "Finish" button, then click OK when you see the original "Start Menu Programs" settings.

The actual item that gets added to the Start Menu is an alias, or shortcut, as aliases are called in Windows. Although it's possible in Windows 95 and NT to add an original folder or program into the Start Menu by dragging and dropping it there, we don't think this is a good idea. If you forget and delete the item, you might actually lose the real application or documents.

Rearranging items in the Start Menu (Windows 95/98)

You can move any item anywhere else on the Start Menu (except below the first dividing line in the first level). This is particularly easy in Windows 98 and 95 (not in NT), because all you do is drag and drop.

1. Go to the Start Menu, then open the "Programs" submenu and find the file you want to move (in Windows 98, you can move whole folders, and you're not limited to "Programs").

2. Drag the file to a new position in any level of the Start Menu; as you drag, you'll see a black, heavy line between existing menu items showing where your item will be inserted. Let go of the mouse button when your file is positioned where you want it.

3. In Windows 98, you'll see the file in its new position immediately. In Windows 95, you have to close the Start Menu, then open it again before you see the item.

Rearranging entire folders in the Start Menu (Windows 95/NT)

Warning:
If this is a company computer on a network (any version of Windows), you may not be able to change the Start Menu folder contents. You may also discover some limitations as to what items you can move because some common accessories or applications may be in the "All Users" or "Default User" folder instead. Contact your system administrator for permission to make changes.

This simple drag-and-drop method of moving files in the Start Menu doesn't work for everything and in all versions of Windows. Except for Windows 98, you can't move entire folders that way—you can only reposition the items inside of them. In Windows 95 and NT, you need to work within a somewhat more complicated interface if you want to move folders (in fact, the following method is also the *only* way to organize the Start Menu in Windows NT).

1. Right-click the Taskbar to get the menu, then choose "Properties." In the property sheet, click the "Start Menu Programs" tab.

2. Click the "Advanced" button. You'll get the Windows Explorer window which is divided into two panels, like this:

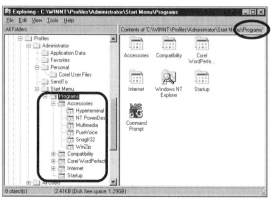

The panel on the right side of this window is just a different way of looking at the contents of the Programs folder shown on the left.

Windows Explorer usually opens with the Start Menu folder selected in the left panel and its contents showing on the right. If it didn't, locate your Start Menu in the "Windows" folder (Windows 95 or 98) or the "WINNT" folder (Windows NT) on the C: drive.

Windows NT multi-users: Look above the Start Menu folder in the left outline view until you find the "User" folder in which the Start Menu is nested. This is your personal Start Menu. If there are other users, their Start Menus are separate from yours so you don't have to worry about making changes to other people's Desktops. **If you're the only user** of your Windows NT computer, the user folder is called "Administrator."

To use Windows Explorer

- The left panel of Windows Explorer is a visual outline of the entire disk drive. The plus symbol (+) to the left of a folder indicates there are files or folders inside. The minus symbol (-) means the folder is open, and you see everything there is.

- Open a folder in the *left* panel by double-clicking it: its folder contents show up in the *right* panel. The example on the previous page displays large icons on the right; use the View menu to choose a view you prefer (it only affects the right panel).

- Select one panel or the other with the Tab key.

- If you double-click folders on the *right*, they'll open and display their contents in the *right* panel. When open, that folder's icon in the left panel will highlight to show that it's open.

Now you can easily move items between the two panels. If you want to move a folder from a submenu up to the first level of the Start Menu:

1. In the *right* panel, double-click on the "Programs" folder. This displays the contents of the folder on the right, and shows the hierarchy of that folder in the *left* panel.

2. Keep double-clicking on the *right* until you find the item you'd like to move.

3. From the *right* panel, select the item you want to move and drag it over to the *left* panel. If you'd like to put the items in the first level of the Start Menu, drag to the "Start Menu" folder and let go. You'll see your file or folder on the left side.

4. Close the Windows Explorer window, then click the OK button in the property sheet to close it.

5. Click the Start Menu button, and you'll see your folder or file.

Tip: The Windows Explorer window is actually a viewing tool you'll use in many other situations.

To launch it whenever you might need it, right-click the Start Menu button and choose "Explore."

Advanced tip: You can create new folders to organize your files into categories. In Windows Explorer, select the folder in the left panel where you want the new folder to appear. Go to "File," choose "New," then choose "Folder." Give your folder a name, and start moving files into it.

Deleting items from the Start Menu

There are a lot of items in the Start Menu that you'll never or rarely use, and they take up valuable space. Deleting is easier than moving or adding. If you change your mind later, you can always replace items by following the steps on the previous pages.

To delete an item from the Start Menu

1. Right-click the Taskbar to get the menu, then choose "Properties." In the property sheet, click the "Start Menu Programs" tab.

2. Click the "Remove…" button.

3. In the scrolling window, select the item you want to remove. (Notice that you need to highlight the item name—clicking on the icon itself won't work.)

   You'll see the "Confirm File Delete" dialog box.

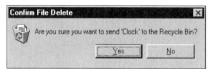

   Remember, items in the Start Menu *should* only be aliases, not the real folders, so you can usually answer "Yes" to this question. *As long as your Recycle Bin isn't set on automatic* (see Chapter 10), you can retrieve any deleted Start Menu items that turn out to be original files instead of aliases and put them somewhere else on the drive. To make sure the files are aliases before you remove them, look carefully at their tiny icons in the window to make sure they have the shortcut arrows in the icons.

4. Click the "Close" button, and your Start Menu is slimmer and trimmer.

Part Four

Applications, Folders, and Files

Nobody can be exactly like me.
Sometimes even I have trouble doing it.

—Tallulah Bankhead

Installing and Using Applications

Applications are like islands in an operating system. They have their own internal rules and capabilities. Once you're safely working inside of an application, many of the differences between the Mac and the PC are less noticeable. Getting to that point is less than half the fun, but it doesn't have to be an unpleasant adventure. This chapter will help you get your applications installed, launched, and integrated into your Desktop.

Can you install this application?

Unlike the Mac, whose system versions are created in numerical order (for example, System 7.5 arrived after System 7.1 and built on its existing capabilities), the term "Windows" is an umbrella for operating systems that look more alike than they really are. Just because a piece of software says it's written for "Windows" doesn't mean it will run on the Windows version you own. That's even more true for Windows NT and its upgrades. Some companies are already working with the next Windows *beta* while others have never upgraded from 3.5 to 4.0.

beta: A version of any type of computer product that is in the process of being tested for problems and improvements.

compatibility: The ability of two pieces of software and/or hardware to perform their functions together without crashing the computer.

We recommend that you read the "System Requirements" fine print listed on the box of a Windows application before you buy it and try to install it on your computer. If you're purchasing from a mail order house and can't look at the box, call the software vendor's 800 number and ask them about system version *compatibility*. And you certainly shouldn't download any software that doesn't specifically support your operating system.

That being said, there are some ground rules regarding what's likely to work and what isn't. *System utilities*—any software that deals with disk optimization or management—are very specific to the operating system. Installing one for the wrong OS could permanently trash Windows, forcing you to spend a lot of time reloading and recon-figuring. When in doubt, wait until you have definitive information.

It's even more important to do a careful check if you want to load a game. Games are at the extreme edge of Windows application writing, and the flashier they promise to be, the more likely they are to be using dubious portions of the operating system. It's 95 percent certain that a Windows 95 game will not run on any version of NT—games must be written with the NT system and its security quirks in mind.

A 16-bit application—any application written for an older version of Windows, which includes many currently-downloadable shareware applications—will probably run on Windows 95 and 98 but probably not on NT.

Windows NT and applications

If you can get a 16-bit application up and running on Windows NT, it may crash frequently or display strange quirks. Experimenting with 16-bit applications won't corrupt your system because NT puts them in a little NT corral where they can't do any harm when they fail. It might be worth the effort to try the application if you can't find or afford a new version. For example, Quark 3.32r5, a 16-bit application, runs quite nicely on NT—as long as you don't need to use PostScript Type 1 fonts.

Normal Windows 95/98 applications, on the other hand, frequently do work on NT 4.0. What's a "normal" application? It's one that doesn't rely on a specific piece of hardware. For example, you can feel pretty confident that a Windows 95 accounting program or HTML web authoring program will work on NT. But you should mistrust a program that's meant to work with something like a MIDI interface card because NT handles hardware (such as a card) very differently from the way Windows 95/98 does.

HTML: **The hypertext markup language used for creating web pages.**

MIDI **(pronounced "middy"): Stands for musical instrument digital interface. MIDI is a standard that describes a way for computers and musical instruments to interact.**

Installing an application

Installing software on a PC is a mysterious process compared to a Mac, where it's easy to see where the things you install are being put. For the most part a Mac program lives in its own self-contained folder with perhaps a sprinkling of extensions and preferences that are easy to track down. In Windows, software actually writes changes to the system. Sometimes it replaces a special kind of system file called a .DLL (dynamic link library) with another one of the same name but slightly different code. Frequently it adds more .DLL files to the system. That's why you can't just copy or backup a program from one computer to another the way you can on a Mac.

DLL: Dynamic Link Library. DLLs are modular program pieces, like Mac extensions, but frequently used by more than one applications. Some DLLs are part of the Windows system; some are specific to a developer or even to one application.

The nasty process of writing directly to the system is why installations sometimes completely trash your Windows computer. (It's also why you can lose access to some applications if you upgrade from Windows 95 to 98, since the upgrade installer will frequently overwrite those application .DLL files.) You should back up the most important aspects of your system before you start installing new software, and should back up once again after you've installed successfully so you won't have as far to go if the next installation goes bad. Backing up system files is a little complicated, and it's different for Window 95/98 and NT. See Chapter 28, *Preventing Problems*, for tips on how to backup your system.

The actual installation process is handled by a special program, frequently called a Wizard. The Wizard interface is very different from the Mac installer, but both programs accomplish the same things. When installing from a CD, the Wizard either starts up automatically or is clearly marked on the CD startup screen. Running a Windows installer isn't any more difficult than a Mac installer, particularly if you accept the "easy install" option.

Add/Remove Programs control panel

Shareware programs that you download from the Internet don't always come with installers. And some software, including Windows itself, comes with goodies and extras on the CD that aren't part of the Wizard process so they don't get installed automatically. You can manually install these items in your computer system using the "Add/Remove Programs" control panel.

To add a program or utility to your computer

1. Open "My Computer" and double-click "Control Panel" (or from the Start button, go to "Settings," then "Control Panel"). Double-click "Add/Remove Programs." You'll get the property sheet shown below.

Control Panel   Add/Remo...
                 Programs

The Control Panel folder stores the "Add/Remove Programs" file.

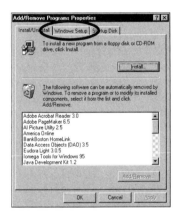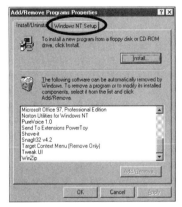

(There's a third tab in Windows 98 called "Startup Disk," which isn't really for program installations.)

2. **If you want to add goodies from your installer disk** that you didn't load originally, choose the "Windows Setup" tab. This process will be a lot like loading from a Mac system install disk. As you scroll down the list of options, some categories will allow you to pick and choose individual items within them. Others, like "Accessibility," will install the entire package.

—continued

3. **For any other program you want to add that doesn't come with its own installer, such as shareware you downloaded,** choose "Install/Uninstall," then click the "Install" button. You'll get this big and mostly empty dialog box:

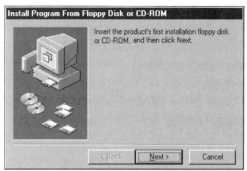

The installer looks first for programs on the A: drive (the floppy drive), which is a little silly since most applications either come on CDs or are downloaded.

Tip: It can be so confusing to sort through all those DOS-named .EXE files or to navigate through your hard disk hunting for a specific application. To make your life easier, create a folder on your Desktop called "Downloads." In your browser, make this folder your default destination for all downloaded files. Back up the contents of this folder to a Zip or Jaz disk on a regular basis in case you need to reinstall any of the applications, then delete these original installers to save disk space.

4. Hit the "Next" button, and the installer will try to find an application on the A: drive; if it can't, it will then head for the CD drive as a second choice. If the installer still doesn't find a program to install, it will look for any file with an .EXE extension on the first level of any hard disks and then removable disks. It may find many possibilities depending on how you organize your hard disk, so check the name of any file it finds before continuing.

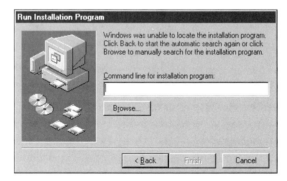

5. If the installer can't find anything to install, you'll get this dialog box:

Now it's your turn to locate the program using the "Browse" button to look through "My Computer." When you find the application, click "Open," then "Finish" on the next screen. The computer will do the rest.

Where the application gets stored

You always know how to find an application on a Mac once you've installed it. Most applications install into their own folder right on the top level of the hard disk, unless you specifically ask that they be placed somewhere else. Thus on a Mac it's easy to find an application to make an alias of it, or to move it someplace else, or to launch it by double-clicking its icon.

Windows is also predictable, although not as easy to control. Most applications are installed in their own folders inside the "Program Files" folder at the top level of your C: drive. Some developers, like Adobe, create their own program folder on the hard disk and install all of their applications inside of it. Most Windows installers do not give you an option of where you want to store the application.

Which file is the actual application?

In Windows 95 and NT, you can recognize which of the many files in an application folder is the actual program because it has an extension of .EXE at the end of its name (the name itself rarely gives you a clue!). In Windows 98, the extensions are often hidden so it's even more difficult.

To find the application file in an application folder

1. Open the folder in which you know the application was installed.

2. From the window's View menu, choose "Details."

3. Click the column heading called "Type" to sort the files by the type of file. Folders will appear at the top of the list, but the rest of the contents will sort by type alphabetically, with the type "Application" at the top of the list.

4. Sometimes a folder has more than one application in it because the main application has separate adjunct parts. Fortunately, most application developers name these files logically so you should be able to recognize which one is the "main" application. If the names aren't useful, double-click an .EXE file to see what it is before you drag a shortcut of it to the Desktop or add it to the Start Menu.

Putting an application alias in the Start Menu

Most installers automatically put a shortcut to their application in the appropriate section of the Start Menu (usually the "Programs" section). Sometimes the installer will ask you before it does this. Less frequently, it gives you the chance to decide exactly where on the Start Menu this shortcut should be placed. Even less frequently, the installer will ask if you want a shortcut to the program right on the Desktop. Since it's not as easy in Windows as it is on the Mac to locate an application file, and there are lots of steps involved in adding a shortcut to the Start Menu (see Chapter 15), you should answer "Yes" to any dialog box that offers one of these options.

Memory and applications

As a good Mac user who knows that some applications and projects need more memory than others, you're probably wondering, "How can I assign the appropriate amount of memory to my applications?"

You can't.

Windows does not let you monkey with the memory. Believe us: in Windows this is a very, very good thing.

You should know just a little about how application memory works on your PC because you *can* have an indirect but serious effect on it. Windows applications are much more dependent on how you manage your files and maintain your hard disk than Macs are because Windows relies so much on virtual memory.

There are two kinds of memory we're concerned about here: the physical memory chips (random access memory, or RAM) that you install into the computer box, and **virtual memory,** which is when the computer pretends that a certain amount of your hard disk space is temporary memory. Windows depends on virtual memory to manage applications. When first installed, Windows looks at the hard disk and does some calculations to figure out what percentage of the free space on the disk it can use as a temporary holding space. Based on these calculations, Windows creates a "page" (95/98) or "pagefile" (NT), which is a fixed address at the root of the hard disk that Windows uses for active programs.

When memory begins to get tight because you have a lot of applications open, the system moves information into this special space. It does this on a "first in, first out" basis, swapping out applications or files that you may have open but haven't used recently.

The good thing about this method of managing system resources is that it's a lot harder for an application to run out of memory and refuse to perform, especially if you have a really large hard disk with lots of empty space. The bad thing is that hard disks get fragmented, which means that nice, open stretches of free space get chopped up into smaller fragments as files are deleted and overwritten.

If the page file is on a fragmented hard disk, the system will slow way down as it tries to find all the pieces of applications and reload them into real memory when they're needed. Good disk management, in the form of *disk optimization,* is even more important in Windows than it is on the Mac. Check out Chapter 28, *Preventing Problems,* for more about this.

disk optimization:
The process of defragmenting files and prioritizing them for quick access.

Launching an application

The most straightforward way to launch an application in Windows is to **click the Start Menu,** slide up to Programs, and then over to wherever you or the installer placed the shortcut to your program in the menu. (See Chapter 15, *Customizing the Start Menu,* for more information about placing shortcuts in the Start Menu.) Just click on the program name in the Start Menu.

You can also **double-click an application's icon** to launch it (if you can find the folder it's in and then figure out which icon is the actual application), or double-click a shortcut you've made of it (for shortcut information, see Chapter 17). Sometimes, as we mentioned on page 232, when you install an application it offers to make a shortcut for you and put it on the Desktop, and to put the application name in the Start Menu as well.

You can **double-click on a document file to launch an application,** too, if that file meets one of three criteria:

native format: **The file format that is unique and specific to the application itself.**

- The file is in the application's *native format.*
- The file was on that application's format list when the application was installed (this is determined by the software company, not you or Windows, so don't worry about it).
- You've told the computer the file and application are connected. See Chapter 18, *File Formats and their Icons,* to learn how to do this.

If a file meets one of these three conditions, then you can **drag that file and drop it on the application's icon,** just like on your Mac. If the application is already launched but minimized on the Taskbar, you can sometimes drag the file over the application's button and hold it there; depending on which application it is and what is already open in it, you might be able to open the file this way.

Tip: **If you select several files that you'd like to open in one application, and then double-click to open them all, only the one you actually clicked on will launch! To force Windows to open all of the selected files, hold down the Control key when you double-click.**

You can also **launch an application with a whole group of selected files** by dragging them all to the application's icon or alias/shortcut.

Multiple application copies

One of the creepiest things about using applications in Windows is how it opens multiple copies of the same application. If you launch any Microsoft application (including Windows accessories), minimize it so you can work on something else, then double-click on its application icon or double-click a file, Windows won't bring the open application forward—no, most of the time it launches a complete second copy of the application as if it were another program altogether!

Cyndi's husband, who's an ace Visual Basic programmer, treats this "feature" very nonchalantly since it doesn't seem to cause a system crash. Cyndi sees it differently—she can think of some potentially useful ways to use this feature (like run a search-and-replace on one long Word document while writing away on another), but it still makes her nervous wondering how the computer keeps each open version straight.

Visual Basic: A Microsoft-specific programming language.

Launching an application in the background

Applications are getting bigger and bigger so they tend to take a long time to load. You can take advantage of Windows' ability to handle multiple tasks by launching the second application in the background while you continue to work. To do this, hold down the Control key when you double-click the application's icon.

Cycling through open applications and windows

Windows has a keyboard shortcut that lets you cycle through anything that's a button on the Taskbar:

1. Hold down the Alt key and tap the Tab key once lightly, but keep the Alt key down.

2. A little box appears in the center of the screen displaying the icons of running applications and open windows.

3. Tap the Tab key again until the icon you want is selected, then let go of both keys. Your chosen application, document, or window will display on the screen.

Quitting an application

There are several ways to quit your application.

- Go to the **File menu** and choose "Exit" or "Quit." The choice of terms depends on how Mac-like the application is. **OR:**

- Press **Alt F4.** In some programs, you can also press Control Q, just like you would on your Mac. **OR:**

- As we mentioned in Chapter 7, Windows doesn't know the difference between "Close" and "Quit." So you can **close** a window from the little X in the upper-right corner of the window, but if it's the last window on the screen, that little X **quits** your application. This is particularly a problem when you're surfing the World Wide Web in a browser—you close the different windows you had open and if one of them happened to be the last one, you just quit your browser. **OR:**

- If an application is minimized on the **Taskbar**, you don't have to display it again to quit. **Right-click** on its minimized button, and select "Close" from the little menu. Close, in this case, doesn't mean "close a window," it means "quit this application."

The Taskbar is handy to use for quitting applications.

The Startup folder

You might have an application you use every time you sit down at the computer, or a folder you always work from. On the Mac, you can drag an alias of that file or folder to the Startup Items folder inside the System folder. Windows has a Startup folder too. You can see it in the Start Menu, under Programs (shown to the right).

To make a file launch at startup

1. Right-click a blank spot on the Taskbar to get the pop-up menu, then click "Properties." Click the "Start Menu Programs" tab.

2. Click "Add," then click the "Browse" button. Navigate through your disk until you find the program you want to launch on startup, then double-click to choose it.

3. Click the "Next" button, then scroll all the way down through the options in the Start Menu until you see "Startup"; double-click on it. In the next screen, click the "Finish" button.

You can put files, folders, applications, sounds, etc., in the Startup folder.

Temporarily prevent startup items from starting up

You can temporarily prevent all of the items in your Startup folder from launching: hold down the Shift key while Windows is loading up (this is like holding down the Shift key when you don't want extensions to load on a Mac). Then after Windows boots up you can manually launch the one or two programs you actually need.

Delete items from the Startup folder

Eventually, you might change your mind about your startup items and want to disable some of them permanently. Or maybe there were startup items installed on your computer when you got it and you want to remove them. The items are all just shortcuts, so if you want them back you can always put them back later.

1. Right-click a blank spot on the Taskbar to get the pop-up menu, then click "Properties." Click the "Start Menu Programs" tab, and then click "Remove."

2. In the next screen, scroll down until you find the "StartUp" folder in the window. Click its plus sign to display the items in the folder. Select the name of the program you want to remove, then click the "Remove" button.

3. Click "Yes" in the last dialog box, and the selected shortcut will be removed to the Recycle Bin where you can delete it.

If you see a plus sign next to the StartUp folder, click it to display the contents.

Uninstalling applications

When you don't want a Windows application taking up space on your hard disk anymore, you can't just drag it to the trash and forget about it like you can on your Mac. Windows *really* doesn't like that. There are some nasty things called .DLL files that the application initially installed, and they will continue to make a mess of the system and bloat your startup. Maybe you don't care about having a neat and trim system, but this is a situation that can cause you problems later. Awful things might happen if you load something new that happens to conflict with the program you thought you'd thrown away.

DLL: **Dynamic Link Library. DLLs are modular program pieces, like Mac extensions, but frequently used by more than one applications. Some DLLs are part of the Windows system; some are specific to a developer or even to one application.**

To prevent an unnecessarily ugly scene, you should always do a thorough **uninstall** of the application. There are three ways to do this. The much preferred way is to put the **original CD installer disk** for the application into the CD-ROM drive, and use the application's own "Uninstall" option. The programmers who wrote it have the best idea of what ought to be there, and you should follow their advice.

Locating the original CD, especially if it's registered for several users, is not always easy. If your application loaded **uninstaller software** when it loaded the program, its uninstaller should appear in the Add/Remove Programs control panel.

Some applications load the uninstaller along with the software and will put that uninstaller right into the Start Menu, as shown here.

To uninstall using the Add/Remove Programs control panel

1. Open "My Computer," then double-click on "Control Panel" (or from the Start Menu, go to "Settings," then "Control Panel").

2. Double-click "Add/Remove Programs." In the property sheet, select the "Install/Uninstall" tab.

3. Scroll down the list of applications until you find the one you want to remove. Select it and click "Add/Remove...."

4. Click "Yes" in the little dialog box asking if you're really sure you want to do this. The program's component names will whiz along the screen as they're erased.

Unfortunately, some programs don't come with Uninstall programs. If the application you want to eliminate doesn't have one, invest in an **uninstaller software program.** There are many dedicated programs to do this task because uninstalling in Windows is complicated and quite beyond the average user. This type of program will not always do as thorough a job as an uninstaller created by the original software company, but when it's the only alternative you have, you'll use it.

Creating Folders, Files, and Aliases

Folders and files are Desktop building blocks that we don't think about very much. Like everything else when we compare Macs and PCs, they're a bit more step-heavy in Windows than on the Mac. In this chapter we look at creating the three basic types of Desktop tools: folders, files, and aliases (which are called "shortcuts" in Windows).

Creating a new folder

There are two ways to make a new folder. Both methods will work when you want to make a new folder inside of an open window. Don't bother trying to make new folders in the windows for "My Computer" or "Control Panels"—you're not allowed.

To create a new folder in an open window

- From the window's "File" menu bar, click "New" ("New" is not always at the top of the menu like it is on the Mac), then click "Folder." A new folder will appear in the window, ready for you to rename.

To create a new folder in an open window or on the Desktop

- **Right-click** on the Desktop or in a blank place in an open window to get the pop-up menu, click "New" (it's toward the bottom) then click "Folder." A new folder will appear on the Desktop or in the window, ready for you to rename.

The "Folder" option is at the top of the submenu.

To create a new folder in a Save As dialog box

- Click the "Create New Folder" button that's at the top of the dialog box (shown to the left). A new folder will appear in the window, ready for you to rename.

This is the "Create New Folder" button in the Save As dialog box.

To rename the folder

Your new folder will be highlighted with a blinking insertion bar at the end of the name, as shown to the left.

- The new folder knows you want to rename it—that's why it's highlighted. Just type the name of your choice and whatever you type will replace the highlighted name.

  If the name is unselected (unhighlighted), just click once on the file to select it, then click once on the name or press the F2 key to make it editable.

The new folder appears in the dialog box (left) or window (right) ready for you to rename it. Just type.

To use a keyboard shortcut to make a new folder

Can't. Well, you can make a new folder using the keyboard by opening the menu and choosing the menu items with the keys, but there isn't any combination that will instantly put a folder in your window.

To use the keys in Windows 98: Press Alt F to open the File menu, then press N to select the "New" choice, then press F to select "Folder." Type to replace the words "New Folder" with the name you want.

Creating and saving a new file

Creating a new file in Windows is essentially the same as creating a file on the Mac. The only new thing to learn is how to navigate the dialog box, and even that's quite similar once you understand Windows' interpretation of the Mac's system.

First we need to open an application so we can make a file. Let's open WordPad because it's small and quick.

1. Click the Start Menu button at the bottom-left of the screen, slide up to "Programs," over and up to "Accessories," out to "WordPad," and click once on WordPad. whew.

   WordPad isn't a very big application so you shouldn't have to wait long for it to open. Notice that the cursor does change briefly from an arrow to an hourglass—the hourglass is Windows' version of the Mac wristwatch that lets you know the computer is busy. Unlike the Mac wristwatch, however, the hourglass will not reliably appear when there's work going on behind the scenes, so avoid pushing buttons or trying to reset when you're working in larger programs or files. You may just have to wait a little longer than you're used to without a visual clue as comfort.

2. On the empty WordPad page, type a few lines of text to create a document.

3. Now **save the new document:** From the "File" menu, choose "Save." Notice in the File menu that WordPad, like many Windows applications, has some familiar keyboard shortcuts like Ctrl S for Save (ignore the + sign you see in the File menu shortcut) and Ctrl P for Print.

   The default folder for saving this file might be the Windows system folder (labeled "Windows" in Windows 95 or 98, "WINNT" in Windows NT), since that's where WordPad is stored. Don't save your file there. Once you switch to the folder you want to save this document into, Windows will open to that particular folder next time (until you close the application).

—continued on next page

4. To choose a different folder to save the file into, click the downward arrow next to the folder that's currently selected in the "Save in" edit box (shown circled, below). You'll get a pop-up list of possible drives and folders:

 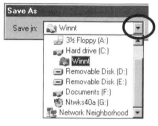

Press the downward arrow to get the list of other drives and folders.

5. Click once on the name of the drive or folder you want to open. It will open and display its current contents in the window.

Click this button to go up one level to the folder or disk in which the currently displayed folder is stored.

There's an **alternative way to navigate** through a Save As dialog box. Next to the "Save in" edit box is the "Up One Level" button (shown to the left, and you can see it in the dialog box above). Click this button to go up one level in the disk folder hierarchy. Keep clicking and eventually you will reach "My Computer" where you can choose a different disk drive, if necessary.

6. Name the file. The "File name" box should be highlighted; if you are using Windows 95 or NT, you'll see "*.DOC" or "*.TXT" already in the file name box. The asterisk (*), or star, is a generic placeholder telling you that any file name you want to type will be inserted in that spot. The three letters, like .DOC and .TXT are "extensions," which are codes that tell the operating system what types of files you're making. We discuss extensions in detail in Chapters 22 and 23.

7. Just type over the extension and the asterisk (*). The system will automatically add the extension to the file name you type, even though in Windows 98 you don't see the extension in the file name box, as shown in the example above.

8. Click the "Save" button. That new file is now saved into the folder and/or disk you selected, just like on your Mac.

Creating aliases (shortcuts)

It's nice to be able to get at your files quickly. It's also nice to avoid the Start Menu and all its submenus when you can. The easiest way to do that in Windows is with *shortcuts*, which function pretty much the same as *aliases* on the Mac.

It's easy to tell a shortcut from an original file by the arrow that gets added to the lower left of the icon.

- Shortcuts can sit anywhere, including directly on the Desktop (but you can't put them in "My Computer" or the Control Panel folder).

- A shortcut of a document will launch the application it was created in.

- You can launch shortcuts from other disks.

- Shortcuts to network files and disks won't work if the network link is down.

- If you rename a shortcut, it will still find the original file.

- If you rename the original file, its shortcut will still find it.

- Once you make a shortcut, you can move it anywhere.

- If you move an original file to somewhere else on the disk, the shortcut will still find it.

- You can make more than one shortcut to the same original.

- You can safely throw away any shortcut and it will not affect the original file.

To make a shortcut to any file, folder, or application

- **Right-click** the file, and from the menu that pops up, choose "Create Shortcut." Move the shortcut anywhere you want.

- **OR:** Right-click the file and drag it to the Desktop or to any open window where you want the new shortcut to appear. When you let go, you'll get a menu. Choose "Create Shortcut(s) Here."

- **OR:** To create a shortcut from any of the files that are in the folders "My Computer" or "Control Panel," hold down the Control and Alt keys and drag the file to the Desktop or a window. It will instantly and automatically create a shortcut.

- **OR:** To create a shortcut to any **application,** drag the application icon to any other folder. Windows automatically makes a shortcut because it doesn't want you to move the actual application.

Shortcut to
Mary Sidney

Shortcuts (like Mac OS 8 aliases) have little arrows in the icons.

alias/shortcut: An icon that represents a file of some sort. You double-click the alias and it goes to get the real file.

Why shortcuts? Many files cannot be moved from their folders. For instance, program files have to be kept in their program folders, and control panels have to be kept in the control panels folder. So you can make aliases to these items, and put the aliases on the Desktop. When you double-click the alias, it goes and gets the original file for you, without you having to dig down through all of the folders.

Right-drag a file to create a shortcut.

Get rid of the extra words "Shortcut to"

In Windows 95 and NT, the shortcut name label will always begin with the phrase "Shortcut to." Because it's at the beginning of the name, not the end, "Shortcut to" is often the only part of the name that's visible.

Shortcut to   Shortcut to   Shortcut to
Shakespea...   Shakespea...   Shakespea...

With the "Shortcut to" label, you can't tell that these are three different files!

You'll get very tired of editing this phrase away. We suggest you try a piece of software called PowerToys from Microsoft, as described below.

To get rid of "Shortcut to" forever

Windows 98 users: Microsoft includes Tweak UI on the Windows 98 disk inside a "powertoy" folder (which is inside "reskit," which is inside "tools"). However, all of the other Power Toys are missing. You still need to download this package to use its other utilities.

1. Download "Microsoft Power Toys" from the Microsoft web site (www.microsoft.com).

2. Run the Power Toys installer, which is fast, easy, and quite painless. This package is very useful for more than merely eliminating an irritating phrase, so you should definitely load all the Power Toy options.

3. Power Toys installs a new file in your Control Panel folder called "Tweak UI," which is your magic bullet for changing shortcut names. Find this file and double-click it to open its property sheet.

Tweak UI

Tweak UI is installed in the Control Panel folder.

4. Click the "Explorer" tab. In the Settings toward the bottom, uncheck "Prefix 'Shortcut to' on new shortcuts." Click "Apply." Your system will do a mini-reboot because this change needs to be written to the system and the Windows Registry. When your computer revives, any file name that included "Shortcut to" has been changed, and new short-cuts you create will be spared the additional text.

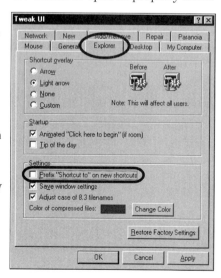

Lighten the shortcut arrow with Tweak UI

The Tweak UI property sheet is also the place to change the look of the shortcut icons themselves by making the tiny shortcut arrow lighter in shade, as shown to the right.

Explorer

This shortcut has a "light" arrow.

Don't get rid of the arrow completely because it's the only way you can tell the difference between the real file icon and its alias (shortcut) on the Desktop. But the light arrow is a pretty good option—it's unobtrusive, but just enough "there" to prevent you from mistaking one type of file for the other.

1. Open the Tweak UI property sheet by double-clicking its icon in the Control Panel folder.
2. Click the "Explorer" tab.
3. In the "Shortcut overlay" section, click the "Light arrow" button. Click OK. The system will reboot and change all icons.

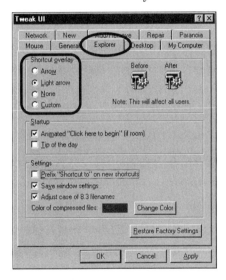

Shortcuts and original files

A Windows computer easily recognizes the difference between a shortcut and the original file. Try this to see something unexpected:

1. Open any window (except "My Computer" or Control Panel).

2. Right-click an icon and make a shortcut for it in the same folder.

3. Click on the still-selected shortcut name, and select and delete the words "Shortcut of." Now you have two files with the same name, right?

On a Mac, you would get an error message because you can't have two files with the same name in the same window. On your PC, you can. How is this possible? It isn't, of course. The two files don't really have the same name, as you can see in their property sheets:

1. **Right-click** the shortcut to get the pop-up menu, and click "Properties." Leave the property sheet on the screen.

2. Right-click the original file, and click "Properties." Leave the property sheet on the screen.

3. Move the two property sheets side-by-side as shown below:

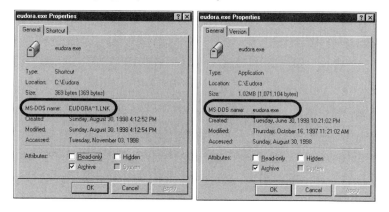

Notice that the MS-DOS names of the files are completely different and have totally different extensions (the three letters after the period). These extensions define the types of files they are: LNK indicates the file is a shortcut, and EXE indicates it's an application. If two files aren't the same type, even if they have exactly the same long file name, Windows will always see them as two completely distinct items.

Use the shortcut to find the original file

Sometimes you need the original file, not the shortcut. The original might be buried deep within a number of folders, or you might not even know the original's name since the names of files can be so obscure in Windows. The shortcut icon can help you find the original file.

To find the original file from its shortcut icon

1. **Right-click** on the shortcut icon to get the pop-up menu, and choose "Properties."

2. Click the "Shortcut" tab.

3. Click the "Find Target" button. Windows will open the folder that contains the shortcut's original file and will highlight it for you.

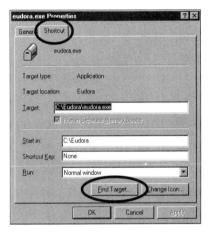

The word "Target" comes up a lot in Windows because it's the Windows name for "original," or the file on which you want to focus.

PowerToys, as mentioned on page 244, has an option called "Shortcut Target Menu" that makes it easy to find the original file. Once you have that option installed, you can find the target of any shortcut by right-clicking the shortcut icon and choosing "Target" from the menu that appears.

Use aliases (shortcuts) to make your Windows Desktop look like your Mac Desktop

Below is an example of aliases rearranged on the Desktop so files are in similar places to where you find them on your Mac Desktop. The most significant changes are the drive icons: Robin made an alias for each drive in the "My Computer" window, then moved them all to the right-hand side, which is where the Mac puts drive icons.

Robin also keeps an alias to the Control Panel folder and to the Display properties right on the Desktop, as well as aliases to her most frequently used applications and folders. The Recycle Bin (not an alias) is in the bottom-right corner where the Mac trash can is usually kept.

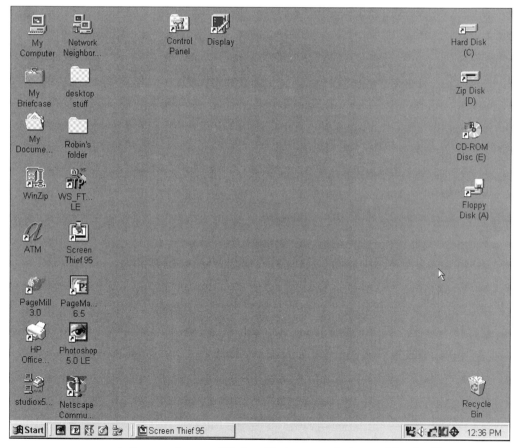

Rearranging your Windows Desktop to make it more Mac-familiar can be comforting.

File Formats and their Icons

It's a good thing our files display a variety of icons. The icon tells us so much in one glance: the type of file, what kind of application the file needs to open, and sometimes the actual name of the application in which it was made.

Recognizing these icons in Windows will make your life easier because you'll be able to match files with their functions. Later, recognizing icons will help you figure out what's happening to the files you transfer between the Mac and PC. Eventually, icons may even help you troubleshoot minor problems in Windows. This chapter is devoted to Windows' methods of recognizing and dealing with files.

Windows file formats

Every file on your computer has a "format"—a particular way of arranging its internal information so the computer knows what to do with it. A **system file** has to be in a format for the CPU to recognize it. An **application** has to be in a format for the operating system to understand and run it. And a **document file** has to be in a format that an application can understand and open it so you can use it.

Some file formats are unique; they can only be created by one application, and often can only be opened and used by that one application as well. These are called **native file formats;** they "belong" to the application that made them. Other file formats can be created and understood by several applications in the same category—like TIF files for imaging programs or DOC files for word processors. Some document file formats (like EPS or TIF files) are readable by more than one type of computer operating system.

In Windows, there are two ways to recognize a specific file format: by its **extension** (see Chapter 19) and by its **icon.**

Windows file icons

There are basically three kinds of files: application files, document files, and system files. Of course, just like on the Mac, within these categories there are subcategories: some system files are really modules or enhancements; some document files are created by system accessories, others by third-party applications. But in general, you can recognize three basic types of file icons, each representing one of the major categories of file types.

Application file icons

Illustrator.exe

W95target.exe

Application icons

There is no standard look for a Windows application icon, just as there isn't a standard look for a Macintosh application. Application icons in Windows are either a little picture or a miniature open folder window, as shown to the left. If Windows is set to show file extensions, you can always recognize an application by its **.exe** extension.

If you double-click an application icon, you'll launch that program.

Document file icons

Just like on the Mac, document icons are usually descriptive little pictures that relate in some way to their function and/or to the application they were created in. Most (but not all) Windows documents are rectangles with their upper-right corners "folded down."

Dad.eps

Document icon

If you double-click a document icon that Windows recognizes, it will launch an application and open that document within it. If you double-click a generic or unrecognized icon, Windows will ask you to find an application to open the file with.

System file icons

A Windows system icon usually has a picture of a gear on it. There are several variations of system icons, depending on what kind of system file it is and what the file actually does.

System icon

Don't bother double-clicking on system icons unless you really like to look at programming code.

Accessory file icons

Each of the document icons shown below represents a native file format for a Windows accessory. These are basically regular document files, as described above, because "accessories"are simply small applications that are shipped with Windows. We wanted to show you these because they are common icons in Windows but are unfamiliar to Mac users.

Bitmap image (MS Paint file)

WordPad text file

Sound clip

Video clip

Clipboard file

Notepad text file

Icon image (displays its own image)

Scrap file (made with WordPad)

Imaging viewer file (generic graphic file)

Application files and their icons

zed.psd

Mac Photoshop icon

zed.psd

Windows Photoshop icon

Applications that are developed for both platforms typically create files whose icons are identical or very similar on both Windows and Mac. When a Windows' file icon doesn't match its Mac counterpart, usually it's because Windows believes that a different application is the file's "owner." When this happens, Windows replaces the original icon with the "owner's" icon. This can make you crazy, so the following pages explain how Windows decides which application owns a file format and how you can change the owner.

This icon switch shouldn't happen to native file formats (see page 250 for an explanation of "native file format"). For example, Photoshop always opens a native Photoshop document (.PSD) because no other application can read that file format. So a native Photoshop file will always display the familiar Photoshop icon if Photoshop is installed on the computer and if the Windows file has the correction extension.

However, Photoshop creates many file formats that can be read by a wide variety of applications. In Windows, the type of icon the different file formats display can change. For example, if you save a Mac Photoshop file in .PCX format, the Mac will still recognize it as a Photoshop file. Transferred to a PC, the .PCX file could end up with any of several icons, depending on how that specific Windows computer has been told to recognize the file. Unless Windows knows that Photoshop is the .PCX file's owner, the file won't display a Photoshop icon, and when you double-click the file it will probably open the Windows accessory called Paint, not Photoshop. (Of course, you can always launch Photoshop, go to the File menu, and choose "Open" to open that file.)

What icon will a .PCX file have instead of the Photoshop icon? It might have the same icon as a .BMP file because Windows thinks it should be opened by the Paint accessory. If it's not recognized as a Paint graphic, Windows might give it a generic picture icon and open it in the accessory called Imaging, which is Windows' viewing application for unknown files. To prevent yourself from going mad, you need to understand why it's doing this and how to control it.

How do applications find their files?

What makes a file "belong" to an application, or what tells a computer that an application "owns" a type of file?

On a Mac, the *name* of a file has no visible connection to its file format. Instead, Mac files contain two hidden four-letter information labels— Type and Creator—which identify them to the system. For example, an EPS file created in Photoshop on a Mac contains this identification:

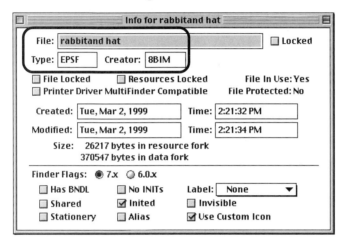

Each Creator label is unique to the program it represents. Because of the Creator information, a Mac can tell the difference between an EPS file created in Photoshop and one created in FreeHand and will open the proper application to edit the file when you double-click the icon.

Windows works very differently. An extension (the code at the end of a file name, such as .EPS) is automatically added to the file name when the file is saved. However, an extension only defines the file's *type*, not its *creator* application. As a result, once you close a document the connection between it and the application it was created in is broken. To reconnect the document file and the application, Windows has to be told, either by the application or by you, the user, that these two things belong together. To tell Windows this information, see the next page.

Connecting files and applications

The first time you double-click a file of a type that Windows can't match with an application, you'll see the "Open With" dialog box:

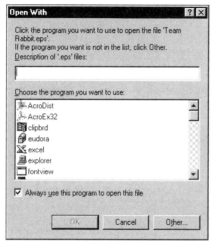

In this example, we're trying to open a file that was created in QuarkXPress and that has an .EPS extension. The list window displays the name of every program Windows recognizes as creating file formats, but doesn't show QuarkXPress installed on this system.

To connect the file format to an application that can open it

- In the "Open With" dialog box that automatically appears when you double-click an "unknown" file format, scroll down the list until you find the right application, then click to select it. In the example, we know that Adobe Photoshop can open EPS files, so we'll choose Photoshop. Unfortunately, if you don't already know which of your applications can open the file format, there's no way this list will tell you. You have two choices:

  - Check the software documentation for a list of file formats your program can create, import, and open.

  - Make an educated guess.

Always use this program?

In the "Open With" dialog box, notice the little checked box labeled, "Always use this program to open this file." As a Mac user, your instinct is to leave that box checked. After all, in Windows you'd like it if all your EPS files would automatically open without showing this dialog box again. But leaving the box checked means you've just identified Photoshop as the mother of all EPS files—Photoshop will be the default application whether you click on a Photoshop EPS, an Illustrator EPS, a FreeHand EPS, or even a QuarkXPress EPS. What if this is one of the only times you'll be launching an EPS file in Photoshop? Why permanently associate all EPS files with one application?

To avoid this problem, **uncheck the box.** You'll see the "Open With" dialog box every time you double-click a file that doesn't have a specific owner, but at least you'll be able to avoid starting up unwanted applications.

Finding out if a file is owned

If you're working at a computer whose defaults have been set by someone else, you might want to find out if the file type you need to open has been linked to a program yet.

To find out a file type's owner

- **Right-click** on the file, and in the pop-up menu that appears you'll either see "Open with…" or "Open…" at the top of the list. Whichever of these commands you see gives you a clue about the file:

"Open with…" means the file is currently unconnected to a specific program.　　*"Open" means there is a program linked to the file, although it doesn't tell you which one. You have to actually select "Open" from the menu and see which application launches.*

Changing file format assignments

You can change the application that currently opens a file type. For example, you might want .TIF files to open automatically in Photoshop. Remember, once you assign an application, all files in that format will open in that chosen application when you double-click their icons.

To change the application assignment of a file format

1. Open any folder window that contains a file of the sort you want to change. For instance, if you want Photoshop to open all .TIF files, open a folder that has a .TIF file in it.

2. From the window's View menu, choose "Folder Options..." or "Options...." (whichever one you see).

3. In the "Options" dialog box, click the "File Types" tab. You'll see a fairly lengthy scrollable list of every file type that Windows currently recognizes as valid.

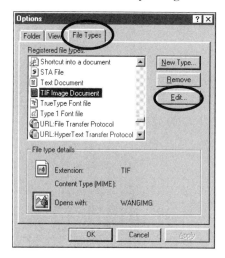

4. Select the type of file you're interested in. Notice the dialog box tells you which application currently opens the selected type of file and shows you the current file icon for that application.

5. Click the "Edit" button to show the "Edit Actions" dialog box. "Actions" are tasks you can ask the computer to perform on files. The actions that already exist show up in the window list.

6. In the "Edit Actions" dialog box, click "Open," then click the "Edit" button. You'll see this little dialog box:

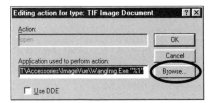

7. Now you need to locate the actual application on your hard disk. Click the "Browse" button to get the "Open With" dialog box:

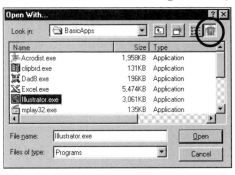

It's easier to find applications in a folder if you click the "Detailed List" button (circled), then click the heading "Type."

8. Use the "Open With" dialog box to find your application. Remember that applications are usually on the C: drive, either in their own folder or in the folder named "Program Files." An application always has an .EXE extension.

9. When you find the application, click to select it, then click the "Open" button. You'll jump back to the previous dialog box, and the path to your chosen application will take the place of the one that had been there before.

10. Click OK, then click "Close" in the property sheet. The application you chose will open this type of file from now on.

Note: Although the application that opens the file will change, the file icon itself may remain the same as before!

Assigning more than one possible application

On your Mac, let's say you made a PICT file in Photoshop. PICT isn't Photoshop's native format, of course, but if you double-click the file icon on the Mac Desktop, Photoshop will recognize and open it.

Windows doesn't work that way. Only one application can own a file type, which can cause some very strange actions. If you create and save a .BMP file in Photoshop, then double-click its icon on the Desktop to reopen it, it will launch the Windows Paint accessory instead because Paint "owns" .BMP files. You could change the assignment, of course, as described on the previous pages so that file opens in Photoshop, but once you've done that *all* other .BMP files will *always* open in Photoshop, no matter where they were created.

There is a nice trick, however, that can be terribly useful if you have a file format like EPS that you often need to open in different applications— create your own "action" that will show up in the file's right-click menu.

1. Repeat the first five steps on the previous pages to change a file's application. When you get to the "Edit Actions" dialog box, this time click the "New" button.

2. In the "New Action" dialog box that appears, there are two edit boxes, or empty lines, as shown below. In the first line, type the name of your new action, such as "Open with Photoshop."

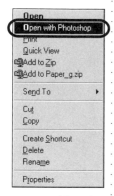

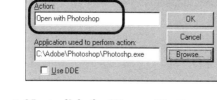

In the edit box, type the name that you want to call the action.

3. Next, click the "Browse" button and use the dialog box to find the application that you want to have as an option for opening the file.

4. When you find the application, double-click its name, and its path will appear in the second edit box in the "New Action" dialog box, as shown above. Click OK, then click "Close."

Once you create this action, your menu offers a choice of "Open," which opens the file in the assigned default application, or in the new action choice.

5. To use this new action, find any file of the type you just changed. Right-click on it, and you'll see your action as a new option in the menu, as shown to the left. You can add as many actions as you like.

System files and their icons

The system files are the ones that help keep the computer running or give you special features. You almost never do anything with a system file. If you've already read Chapter 20, *Finding File Information*, you know that some system files are not visible, which is meant to protect them from accidental damage or erasure. But if you want to see them, you can make them visible.

To see Windows system icons

1. In any open folder window, go to the View menu and choose "Folder Options…" or "Options."

2. In the Options property sheet, click the View tab.

3. Click "Show all files." Click OK.

Types of system files and icons

System program file: An icon with a yellow machine gear on it is an integrated part of the Windows system. Deleting, moving, or changing a file like this could have disastrous consequences. Look, but don't touch files with this icon, at least until you become much more experienced.

 System program file

System batch file: An icon that looks like a spiral notepad with a gear in the lower-right corner is an editable text file you can open and read using the Windows Notepad. Although the text in the file may look like normal text, they're actually batches of commands and default program settings that Windows uses to run "action sequences." If you know what you're doing you can use batch files to change how Windows launches applications, change the size of a newly opened window when its application loads, and a host of other things. It's not a good idea to randomly experiment with these files.

 System batch file

Generic or unknown files: A file that displays the Windows logo icon is one that Windows can't match with a specific application or function. It uses the same generic icon for files that need to be treated with care (but don't have gears on them) and generic data files. These is one of the most frustrating things about Windows and its icons. On the Mac, every visible file displays an icon that tells you something about what the file does—if a file has no icon, it's either damaged or in a foreign file format. But Windows is much less discriminating. Mac files that haven't been prepared properly (as described in Chapter 22) will also display this icon when moved to a Windows Desktop.

 Generic or unknown file

A good guideline for whether a generic file is just homeless or an incognito system file is whether or not it has an extension, that code at the end of a Windows file (see Chapter 22, *Transferring Files*, for details about extensions). A file without an extension will always be some kind of data file that was either made on a Mac or improperly renamed in Windows. (By default, Windows 98 hides the extensions that it understands. To see all of the extensions, open a folder window, and from the View menu, choose "Folder Options...." Uncheck the option "Hide file extensions for known files.")

System controls and helpers

Tweak UI   Tweak UI

On the left is a generic Windows control panel; on the right is the same control panel when it's properly installed as part of the Windows system.

Windows comes with many files that are not integral to the system but that do add functions and capabilities. If they were removed, most wouldn't cause a system crash. Sometimes they wouldn't be missed at all because no other files or applications depend on them. Some of these types of files show up with unique, descriptive icons.

Many control panels fall into this category. A control panel file that's stored in a regular folder may display a generic icon, but when you install it in the Control Panel window it suddenly puts on a colorful logo, as shown to the left.

Even though many of these system controls and helpers don't show up in the Start Menu, you can usually launch them by double-clicking their icons. Others can be inspected using Quick View, Windows' all-purpose content viewer (we explored Quick View in Chapter 14, *Mac Desk Accessories à la Windows*).

TrueType font file   *Screensaver file*   *Help file*   *Generic or DOS-related program file*

Paths and Long File Names

Disk organization and file-related tasks in Windows are very different from what we're used to on a Mac. These differences aren't merely window dressings—beneath the user interface, Macs and PCs have very little in common. The current versions of Windows may be easier to handle than their predecessors, but they're still based on DOS or DOS-related computer code. This underlying Disk Operating System will always dictate what the user can do with files.

In this chapter, we'll look at what the DOS rules are and why they're different from the ones we're used to on the Macintosh. We'll spend some time on file-naming issues, leading you through the Windows disk and folder architecture and why it's important to understand this different way of doing things.

The tree structure

Often when talking about the PC, people use the analogy of a tree to describe a disk's structure. Each disk drive (A:, D:, F:, etc.) is a separate tree. The system files are like the roots, folders are like tree limbs, and documents are like leaves—integral parts of the tree and its structure. If you move some types of Windows files to different disk trees, you might jeopardize the integrity of both the file and the tree on which it used to be located.

Windows folders are often called "directories" by PC users because that's what they were named in DOS. Newer Windows users use the term "folders," just like Mac users do.

If you apply the tree analogy to the Mac, you'd have to think of all Mac files as tree ornaments. Even the application files are self-contained and separate from the disk "tree" they're on, and they can be repositioned anywhere you like without affecting that tree or any other ornaments. Thank goodness.

Paths

The route you take through the Windows tree to the file or folder you want is called a **path.** In Windows the path is more than just a road map from one place to another on the disk—it's actually part of the "true" name of any Windows object.

Your Mac uses paths, although they differ from Windows in that they are not physically part of the name itself. The Mac path simply tells the computer and you where the file is stored. For instance, in the example on the opposite page there is a word processing document that is inside a folder that's inside a folder that's inside a folder that's on the hard disk. The computer keeps track of the "path" to get to that document. Windows does the same thing.

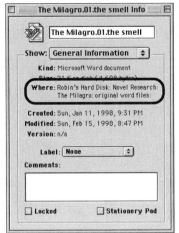

In the Mac window *shown above, you see a file called "The Milagro.01.the smell." In the hierarchy in that window's title bar, you can see this file is stored in a folder called "original word files," which is in a folder called "The Milagro," which is in a folder called "Novel Research," which is on "Robin's Hard Disk." **That list of folders within folders is the path.** You can see the path spelled out in the Get Info box to the right: each folder level is separated with colons.*

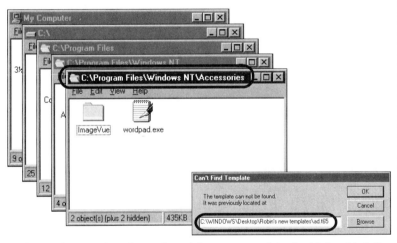

If people were named like DOS/Windows files, we'd have to sign our names like this:

EarthUS:\Massachusetts\
  Boston\CynthiaBaron.hmn

In the Windows window *shown above, left, you see a path in the title bar (circled). Each item in that path is a folder separated by a backslash (\), going back to the hard disk which is called C:. In the illustration you can see the folders that are nested into each other, and you can see how the path is directly related to the folders.*

In the illustration on the right is an example in a dialog box of the path where the computer previously found the file Robin's looking for. Notice it is just a list of the folders inside of folders, just like on the Mac (except the Mac shows us this path in a dialog box through the drop-down menu).

Path names and title bars

By default, Microsoft doesn't display the path name in the Windows title bar, probably because it can be pretty intimidating. We understand and agree, but being able to see the whole path to a folder can be extremely useful. Often when you install applications or make other additions to Windows, you need to know the path to and from files and applications.

Note: The application "Windows Explorer" has nothing to do with "Microsoft Internet Explorer"!

Microsoft is so sure that you'll need to know file locations that it provides a whole application called Windows Explorer just to view and manipulate the disk tree. Using Windows Explorer is a little intimidating itself and doing so is overkill if you just need to know the path to a specific folder that's already open. Rather than make you deal with Windows Explorer all the time, we think it's easier to change the title bar display if you need to know a path.

This title bar does not give you a clue to where this folder is stored. It displays just the name of the folder itself.

This title bar tells you exactly where the folder is stored. It's displaying the path.

To show paths in window title bars

1. In any open window, go to the "View" menu and choose "Options…" ("Folder Options" in Windows 98).

2. In the property sheet, click the "View" tab.

3. Click "Display the full path in the title bar," then click OK.

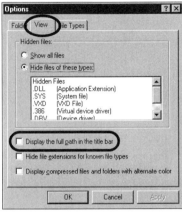

Windows 95/NT

Windows 98

To fit more text into the title bars

Displaying lengthy paths can clutter up the title bar when you get into heavily nested folders. But it's possible to fit more on the title bar simply by choosing a narrower font. Use the Display Properties as explained in Chapter 12 on page 179.

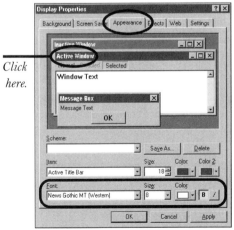

Click here.

Right-click on the Desktop and choose "Properties." Click the "Appearance" tab. Click on the title bar in the preview picture, then choose a font from the menu near the bottom of the property sheet. The preview will show you what it looks like so you can change your mind if it's awful.

Extensions and long file names

The basic disk operating system, called DOS, imposes an eight-character limit on a file name, plus a three-character extension. This is the famous "eight dot three" or "eight.three" you often hear about. It looks like this:

calendar.jpg

In this example, the three-letter "jpg" is the extension and is the most important part of the name because it tells the system what type of file you've made and which application can open it. (We talk more about extensions in Chapter 22, *Transferring Files*.)

Mac users once felt quite superior over this limited DOS naming capability. Mac names can be up to 31 characters long and are far less restrictive in the use of punctuation and other characters. But times have changed. Now Windows users like to turn around and sneer because they have "long file names."

Let's get one thing straight. It would sometimes be useful if the Mac could support twice as many characters in a file name as it does. On the other hand, long file names, although a tremendous improvement over the old DOS names, are rather overrated. In practical terms, using more than 60 characters to name a file is kind of silly. With 255 possible characters, long file names are disk management Gargantuas.

Gargantua: An amiable giant with a large appetite in Rabelais' satirical novel, 1534.

Why are long (like 255 characters long) file names overrated?

- You have to actually read a long file name, not just glance at it in recognition. Unless you're leaving yourself messages this way, very long names are less efficient.

- On the Desktop, that long file name will get cut down to a small fraction of its full length. In the large icon view, the name will get trimmed to two lines centered under the icon, which works out to about 25 to 30 characters.

- To the Windows operating system, the long file name is not even the file's real name. Despite the fact that they knew DOS's wacky limitations, Microsoft couldn't design Windows from the ground up. The first people who ran out to buy Windows 95 were DOS/Windows 3.1 users with a major investment in existing files and software. Not even Microsoft could leave that massive installed base twisting slowly in the wind. They had to make sure files would be backward-compatible; that is, the files needed to be able to read and be read on both old and new systems.

So every Windows file or folder actually has two names, the legal name (the eight.three name the system sees) and the stage name (the one you use). If you doubt that this is the case, try changing the name of your hard drive to something longer than eleven characters (that's 8+3). Because hard drives are a part of the operating system, they can't use a stage name.

If you make a shortcut (alias) to your drive, as explained in Chapter 17, you can make the name longer than eleven characters.

Want to see what a file's real system name looks like?

- Right-click on a file to get the pop-up menu, and choose "Properties."

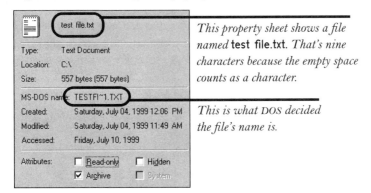

This property sheet shows a file named **test file.txt**. *That's nine characters because the empty space counts as a character.*

This is what DOS *decided the file's name is.*

So why didn't DOS rename this file **test fil.txt**, which would be eight.three (including the blank space)? That would be bad enough, but at least it would make sense. Here's why the name was automatically changed to **TESTFI~1.TXT**.

- DOS doesn't like spaces. They're illegal characters because DOS uses them as separators in its *command lines.*

command lines: DOS is a text-based operating system. You communicate with it by typing codes, one line at a time—thus a command line is an instruction from you to DOS telling it to do something.

- DOS sees no difference between upper- and lowercase letters. No keystroke combinations—not even with the Shift key—are allowed (even if you type in lowercase letters, DOS will read it as uppercase). Besides, not having to deal with the complexities of caps versus lowercase makes for smaller, faster programming. And DOS doesn't give a hoot that words in all caps are harder to read.

- Because a DOS name can only have eight characters, Windows needed a way to deal with files whose first eight characters are the same, such as:

  pumpkin1 smiling.tif pumpkin1 after.tif
  pumpkin1 glow.tif pumpkin1 flicker.tif

Windows makes the DOS name by truncating (cutting off) all of the characters in the long file name except the first six. To these six characters, Windows adds a tilde (~) followed by a number, called the "tail number." In a list of files like the ones shown below, the DOS names will all have the same first six letters (PUMPKI) with different tail numbers. The oldest file will end with ~1 and the newest file with ~4. The tail numbers will increase each time you make another file with the same beginning name and put it in the same folder. If you've made more than nine files with the same first six characters, the tenth file will have only five real characters and two digits after the tilde (like PUMPK~10). Here's how the pumpkin files look with their names truncated:

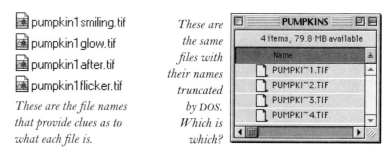

pumpkin1smiling.tif
pumpkin1glow.tif
pumpkin1after.tif
pumpkin1flicker.tif

These are the file names that provide clues as to what each file is.

These are the same files with their names truncated by DOS. Which is which?

PUMPKINS — 4 items, 79.8 MB available

Name
PUMPKI~1.TIF
PUMPKI~2.TIF
PUMPKI~3.TIF
PUMPKI~4.TIF

The way Windows deals with DOS file names is relevant to you whether you need to deal with these files on a PC or a Mac. Files that end up on a system which is unable to read long file names will use the DOS name instead. You might think that such a situation is unlikely, but you could run into it tomorrow. Any Mac running an operating system earlier than OS 8.1 (which includes OS 8.0) can only see truncated names. Any Windows 3.1 computer is in the same situation. You probably know lots of Mac users who are still working on some version of System 7 or Mac OS 8.0. We can vouch for the fact that thousands, perhaps millions of people have not yet upgraded to Windows 95, let alone 98 or NT.

Long file names and paths

We've implied that there's a connection between the way long file names work and the concept of paths. Let's explore this in a little more detail.

Earlier, we told you that the path to the file counts as part of the long file name. We mean that literally. Of the 255 characters available to long file names, three of these characters belong to the drive letter designation:

> C:\ (letter, colon, backslash)

So even if a file is just going to sit on the Desktop, it is actually limited to 252 characters. Now, we'll make a file with a useless and overly-long file name, and then nest it deep within branches of folders. When we tried to copy this file into the ninth folder in the series (nine levels down is deep, but not outrageously so) we got this message:

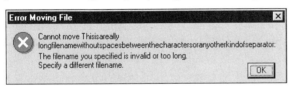

As you can tell by the file name in the dialog box above, we really did cross the line into silly. But silly is exactly what you should consider a really long file name because *the name of every folder you put the file into* will become part of the path name and thus part of the file name. If you can't move a file anywhere you might need it on a disk, then you can't afford to make a really long file name. You'll end up having to rename it anyway.

In case you're wondering, this can't happen on a Mac. As we implied with the analogy of the tree ornament, the Mac OS keeps track of folders and paths using a totally different system. It keeps the folders and their positions on the disk separate from their given names. You can have 31 characters for each and every Desktop item, no matter how deeply nested they are inside other folders.

Renaming files and folders

Renaming a file in Windows is very similar to doing it on the Mac.

1. Click on the file you want to rename.

2. Click again directly on the name itself, or press the F2 key.

3. Type to rename.

Once the file name is selected and that insertion point is flashing, you can use the arrow keys to move the insertion point, use the Backspace key to delete a few characters, copy and paste, and do basically anything else you would to rename a Mac file. All of the Desktop shortcut keys for cut, copy, paste, and undo work perfectly well on file names. Just make sure the file *name* is selected or you'll copy and paste the file itself rather than just its label.

A little warning: You can't always rename a folder if its window is open on the Desktop. Windows 98 allows you to rename an open folder, but Windows 95 gives you a warning screen with the option to cancel the renaming if it thinks the change might cause problems. In Windows NT you'll get a message on the screen telling you there's been an error renaming the file. If either of these things happens, just close the folder window and make the name change, then reopen to continue working.

Don't forget the DOS name

If you edit a long file name to add an identifying number for yourself, it's best to add the number at the *beginning* of the name. Otherwise the MS-DOS name won't adapt because the first six characters would still be the same. For instance, let's say you are writing a novel and are numbering the chapters. They're not in order yet because you are skipping all over the book writing different chapters. So you write a few chapters and happily name the files Chapter6.doc, Chapter3.doc, Chapter12.doc, etc. Remember, DOS renames them in the order they were *created*—it doesn't give a hoot what number *you* gave them. So your Chapter6.doc will become (to DOS), CHAPTE~1.DOC, and your Chapter3.doc will become CHAPTE~2.DOC.

So to keep these files in an order in which they make sense (if you ever find yourself having to use their DOS names), put the chapter number at the beginning of the name, like this: 3Chapter.doc, 6Chapter.doc. Then the DOS names will be 3CHAPT~1.DOC, 6CHAPT~2.DOC and you'll still know what they are even if DOS changes the tail number again.

Renaming numbered files

You need to consider both the long versions and the DOS versions of file and folder names when the names have sequential numbers, particularly if you are importing frames for animations, which often require files to be imported in a specific order. If these animation images will be used on computers that can't read long file names, keeping the DOS numbering straight could be very important.

For example, look at these four sequentially numbered files:

crackers1.BMP

crackers2.BMP

crackers3.BMP

crackers4.BMP

We mentioned earlier that the MS-DOS tail number (the number after the ~) is assigned when the file is made. When several files share the same first six characters, the tail is added *in the sequence that the files were created in the folder.*

In the property sheets for the files named above, the long file name number and the MS-DOS tail number are the same, as you can see in the illustration below. This happened because *the files were modified in numerical order;* that is, crackers1.bmp was modified before crackers2.bmp. The long file name has nothing to do with the number after the ~, because MS-DOS only reads the first eight characters.

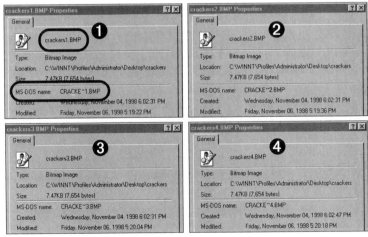

Notice the numbered modification dates in these property sheets. The files were created and modified in order so their MS-DOS tail numbers are correct.

Let's look next at another group of files, below. The illustrator worked backwards in editing them, from the last illustration in the animation sequence to the first, renaming them with numbers at the *ends* of the names in the correct sequence for the animation. Now the long file names and the MS-DOS names (examples circled, below) don't match. The long file names are in the correct order, but the MS-DOS names are in the order in which they were renamed.

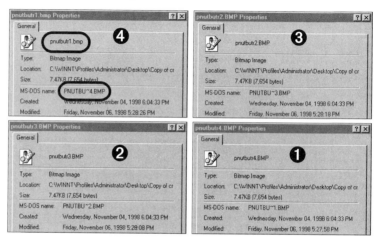

These files are now out of sequence because MS-DOS names are based on the file's order of creation, modification, or renaming.

It isn't possible to change the DOS file name directly, so the only way to solve this kind of numbering problem is to rename the files once again using "Save As" in the application, but this time save them in the correct sequential order. Since this is such a terrible waste of time, it's better to avoid the situation by putting your numbers at the *beginnings* of the file names when you originally create the file.

DOS has a short memory

MS-DOS doesn't remember a previous file name or tail number. If you change the first six characters of a long file name from something that's shared by many files to something unique, the final number in the DOS name will revert to 1. For example:

Original file name	MS DOS name	Renamed file name	New MS DOS name
Crackers4.doc	CRACKE~4.DOC	NewCrackers4.doc	NEWCRA~1.DOC

Finding File Information

Getting information about documents, applications, and folders on your Windows computer is so necessary, yet it's much less straightforward than on the Mac. Simply hunting down a system file or locating all the pictures you edited yesterday can be a bit of an adventure. In this chapter, we explore the Windows Find utility to make finding files and finding out about them a little less mysterious.

Getting file information

There is no "Get Info" box in Windows, but you can get certain pieces of information about a file, like the file type, size, and creation date, through its **property sheet.**

To get information about a file

- **Right-click** on a file to get its pop-up menu, and click "Properties." You'll get the file's property sheet, as shown below.

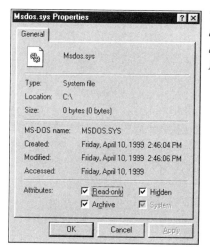

This property sheet gives you a little bit of information, although not as much as a Mac user is accustomed to.

A file's "Attributes"

There's an unfamiliar group of options at the bottom of the property sheet called "Attributes," which are elements that describe a file's character. This is what each one means:

Read-only	Read-only files can't be erased or altered by mistake, but they can be opened and read. Folders can be read-only, but making them so doesn't protect the files inside them.
Archive	A checkmark here indicates this file has been changed since a backup program has been run on the disk.
Hidden	Hidden files don't display in folder windows or in Windows Explorer. Although all system files are usually hidden, not all hidden files are system files. Some of them are system utilities or library files. See page 280 about displaying and hiding hidden files.
System	A checkmark here indicates Windows needs this file to run the system properly.

Locking and unlocking a file

You can lock a file in Windows just like you can lock a file on a Mac. Locking will prevent you or anyone else from accidentally deleting or changing the file. Keep in mind, however, that this attribute is no protection against deliberate malice or cluelessness—anyone can easily unlock the file. And if you drag a read-only (locked) file to the Recycle Bin, you'll get a dialog box asking if you really want to delete it. Answer yes or simply hit the Enter key, and the file is unlocked and gone.

To lock or unlock a file

- **Right-click** on a file to get the pop-up menu, and click on "Properties." At the bottom of the property sheet, under "Attributes," check or uncheck the "Read-only" box.

Hiding or showing a file

You can hide any file so it won't display in any Desktop window, nor will it appear in any Open or Save As dialog boxes, nor can you find it through a file search.

If you're going to hide a file, make sure you read page 280 to show all hidden files, or you might panic unnecessarily when you can't find this important file!

To hide or show a file

- **Right-click** on a file to get the pop-up menu, and click on "Properties." At the bottom of the property sheet, under "Attributes," check or uncheck the "Hidden" box.

To show all hidden files, see page 280.

Finding files

Finding files is a basic need on both the Mac and Windows platforms. Although the Windows' format for the Find dialog box is completely different from the Mac's, most Mac users will find its basic parameters understandable.

To open the Find dialog box

- Click the "Start" button, click "Find," then choose "Files or Folders…." **Or** press F3. The Find dialog box will appear:

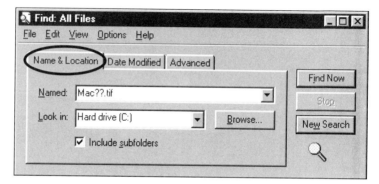

Searching by name and location

The "Name & Location" section is set by default to search everything in "My Computer." Use the "Look in" menu or the "Browse" button to narrow the search to one specific drive or even one folder.

You don't need to type a file's extension, and it doesn't matter if you type caps or lowercase.

Using wild card characters

Unlike a Mac, you can't use "qualifiers" in Windows to include or exclude information from a search, such as searching for a file that "starts with" or "ends with" or "is not." But you can use wild card characters that substitute for unknown letters or numbers.

The asterisk (*) is a wild card character that loosely translates to "put as many characters in a row as you'd like here." For example, if you want to search for every TIF file on your disk, enter ***.TIF**. If you want to find every file that begins with "mac," enter **mac*** instead. If you want to narrow that search down to find every TIF file that begins with "mac," enter **mac*.tif**.

TIF: Tagged Image File Format, a platform-independent graphic file format.

The question mark (?) wild card character means "insert exactly one character here." This symbol is particularly good for finding files with the same name but a sequential number. For example, to find the files Mac001.TIF through Mac149.TIF, enter **Mac???.tif**. Using this character prevents you from finding extra files that start with the same first characters, like "Macaroni.TIF" or "Mac01.TIF."

Search by the date a file was modified

The "Date Modified" section allows date-based searches, although once again its flexibility is a little limited. You can specify a range of days or months, but not weeks. You can't search by excluding dates either, such as looking for a file that was not created while you were on vacation.

Search by size, content, and file type

The "Advanced" tab is where you can get a little more precise in your search, but it's still pretty limited. Searching by content ("containing text") is very time consuming, of course, because Windows has to search the contents of every file on your computer, so you have to have a pretty desperate reason to do this. Searching by content has been eliminated from Windows 98.

Searching by file type is the nicest thing about the Windows Find dialog box because Microsoft provides a menu of every kind of file it recognizes. This doesn't help much if you want a file with a generic icon, but it can be a handy feature in other circumstances.

Searches you can't do

Windows Find works well for simple text- or date-based searches, and it does a good job searching for recognized file types, but it has no ability to search based on system parameters or file attributes (like searching for all files created by a specific application) the way you can on a Mac.

You can't find invisible files; you have to make them all visible first (see page 280).

Strangely enough, you can't search for files with custom icons the way you can on a Mac. This is something that an operating system with an overabundance of themes and schemes could really use.

Nor can you search by software version number, which would be very useful for finding pesky files for programs that don't uninstall completely.

Mac tip: In Find File, hold down the Option key and click on the "name" menu— you'll get an extra set of options so you can search for things like invisible files, custom icons, or content.

Multiple searches at the same time

You can speed up your searching by taking advantage of something that on the Mac would be seen as a really nasty bug: launching the same program several times.

1. Launch the Find dialog box as many times as you have searches to do. The windows will open on top of each other so you'll need to rearrange them on the Desktop (this is a good use for the "Arrange Horizontally" option we showed you in Chapter 8, *The Taskbar and Start Menu*).

2. Type your search into each of the Find dialog boxes.

3. Click the "Find Now" button for each search and sit back while the hunt takes place.

Be sure to close all of the Find windows when you're done because Windows thinks they're separate applications, not one application with different windows—each Find window takes up the memory of the entire application.

Using a found file

Once you find a file, you can treat its name in the Find listing exactly as if you had the icon in a regular window: launch it by double-clicking; drag-and-drop it into another folder; delete it by dragging it to the Recycle Bin; and even right-click on it to get its property sheet.

Sorting the list

The results of your search appear in a list on the bottom half of the dialog box. This list has similar column headings as a window when viewed in detail, and just as you can in a window view, you can click a column heading to sort all of the items in the list by that heading. Click the same heading again to sort them in the opposite order. This is invaluable when you're looking for a certain file type like "application" or "shortcut" and you've got a long list to look through.

Open containing folder

Select any found file, then from the File menu choose "Open containing folder." The folder in which your selected file is stored will open.

Saving a search

If you're likely to search again using the same criteria, you can save your search information as a file.

1. Open the Find dialog box. Before you run the search, go to the "Options" menu and choose "Save Results."

2. Run your search.

3. When the search is finished, go to the "File" menu and choose "Save Search." A little file that looks like one of the icons below will appear on your Desktop, named with a description of your search criteria.

Files named
windows

Saved search icon,
Windows 98

Files of type
TIF Image ...

Saved search icon,
Windows 95 and NT

When you want to run the same search, double-click on this icon. It will launch the Find utility, and the original search criteria will appear, as well as a list of the files that had been found as a result of that search.

Showing all the files

Windows has lots of hidden files, files that are actually in the folders but you can't see them. When visible, they clutter up the windows and make it more difficult to see the contents. So why would you want to show all of them?

- You can't search for a file if it's hidden. If you're on the phone with tech support because something strange happened with your system or an application, they may ask you which version of a particular .DLL you have. If you can't find this file, you can't tell them.

- You can't copy hidden files. If you plan to copy an entire system or application folder, you want to make sure the hidden files copy also or the folder will be incomplete.

- Perhaps you've hidden files yourself to keep your children from having easy access to certain documents on your shared computer. If you want to search for these files, they have to be visible.

To see all the files in your Windows system

1. Double-click "My Computer," then double-click the C: drive icon.

2. From the "View" menu of the C: drive window, choose "Large Icons." Take a look at the files and folders in the window. Then:

3. From the "View" menu, choose "Folder Options…" or "Options…."

4. In this Options dialog box, click the "View" tab, as shown on the opposite page.

5. To make the hidden system files visible, click the "Show all files" button, then click the "Apply" button.

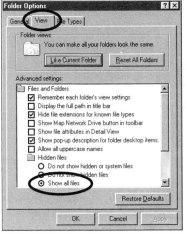
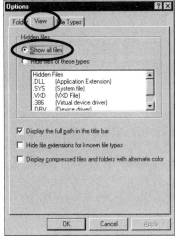

Windows 98   *Windows 95/NT*

Suddenly you'll see more icons in your folder windows, some with incomprehensible names. This is a global setting, so all folder windows that had hidden files will now display additional files and folders.

6. Uncheck the box or radio button if you want to hide the files.

In Windows 98, the hidden files that are now visible appear as "ghost" icons—visible but grayed back slightly.

Logo.sys   Config.sys

The file on the left is an example of a ghost icon. The file on the right is what you typically see.

Finding other sorts of items

Experiment with the other options in the Find menu.

Besides finding files or folders, Windows offers several other Find options in the Start Menu. Some of these functions are more useful than others, and some only work with certain versions of Windows.

Find "Computer..."

If you're connected to a network, you might want to find a file that's stored on another computer on the same network. First, however, you need to find the computer before you can find the file on it. Use Find "Computer...."

Find "On the Internet..."

You need to have Internet Explorer version 3.0 (or later) or Windows 98 for this option. This will not launch Netscape even if Netscape is your default browser. This option launches Internet Explorer and displays a website where you can search using several search engines. When Cyndi used this function for the first time, she couldn't help but giggle: Internet Explorer took her directly to Netscape's search page (home. netscape.com/home/winsearch.html).

Find "People..." (Windows 98, OSR2 version of Windows 95)

The "People…" feature searches your hard disk's address book, or connects to the Internet and offers you several people-finding search engines to locate names, email addresses, and regular mail addresses. To see your options, click the down arrow in the "Look in" box.

To search your hard disk, click "Find Now." To search on the web for people, click "Web Site."

The logo at the bottom of the dialog box changes depending on which search engine you choose.

Type a name or email address in the edit boxes before you click "Web Site," and that text will appear automatically in the people-search you choose.

QuickFinder (Windows NT only)

Don't bother. QuickFinder is a utility on NT systems that does the same searches the regular Find utility does, but it's messier.

Part Five

Going Back and Forth

Nothing in life is to be feared.
It is only to be understood.

—Marie Curie

Mounting PC Media and Reading PC Files

Macs are very good at mounting and reading a variety of storage media (disks, removable cartridges, CDs) that were formatted on a PC. In fact, if you're using a Macintosh with a recent version of the operating system (and of course you should be if you're working cross-platform!), you have all the tools you need to mount PC media, read PC directories, and even open and read files.

In this chapter we concentrate on getting to know the tools you have for reading and writing across platforms. Of course, we assume the files on the PC media have been prepared properly for use on a Mac. See Chapter 22, *Transferring Files*, if things don't go as you expect when you open files.

Mounting removable media

If you have a Mac running any version of System 7 or later, most PC disks and CDs will mount effortlessly on your Mac. Just put the disk in and it mounts. It's really quite amazing.

There are a few exceptions to the ease of mounting PC disks. If you have trouble, see if one of the following exceptions might be your problem.

SCSI drivers

File Exchange and PC Exchange are Mac control panels that we explain on pages 289–294. Right now what you need to know is that Exchange needs its own SCSI drivers to correctly manipulate files on DOS media. Although Exchange accepts Iomega's drivers (so Zip and Jaz disks work as easily as floppies), other removable media need special handling. **If you are about to attach a Syquest, optical drive, or other exotic device to your Mac and hope to read PC files, follow these steps:**

1. Don't load the drive's own software driver. Attach the drive, restart, then open the File Exchange or PC Exchange control panel.

On the left is the File Exchange control panel on the Mac (PC Exchange, on the right, is the older version). For more details on how to use this, see pages 289–294.

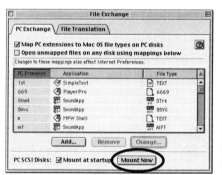 

2. In the File Exchange control panel, click "Mount Now."

2. In the PC Exchange control panel, click "Options…" to get this dialog box:

PC Exchange is a SCSI detective, looking through the SCSI chain for mounted drives.

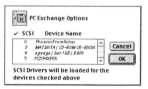

Select the SCSI device that holds your PC files, then click OK. Special drivers will load for this temporary operation.

The FAT 32 format

Mac OS 8.0 or earlier can't read Windows' disks created in the FAT 32 format (explained below). If you do need to read a FAT 32-formatted disk on your Macintosh, you must upgrade to at least Mac OS 8.1.

FAT 32 is a new way to format a PC disk. Until recently, big hard disks had to be partitioned (chopped into smaller virtual pieces) because Windows couldn't recognize a disk bigger than 2 gigabytes. FAT 32 solves this problem.

However, only Windows 98 can create this type of disk, so you probably won't run into difficulties with FAT 32-formatted disks frequently. Until this new format becomes a standard, many Windows users will avoid using FAT 32 for anything other than formatting their internal hard disks because of compatibility issues.

Non-English characters in file names

PC/File Exchange has a problem with non-English characters. If you need to exchange files with people in Europe, the disk name and the names of files on it could prevent you from mounting a disk or using a file. The special characters like the German "ß" or the Scandinavian "ø" in file names sometimes prevent a non-English DOS disk from mounting. The easiest solution is to ask the PC users who are supplying you with foreign-language files to substitute these non-English characters with English equivalents.

Mounting PC CDs on a Mac

Cyndi says: A few years ago, we upgraded the Novell Netware file server in the university labs. It turned out to be a very difficult experience. At one point, the installers brought a CD with critical installation files on it. The files themselves weren't very big, but the technicians couldn't transfer them to the file server because none of our lab PCs had CD players. While they were scratching their heads, I put their installation CD into a Mac where it mounted without a smidgen of difficulty. Then I took a DOS-formatted floppy disk, put it in the drive, and dragged the critical files onto it. The rest of the installation continued smoothly, with two Novell engineers eyeing the Mac in stunned silence.

There's almost never a problem mounting a PC-formatted CD on your Macintosh. If you do experience difficulties, it's probably because you have either dumped or turned off two Mac extensions that make this possible: ISO **9660 File Access** and **Foreign File Access.** (Isn't it nice to find out what some weird-sounding extension does?)

multisession CD: A CD with information that was pressed onto the disk during two or more separate occasions, or sessions. Older CD drives can only recognize the information from the first session.

You might also have a problem if the CD you're trying to read is a *multisession CD* or has multiple partitions. Older Apple CD-ROM extensions don't support these special situations, so this is another reason to keep your system software current. (Lots of commercial CDs have two partitions: the Windows part and the Macintosh part. Sometimes you might want to see something from the Windows side on a Mac.)

The Mac's File Exchange control panel

Mounting a Windows disk on a Mac is half the battle of working cross-platform, but being able to use the files is just as important. That's what the File Exchange control panel is for (this control panel replaced the PC Exchange in Mac OS 8.0, which replaced Apple File Exchange in System 7.5). Exchange's main mission is to put "Type" and "Creator" codes on DOS files so Macs can read them.

The Macintosh Type and Creator codes are internal information labels that identify a file to the system. The "Type" tells the system what the document's file format is; the "Creator" tells the system in which application the document was created. PC files have to include both of these labels before they will mount and open on a Macintosh.

File Exchange compares DOS/Windows file name extensions with a database of Type and Creator codes. The process of matching up Windows file extensions with the Macintosh codes is called "extension mapping." If you haven't mapped a PC extension to a Mac application in File Exchange (see below), no application will open it.

There are several versions of File Exchange. Only those versions 2.2 or higher are bug-free and capable of dealing with Windows' long file names. If you have Mac OS 8.1, you have v. 2.2; if you have Mac OS 8.5 or higher, you have v. 3.0. Don't try to use a newer version of File Exchange or PC Exchange without upgrading your system—it won't work.

Mapping PC file extensions to Mac applications

Mac OS 8.5's File Exchange comes with about 300 DOS extensions mapped to applications like SimpleText, Movie Player, or Picture Viewer. Mac OS 8.1's PC Exchange, however, can only exercise a fraction of its potential until you create connections between PC file types and Mac applications. You'll want to build a database of extensions and applications so Exchange can do its job correctly.

In both cases, you won't be satisfied for long with the original definitions. In File Exchange, the 300 connections seem like a lot until you begin to work cross-platform, and you'll soon discover that you want it to launch applications that let you *edit* the files, not just *look* at them. The database of extensions you can download for PC Exchange has some missing connections, and new file formats are always cropping up.

Tip for PC Exchange: There's a free file you can download from www.macworld.com's "Macdownload" area called "PC Exchange Preferences." It's a Preferences file with dozens of mappings. Drag a copy of the downloaded file to the Preferences folder in your System Folder. Remember to copy it; don't move the original! Preferences are the first thing to get rid of when a program stops behaving nicely, and if you dump this file without a backup you'll have to download it again.

You'll know that a file needs mapping (and maybe translating too—see the following section on translating files) when you look at a file list and see icons like these:

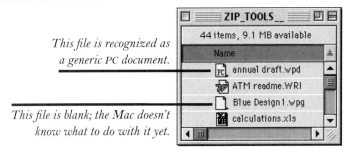

This file is recognized as a generic PC document.

This file is blank; the Mac doesn't know what to do with it yet.

The file with the blank icon may actually cause fewer problems than the one that's recognized as the PC document. The blank icon sometimes means there are several possibilities for opening a file with this extension, but none of them have been mapped yet.

To map an extension in File Exchange or PC Exchange

1. With the PC media mounted on your desktop, open the File Exchange control panel (Mac OS 8.5 and up) or the PC Exchange control panel (Mac OS 8 or 8.1).

2. Click the "Add" button to get this dialog box:

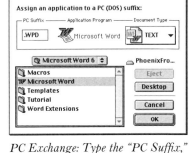

PC Exchange: Type the "PC Suffix," select the application, choose a "Document Type," and click "OK."

File Exchange: Type the "Extension," select an "Application," choose a "File Type," and click "Add."

3. In the "Extension" or "PC Suffix" box, type the DOS extension you want to map.

4. Use the directory list in the dialog box to find the application on your hard disk. When you find the application you want to connect to the PC extension, click to select it.

5. In the menu next to "File Type" or under "Document Type" you'll get a list of all the Mac document types the selected application supports. You'll probably want to choose the most generic document type you can find if you don't see the one that exactly matches your extension. For example, if you need to map a .JPG file, you'll certainly find many programs that will open the JPEG document type. But if you want to open a file generated by word processing software you don't have, choose the TEXT option.

6. After you've chosen your document file type, click the "Add" or "OK" button.

7. Back at the Desktop, reopen the disk window that had the unmapped file. See how the icon has changed?

Tip: To help identify a mysterious PC extension, visit www.whatis.com/ ff.htm. This site identifies every file format in existence by its extension.

Now that the Mac knows which application should open this file, it applies the correct icon.

```
┌─────────────────────────────────────┐
│ □  ══  ZIP_TOOLS __  ══  □ ▤         │
├─────────────────────────────────────┤
│      44 items, 9.1 MB available      │
├─────────────────────────────────────┤
│  Name                            ▲   │
│  📄 annual draft.wpd            ▲    │
│  📄 ATM readme.WRI              ▤    │
│  📄 Blue Design1.wpg                 │
│  📄 calculations.xls            ▼    │
│  ◄ ▥ ▨▨▨▨▨▨▨▨▨              ► ▨     │
└─────────────────────────────────────┘
```

Downloaded DOS files

If you use the Internet to download a DOS file with a readable extension, sometimes the Mac doesn't recognize its type even after you've mapped it properly. You can still use the standard Mac solution to open this file by dragging it over an application icon, but being able to double-click a file is more convenient.

The solution to this unsuccessful mapping quirk is silly but foolproof: Put any disk or cartridge in the Mac and copy the downloaded files to it. Eject the disk, then put it back in. Suddenly, all the PC files whose extensions are known to File Exchange will display their icons. Copy them back to the hard drive and use them safely.

Translating a file after you've mapped it

It's easy to get file *exchange* programs confused with file *translation* programs. You might get your file exchange program all set up and still see a dialog box like this:

That's because extension mapping in a file *exchange* program only helps the Mac recognize a file *type*—it can't change the *format* the file was actually written in. For instance, if you have a file in "Word Perfect for Windows" format, you can't just assign a Microsoft Word file extension to it and expect the file to magically transform into a Microsoft Word document. Often, instead of double-clicking a Windows file to open it, you need to launch the application first, and then open or import the file, and you may need to *translate* the file before you can read it in any of your programs. For translating files, see the following sections.

Using File Exchange (Mac OS 8.5 and up) to translate files

File Exchange combines the application-mapping ability of PC Exchange with some basic file translation functions. The File Translation portion of File Exchange is merely a link to an application that you can assign to do the file translating. If you choose the wrong application or if the application can't automatically translate the file format, File Exchange will not be very useful. No actual file translators come with the Mac OS 8.5 File Exchange, so if you need, for example, to translate Word Perfect documents from the PC into Macintosh Microsoft Word documents, you'll need to buy a commercial product like DataViz's MacLinkPlus Deluxe (www.dataviz.com).

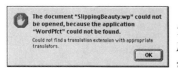

You'll get this dialog box when File Exchange can't find an application with which to open your file in its mapping list.

Customizing File Exchange

File Exchange will automatically launch when you double-click a file that needs translation. If the file type is in the list of mapped applications, the application it's mapped to will open without you even seeing the File Exchange dialog box. When you first install Mac OS 8.5, you should customize some settings to make File Exchange more efficient.

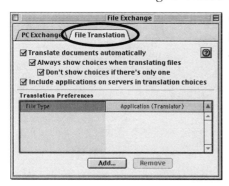

Open File Exchange through the Control Panels under the Apple menu, and click the "File Translation" tab.

- **Translate documents automatically** is already checked, but it's a good idea to also check the boxes below it.

- **Always show choices when translating files** is a particularly useful option when you've just installed OS 8.5 and File Exchange doesn't yet have a good database to work with. There are often several applications installed on your computer that might open and translate a file, and you'd probably like to choose the one you'll use most frequently for a file type.

- **Don't show choices if there's only one** will save time if File Exchange finds only one possible application that matches your file.

- **Include applications on servers in translation choices** is useful if your computer is attached to a network because sometimes software on your Mac is actually being accessed from a server. If you don't check this box, File Exchange won't know these applications are available.

Using File Exchange

Tip: File Exchange mappings are used for files you download as well as those on PC disks. If you want File Exchange to deal differently with downloaded files, select its extension in the "PC Exchange" settings, click "Change," then click "Show Advanced Options." You'll get a second dialog box. Uncheck "Map incoming," and File Exchange will let you choose the application to handle these types of files when you are downloading them.

When you double-click a PC file that's not in File Exchange's Translation Preferences list, you'll see a dialog box like this:

Although this dialog box has a check box labeled "Show only recommended choices," it's always grayed out.

- Click a choice in the list to select it, then click "Open." File Exchange will launch the application and attempt to open— or translate and open—your file.

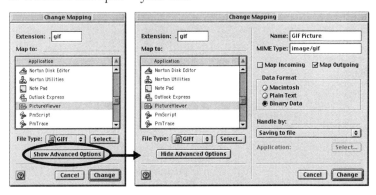

On the left is the standard setting, and on the right are the advanced options.

Using Mac OS Easy Open (OS 8.0 and 8.1) to translate files

If you have Mac OS 8 or 8.1, you have a very powerful control panel, a file translator, called **Mac OS Easy Open.** If you haven't installed it, you should use your original install CD and do so. Easy Open is very easy to use and allows you to customize its actions.

Easy Open is a control panel so you'll find it with the other control panels in the Apple menu.

Customizing Easy Open

Most of the time you'll want to leave the radio button checked on for "Automatic document translation." Doing so will prompt Easy Open to step forward and deal with any file your Macintosh doesn't recognize after PC Exchange's mapping process. The other checkboxes you select will determine how Easy Open works for you.

- **Always show dialog box** makes Easy Open alert you to the fact that the file you're trying to open needs to be translated. If you don't check this box, Easy Open will handle the translation in the background, which is certainly a time-saver, but sometimes it pays to be aware that a type of file isn't already prepared for your Mac. If you'll be receiving similar files frequently, you might be able to ask your PC associates to save their files in a more compatible format. Translations aren't always foolproof, and you'd rather deal with files that maintain more of their original formatting when you open them on your Mac.

- **Include applications on servers** is useful if you're networked because sometimes software on your Mac is actually being accessed from a file server. If you don't check this box, Easy Open won't know these applications are available to open your PC files.

- **Auto pick if only 1 choice** is a timesaver, particularly if you have not chosen "Automatic document translation." If Easy Open only has one possible application that matches your file, it won't bother to check with you before translating.

- **Translate "TEXT" documents** prompts Easy Open to translate unformatted ASCII text documents, which allows you to assign something other than Simple Text as the chosen application.

- Although you won't use the button **Delete Preferences...** very often, it can be handy. Once a file type has been associated with an application, Easy Open opens every similar file with that application, too. But sometimes you—or the software—guess wrong, and your mistake gets repeated over and over. Choosing "Delete Preferences" lets you start from scratch (you'll get a warning dialog box when you click the button, which will prevent you from dumping the preferences by mistake).

Using Easy Open

Once you've set up the Easy Open control panel, you're ready to double-click an unfamiliar PC file. If you've set Easy Open on automatic, you won't receive the "unknown format" dialog box you saw on page 292. Instead, you'll see a dialog box like this:

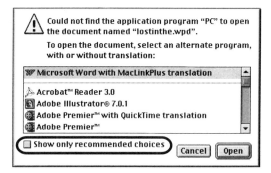

- Click on a choice in the list to highlight it, then click the "Open" button. Easy Open will launch the application and attempt to open—or translate and open—your file.

  The applications that appear *below* the dotted line in the scrolling box represent every application that has even a possibility of opening the PC file. Applications *above* the dotted line are those that Easy Open recommends. If you'd rather not be bothered with applications that aren't recommended, just check the box labeled "Show only recommended choices."

Sometimes the recommended application, like the one in the example, will be followed by the phrase "with MacLinkPlus translation." This is a good sign, and means that Easy Open recognizes the file type and is fairly confident that it's chosen an appropriate application. There are two possible scenarios if this phrase isn't there. The first is that the application can open the file without a translation, perhaps as a simple text file without the original file's formatting. The other possibility is that Easy Open has no translator and is not confident that its chosen application will really be successful. It offers its recommended choice as your best option.

If you want to know in advance what the chances are that Easy Open handles a specific type of PC application, go to your Mac's System Folder and open the folder inside it labeled DataViz. This folder holds all the translator modules:

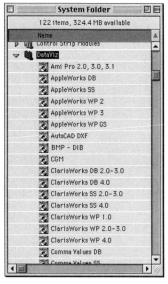

Useful hint: The DataViz translators can take up a lot of memory since they occupy over 7 MB of space in the System Folder. If you are short on RAM and only need to convert a limited number of PC file formats, create a new folder and drag the translators you don't need into it. Move this folder out of the System Folder to store it, or leave this new folder right in the DataViz folder since the application won't read translators in sub-folders. When you need more translators, drag the ones you need back into the main folder.

Other file translators

If the original PC application or version isn't among the translators in the DataViz folder list or if you're using Mac OS 8.5, you have other options. Mac OS Easy Open and MacLinkPlus specialize in converting **text, spreadsheet,** and **database files.** If the file you need to translate falls into one of those categories, contact DataViz (www.dataviz.com) to see if they include its format in the latest version of their commercial product, MacLinkPlus Deluxe.

If you need to translate **graphic files,** neither of the OS 8.x translation options will serve all of your needs. The DataViz products translate some presentation graphics files into readable (but not editable) form, and translate to and from PC and Mac versions of some standard bitmap graphics formats, like TIFF. If your file format isn't among this short list, you'll probably need another application to handle your translating. Adobe Photoshop can open or import a wide variety of graphic formats; launch it and browse through its menu of formats in the "Open" dialog box (click "Show All Files" to get the "Format" menu).

If you deal with **specialized PC graphic formats,** you should probably invest in a dedicated commercial file converter like Equilibrium's DeBabelizer. DeBabelizer can also handle many multimedia formats, as can Apple's QuickTime 3 MoviePlayer, which specifically deals with video and audio formats.

Transferring Files

Mac users don't worry much about file format problems. When you want to view a file, you double-click it, the file finds its original application, the application opens, and voilà—your file is on the screen. Even if you don't have the original program, you can usually find at least one other that will open it. If all else fails, good ol' Simple Text opens lots of files.

But when you start to send files across platforms, the lack of cooperation from Windows (as you may have discovered already) can be very frustrating. Rest assured that it's not *impossible* to send documents from one platform to the other. With some basic understanding of the different ways file formats are handled on the two operating systems, you can share your work successfully on any Desktop.

Why won't some files open?

Two kinds of files can fail to open in Windows: those that were created on a Mac and those that weren't.

This doesn't mean that Windows can't open files, although it sometimes feels like that. PCs have experienced radical changes over their lifetime that the Macintosh environment has not (Macs were built correctly in the first place) so there's a lot more "variety"— good and bad—between the newer Windows software, the older DOS/Windows applications, and the different formats they create.

To avoid problems you need to know something about how both operating systems work with the files you create.

Generic Windows icons

kingdom of lost
Generic Mac icon

Questions
Generic Windows icon

If your Mac doesn't recognize a file type, you typically see the generic, blank icon which is your clue that you might have trouble opening that file. The same thing happens on Windows: if Windows doesn't recognize a file type, it displays a generic Windows icon, and you'll *probably* have trouble opening it. It *certainly* means the file won't automatically launch an application program when you double-click it. And you *definitely* have a problem if you manually launch your application, use the "Open…" command from the File menu, and the darned file still won't open. Too often when you double-click a generic Windows icon you get this "Open With" dialog box:

This dialog box appears because Windows doesn't know what to do with your file. Sometimes you can use this dialog box to force Windows to open the selected file in a certain application, but most of the time that application will just launch and tell you it can't recognize the file anyway. The best way to deal with these clueless files is to prepare them correctly to begin with. Read on and we'll show you how.

Create and name those Mac files correctly!

As we mentioned in Chapter 19, *Paths and Long File Names*, Windows is very fussy about how you name your files. In fact, it's so fussy that if you don't name files correctly the [dumb] system can't even open them. It also has trouble dealing with files that aren't created with exactly the right file formats and options. There are four basic rules to follow so your Mac files will open properly on a PC.

Mac-to-Windows Rule #1: Save in the correct file format

When in doubt, use file formats that are supported on both platforms. If you have to use a different file format from one of those mentioned on the opposite page, make absolutely certain in advance that the specific Windows program you'll be using can open or import what you create.

Use the native file format whenever possible

If both the Mac and the PC have the same version of the same application (for instance, if both platforms use PageMaker version 6.5), the files will have the most compatibility in the "native" file format (the native format is the default format in an application). Native file formats maintain the most information about a document, and you don't have to remember to change the program settings when you save.

query2.p65   query2.p65

This native PageMaker 6.5 file (on the left) transferred over to the PC (on the right) with no problems because both platforms had the same version of the same software.

Save Mac documents in Windows formats

Many spreadsheet and word processing applications allow you to save files in the version that works best with the other platform. Look carefully at your "Save As" dialog box. It probably has options like in the Claris/AppleWorks menu shown below, which let you save your documents in a variety of word processing and platform formats.

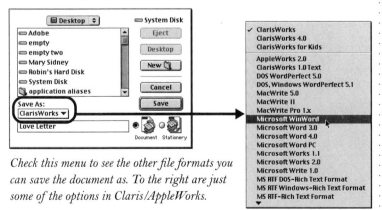

Check this menu to see the other file formats you can save the document as. To the right are just some of the options in Claris/AppleWorks.

For example, one of the most common file transfer problems is sending and receiving Microsoft Office files, particularly Microsoft Word documents. Hard as it is to believe, Windows Word 97 files often don't transfer properly to Mac-based Word versions, and Mac Office 98 files do equally badly in transferring to Windows Word 97. Many people erroneously blame their email and complain of receiving files sandwiched by nonsense characters, with graphics missing, or with charts and headlines suddenly reappearing in edits.

Although it can mean sacrificing some of the enhancements of Office 97 and 98, re-save your files as Word 6.0/95 before transferring them to someone using a different operating system and/or software version. Microsoft has created converters for the latest Mac and Windows versions of Word to make the files easier to read on older software.

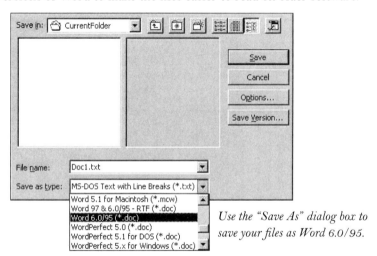

Use the "Save As" dialog box to save your files as Word 6.0/95.

Use a cross-platform format

Below are the preferred file formats for various types of documents or graphic images you might need to send cross-platform.

- **Web browser files**   GIF, JPG, PDF, HTM
  GIF and JPG are the most common image file formats on the web. Adobe PDF files are for viewing formatted documents cross-platform, and they transfer beautifully. HTM documents (HTML on the Mac) are just text files so they are easily read across platforms.

- **Word processing**   TXT, RTF, DOC
  TXT is the safest but you will lose all formatting. RTF (Rich Text Format) retains the formatting code, but it still might look a little different from the original. Most word processors will handle DOC files since they are Microsoft Word compatible.

- **Spreadsheet**   XL*
  The asterisk (∗) is a place-saving symbol; different types of Excel-formatted files use different letters; XLS is the most common. XL* is the universal spreadsheet format so any fairly current spreadsheet program can read it without difficulty.

- **Database**   DBF
  DBF is the format created by dBase/FoxPro. It's recognized by all databases, including Microsoft Works and Claris/AppleWorks.

- **Publishing graphics files**   TIF, EPS, PDF
  TIF is most common for files scanned or created in paint or image editing programs. EPS is common for files created in illustration programs (like FreeHand or Illustrator) and page layout applications (like QuarkXPress, InDesign, or PageMaker). PDF files, which can include text, image, and font information, are increasingly used to provide printers with complete, cross-platform files.

- **CAD, 3-D vector files**   DXF
  DXF is Autodesk's AutoCAD exchange format. Autodesk software products are either the industry standard or a major competitor in 3-D and drafting applications. Most Windows-based programs will read them. Many programs will also convert DXF files to other usable formats.

- **Video**   QTM (QuickTime)
  This is no such thing as a universally accepted video format, but QuickTime is the only major cross-platform solution.

- **Sound**   AIFF, WAV
  Most every serious digital sound package will export and import both the Macintosh AIFF and the Windows WAV formats, but AIFF has a slight edge since recording professionals tend to use Macs.

System-specific file formats

Each platform has its own *interchange format*—types of files that were specifically designed to transfer data efficiently between different applications within its own operating system. On the Mac we have SimpleText for text files and PICT images for simple graphics. On Windows, Notepad plays the role of SimpleText and BMP is the simple graphic format.

Each platform's *text* format travels to the other platform reasonably well: Notepad makes TXT files that Mac programs can read, and SimpleText files open nicely in Windows if you add a .TXT extension at the ends of their names. The *image* interchange formats are not as cooperative: Each operating system's image files rely on their own system's distinct method of seeing graphics, and they contain no special hints to help the other platform make sense of them. That's why the interchange image files don't travel well across platforms. The problems can range from incorrect color displays to the file not opening at all.

What to do about system-specific image files

Dealing with a system-specific image file is very straightforward: Open the application that created it and resave it in a "portable" format—one that will go cross-platform more reliably. Follow the simple chart and directions below.

If your current format is	Change it to
WMF, EMF, CGM in Windows	EPS
BMP, PCX, PIC in Windows	TIF (Windows)
Draw-based PICT file in Macintosh	EPS (Note: see pages 306 and 313)
Paint-based PICT file in Macintosh	TIFF (Macintosh)

To change a file format on the original platform

1. Open the file on the original platform and in the original application. From the File menu, choose "Save As…."

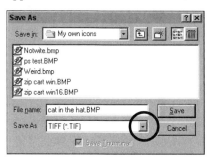

2. Click the "Save As" arrow (circled above), to get a menu with the list of possible file formats in which your program can save files (shown below).

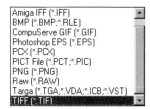

Here's a partial list of possible file formats in Windows Photoshop. In this example TIFF is chosen because the original file (shown above) was a BMP.

3. Click "Save," and you've created a cross-platform file.

If the application you used doesn't have the correct portable file format as an option, it's either very old or very non-standard. Use a program like Adobe Photoshop, Macromedia FreeHand, or CorelDraw instead. As mentioned in Chapter 1, *Preparing to Do Windows*, you really must use current versions of software on both platforms.

Mac-to-Windows Rule #2: Save with the correct options

Part of saving in the right format is saving with the correct options that the program offers. Make the wrong choice and your graphics file may open in your Windows application with the colors shifted or as a blank page. Or maybe the file will appear to be happily working in its new environment, but then refuse to print.

Saving Macintosh TIFF files for Windows

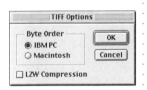

On the Mac, save a TIFF with a PC byte order so Windows will read it properly.

The graphic format TIFF (Tagged Image File Format) was created specifically to cross platforms. It can be saved in a variety of ways to accommodate the different sets of basic system colors that Windows and Macs have. If you create a TIFF file on a Mac and try to open it in most Windows applications, you'll probably get an error message or an empty box. Mac TIFF files should be saved (or resaved) in PC "byte order." If the application you're working in creates TIFFs, it should give you the chance to choose Mac or PC byte order right *after* you choose TIFF as your format and click the Save button.

If you already have a TIFF file that you want to change from Mac to PC, choose "Save As" or "Save a Copy" from the File menu—you'll get the opportunity to change the file to a PC byte order.

Saving Mac EPS files for Windows

The EPS format (Encapsulated PostScript) is a sophisticated PostScript file. The monitor doesn't really display PostScript—it's meant for printing. But of course we want to see the image on the screen, so an application that can make EPS files always offers a choice of "previews," or how you want to see the image on the screen before it prints. If you don't choose the correct preview options when you save the Mac graphic, then in the Windows application you might see the image as a blank page or a gray box with "PostScript header" information (just some text and the name of the file). The default in most Macintosh applications is to make an EPS preview a PICT image. PICTs are generally incompatible with Windows; they're Mac-specific, so the PC doesn't know how to display the picture information.

If the graphic image is going to a Windows machine, you need to save the file with a TIFF preview (not PICT) so it can be seen in Windows. All current Macintosh desktop publishing and illustration programs that can output to EPS let you save your files with a preview that a PC can read, although every program handles this task differently. For example, in Adobe Illustrator, choose the option "Illustrator EPS" when you save the file; you'll get a dialog box where you can choose either 1-bit (for black and white) or 8-bit (for color) TIFF files. Other applications are different; for instance, QuarkXPress has a "Save Page as EPS" dialog box and offers choices of "PC B&W" and "PC Color." PageMaker outputs to EPS through its Print dialog box. Check your software's documentation for exactly how to save a file as an EPS and which options to choose.

If you will be printing your EPS files on a Windows printer or over a non-Apple network, see Chapter 26 on *Printing* for more on EPS settings that can affect how the file outputs.

Mac-to-Windows Rule #3: Beware of shady characters

You've probably noticed that the Mac won't let you type a colon (:) in a file name. That's because the Mac uses this character internally to keep track of the path to a file. You can't use a colon in a file name on Windows, either, nor can you use a number of other characters. Your file might still open in Windows if you've used one of the forbidden characters on your Mac file, but the name will change permanently in Windows. If a file has to go back and forth between the two platforms, name changes will only result in confusion. It's better to stick to the Windows conventions. Don't use any of the following characters in your file names, and read the following page about using periods and spaces.

Illegal characters in Windows	
:	colon (the colon is illegal on both Mac and Windows)
\	backward slash
/	forward slash
|	vertical bar
?	question mark
*	asterisk
"	ditto mark (typewriter quote mark)
< >	less than or greater than

Periods in file names

Tip: If you use extra periods in your Photoshop file names, then choose the preference to have Photoshop automatically add the PC file extension (as mentioned on the opposite page), Photoshop will lop off anything after the first period it finds.

The period is not an illegal character, but if you'll be working cross-platform it's best to use periods only to separate file names and their three-character extensions. As we mentioned in Chapter 19, *Paths and Long File Names*, Windows stores two versions of each file name: the long file name, plus a version that is "backward compatible" to Windows 3.1 and DOS ("backward compatible" means older software can recognize and use the file). If you use a period in the first eight characters of the file name, its long file name in Windows will be fine; but when DOS creates the old "eight dot three" version, it becomes confused by the first period, deletes it, and lops off the real extension. If there's even a remote chance that you or anyone else will need to use the file on a PC running Windows 3.1 or DOS, or on a pre–OS 8.1 Mac, don't put any periods in the file name except the one in front of the three-letter extension.

Blank spaces in file names

Blank spaces are legal characters on both Macs and Windows machines, but each platform reads them slightly differently. On a Mac, you can type a space at the very beginning of a file name, at the end, or anywhere in-between. Sometimes you might type a space at the beginning of a file name on purpose so it will be alphabetized first in a list; other times it happens by accident when you change the name of a file.

Windows ignores spaces at the beginnings or endings of file names and sees only the space characters between words. This can be a problem if you've created two files with almost the same name, the only difference being a blank space at the beginning or end of the file name. If you take these two files over to a Windows machine at different times, one file will replace the other because Windows doesn't see the blank space and so it thinks the two file names are exactly the same.

What if you already have misnamed files?

Now that you know how to name your Mac files for the PC, you might look at your Mac and shudder at all the extra work to do in renaming the files you want to send cross-platform. Instead of renaming dozens of files for the PC by hand, go to www.sigsoftware.com and download a copy of "NameCleaner," a very inexpensive piece of shareware. It does a lovely job of stripping out all the illegal characters in your Macintosh file names. It can't do anything about the file format or the options you chose when you saved the file, however!

Mac-to-Windows Rule #4: Use file name extensions

When you create a file in Windows, the file is assigned a character code called an **extension** that gets tacked on to the end of its name. Extensions are critical to the success of opening a file. The extension tells the Windows operating system which application to open the file in, which icon to use to display it, and allows you to double-click the file to open it. Accidentally delete the extension and Windows develops amnesia— it no longer sees the link between your file and the application that created it, and it can no longer figure out which icon to display so you get the generic one.

Questions.doc

In this example, the ".doc" is the file name extension.

If you want Windows to read your Mac files, give them extensions. The extension must match the actual file type you've created, of course. That is, you can't fool Windows by creating a file in one format (.QXP, for example) and simply adding a different extension (like .EPS, for example)—the file must really be saved in the format that matches the extension.

QuarkXPress (3.3 and above) and all Microsoft Office products create files that are already compatible with both Mac and Windows platforms and will recognize most files from their older version even if those files were created on the other platform. Adobe PageMaker requires that you match the application versions exactly to take files back and forth between Macs and PCs. In all cases, these programs require you to manually add the correct "dot-plus-three" extension to Mac files for the document to be read in Windows. Since all of these programs create files with different extensions depending on what kind of file you're making (regular documents, libraries, tables, etc.) you should consult the application's documentation to match files and extensions.

In Mac Photoshop 4.0 or above, you can have extensions added to the file names automatically: Open the "Saving Files" preferences and make a choice from the "Append File Extension" menu. Read the tip on the previous page.

Macromedia FreeHand 8.0 adds the correct extension for EPS files through its "Save As" dialog box, and for a host of other file formats through its "Export" dialog box ("Export" is in the File menu).

See the following page for extensions you should use on your files.

Extensions you should use

Although some Macintosh applications offer "automatic extensions," you can't take it for granted that an extension will be applied. If you're using older software (which you really shouldn't if you're transferring files cross-platform) or software created by small developers, you'll almost certainly have to do your own extension naming. In some cases, choosing the right extension for a file is pretty obvious. For example, the extension for an EPS file is simply **.EPS**. In other cases, you'd never guess the code in a million years. Below is a chart of the most frequently used file format extensions created by Macintosh-based programs.

Extensions must be separated from the rest of the file name by a period. Don't type any character, not even a space, after the extension.

Note: Fonts are special and must go through a conversion process to travel from one platform to another. See Chapter 24, Fonts, for more information.

Adobe Acrobat file	.PDF
Adobe Illustrator file	.AI (yes, it's a two-letter extension)
Adobe PageMaker file	.PM6, .P65, .T65 (template)
Adobe Photoshop file	.PSD
ASCII (text only) file	.TXT
EPS (Encapsulated PostScript) file	.EPS
GIF graphic file	.GIF
JPEG graphic file	.JPG
Macromedia Director file	.DIR
Macromedia FreeHand file	.FH# (# is the version number)
Microsoft Excel spreadsheet file	.XLS
Microsoft PowerPoint file	.PPT
Microsoft Word file	.DOC
QuarkXPress file	.QXP
QuickTime Movie file	.QTM
SimpleText file	.TXT
Shockwave file	.DCR
Text-only file	.TXT
TIFF graphic file	.TIF

What about Windows files on a Mac?

A Macintosh is by nature more comfortable with Windows disks and files than a Windows machine is with Mac ones, but the Mac needs your cooperation to perform at peak cross-platform efficiency. Help your Mac help you by following the three rules of Windows-to-Mac file naming.

Windows-to-Mac Rule #1: Upgrade to at least OS 8.1

Your Mac will do a better job of handling PC files if you give it the right tools for the job. If you expect to open Windows files frequently on a Macintosh (or put Mac files onto PC disks for transfer), you should *at least* upgrade to Mac OS 8.1. If you really want to be as compatible as possible, use the most current operating system on the Mac.

Earlier versions of the Mac OS ignored the long Windows file names and displayed the DOS names instead. The DOS-named files open on a Mac, but it's often difficult to figure out which file is which. As we explained in Chapter 19, *Paths and Long File Names*, the renamed files get truncated (cut off) to only six recognizable characters with a tilde (~) and a number before the extension. If you are still using Mac OS 8.0 or earlier, you've probably seen this happen when you put a Mac file onto a PC-formatted disk. This nasty name change is permanent.

The exchange software built into the newer Mac operating systems recognizes Windows' long file names and doesn't truncate down to an ugly DOS version. If you can't upgrade your system to OS 8.1, you'll need a third-party solution, like Software Architects' (www.softarch.com) DOS Mounter 95. It works with older operating systems, such as Mac OS 7.5. (Even though it works with current versions, you don't need it.)

Windows-to-Mac Rule #2: Don't double up on extensions

Extensions are those three-letter abbreviations (the "dot-plus-3") on the ends of file names that tell Windows how to open the files, and they can be tricky for the occasional Windows user because some versions of Windows *hide* the dot+3 extensions when they display files in a window! Thus it's easy to forget the extensions are already there since you don't see them, and so you type the dot+3 extension as part of the name. Then a file you named "Yellow Logo.EPS" actually becomes "Yellow Logo.EPS.EPS."

To avoid adding an extra extension to a file name, tell Windows to **display the extensions that are on all of the files:**

1. Open a folder in Windows. From the View menu, choose "Folder Options…" ("Options…" in Windows 95).

2. In the Options box, click the "View" tab.

3. Uncheck the box, "Hide file extensions for known file types," then click OK.

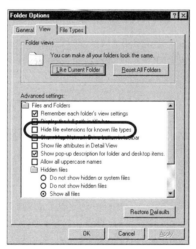
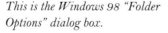
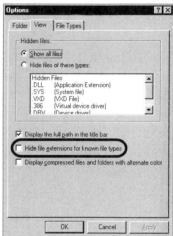

This is the Windows 98 "Folder Options" dialog box.

This is the Windows 95 folder "Options" dialog box.

Windows-to-Mac Rule #3: Watch the file name length

Mac files and folders can have a maximum of 31 characters in their names. A Mac can't read the name of a Windows file that's longer than 31 characters, so it shortens the file name to fit its limit. This file naming is *only* temporary if you *only* open the file to view or print it. But if you make any edits to the file—even just to change the print setup— and save them, the shorter name sticks.

Both Macs and Windows truncate what they can't read in a file name. However, Macs are smart enough to leave the dot+3 extension untouched, so at least the file will still work on a PC.

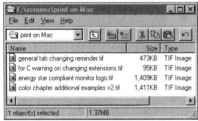
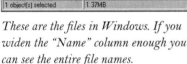
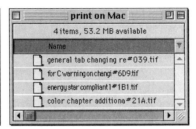

These are the files in Windows. If you widen the "Name" column enough you can see the entire file names.

These are the same files on the Mac. Notice how it truncated the names but kept the extensions.

Saving EPS files on the PC for the Mac

If you don't save your EPS files on the Mac with a PC preview, you won't be able to see the image on your PC—at most all you'll see is a gray box. Fortunately, saving EPS files on the PC so they can be seen on the Mac is easy. Most cross-platform applications offer choices of saving your EPS file in a variety of formats (see pages 306–307). Check your application's documentation to see what choices are provided when you save a file as an EPS and where you can find those choices. Then simply choose a color or black-and-white Mac preview or format instead of the PC one.

Macs are more flexible than PCs. If you make a mistake and choose the wrong type of preview option in your Windows software, you'll probably still be able to see an image of your EPS file on the Macintosh screen, although you may see some ugly color shifting, particularly when the file is printed. (For more about color on Macs and PCs, see Chapter 25.) If your cross-platform program doesn't seem to offer a preview or format choice that's specific to the Macintosh, that probably means its previews are already Mac-compatible.

WINDOWS FOR MAC USERS

Know your application formats

There are thousands of lesser-known or even completely obscure applications for the PC, many of which were created for DOS or earlier versions of Windows. As a consequence, there are hundreds of different file format types, including dozens for graphic files, all with different extensions.

The fact that you don't recognize a file extension shouldn't worry you— it may turn out that your "orphan" file can be read by a more familiar program. For example, Adobe Illustrator for Windows will open many CorelDraw files and many of the old pre–Windows 95 system file formats for graphics. Most spreadsheet and office suite applications can either open or import some competitors' file formats, too.

Don't immediately panic if some files don't open as expected—in Windows or on the Mac—when you double-click; you may have to open an application first, then use the "Open" command from the File menu. (See Chapter 21, *Mounting PC Media and Reading PC Files*, for more information on helping the Mac recognize and open PC files.)

The list on the opposite page identifies a number of extensions you may be unfamiliar with, along with suggestions for applications that will open the files if their original applications aren't available. Many of these files will require a file conversion program (see Chapter 21).

Very unfortunately, extensions in Windows are not always unique; several applications might apply the exact same extension to completely different sorts of files. For example, .DOC is the Microsoft Word document extension, and an alternate extension in Notepad. But .DOC is also an extension for many versions of WordPerfect, WordStar, and Adobe FrameMaker! PDF is a well-known abbreviation (and extension) for Adobe's portable document format, but Novell Netware uses the same extension to tag its printer definition files.

Windows extension	Windows application
CDR	CorelDraw drawing file
CGM	Computer Graphics metafile
CMF	Corel graphic metafile
CPT	Corel Photo-Paint image
DRW	Micrografx Designer/Draw
DWG	AutoCAD drawing file
DXF	Digital Exchange format
FLC or FLI	Autodesk FLIC animation
GEM	GEM graphic metafile
JBF	Paint Shop Pro thumbnail browser file
MSP	Microsoft Paint bitmap graphic
PCS	PICS animation
PCX	ZSoft PC Paintbrush bitmap graphic
PP4	Picture Publisher 4 bitmap graphic
PRS	Harvard Graphics for Windows presentation
PRZ	Lotus Freelance Graphics 97 file
PUB	Ventura Publisher publication
SAM	Ami Pro document files
TGA	Targa bitmap graphic
WB#	Quattro Pro spreadsheet files
WK#	Lotus 1-2-3 spreadsheet files
XY#	XYWrite word processing document

(# is the version number or letter)

Also see the chart on page 310.

Getting Macintosh files onto a PC

Once your files have correct cross-platform formats and names, there are many ways to move them from Macs to PCs. You could use a local network that allows Macs to share files with Windows computers (speak to your company's network administrator). You can send files as attachments to email (see the following chapter, Chapter 23, *Sending Email Attachments*). Or if the Windows machine has an FTP site and you know how to FTP, send your files over the Internet. Of course, the simplest choice is sneaker net—put the files on a disk, walk over to the PC, and insert the disk.

Making a DOS-formatted floppy disk

As we mentioned in Chapter 4, *Starting Up and Using Disks*, a PC won't mount Macintosh disks unless the PC has a special program installed, such as Mac Opener, that makes it possible for Windows to recognize Mac-formatted media. If you suspect that the PC your files will be used on doesn't have a program like this, you'll need a PC-formatted disk for your perfectly named files.

To format a Macintosh floppy disk for Windows

1. Put a floppy disk in your Mac, then click its disk icon to select it.

2. From the "Special" menu, choose "Erase Disk."
   You'll see this dialog box:

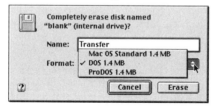

3. From the Format menu in this dialog box, choose "DOS 1.4 MB." Then click "Erase." You'll get a warning that everything on the disk will be permanently erased.

   When your disk is reformatted, its icon on the Desktop will change:

Transfer

This is what a Mac floppy disk looks like, as you well know.

TRANSFER

This is what the floppy disk looks like when formatted for Windows.

Making a DOS-formatted Zip or Jaz disk

You can't use the Mac's "Erase Disk" option to format a Mac Zip or Jaz disk for Windows. You'll need Iomega Tools, version 6.1 or above, which can be downloaded, if you don't already have it, from the Iomega site (www.iomega.com).

To format a Macintosh Zip disk or Jaz disk for Windows

1. Put a Zip or Jaz disk in the Macintosh drive, then click the disk icon once to select it.

2. Launch the Iomega "Tools" (it should be in your Iomega folder). In the "Tools" dialog box, click the "Erase" button (shown below, circled).

Phoenix

This is a typical icon for a Mac Zip disk.

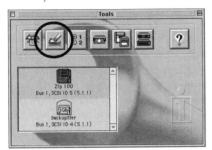

3. The "Erase/Initialize Disk Options" dialog box will appear. From the "Format for" menu, choose "DOS."
   Click the "Long Erase" button.

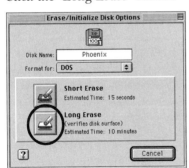

Always use the "Long Erase" option when you reformat a Mac Zip disk for Windows. A "Short Erase" doesn't do a thorough job of changing the disk directory structure, and many times the disk won't mount on the PC even though it displays a PC icon.

4. The dialog box will remind you that changing the disk's format will totally erase anything on the disk. When the formatting is complete, the cartridge icon will change, as shown to the right.

PHOENIX

This is a typical icon for a PC Zip disk.

Checklist for transferring files

For successful cross-platform file transfers, use this checklist:

❏ Use current system and application software.

❏ Don't use system-specific file formats.

❏ Use native file formats for identical applications on both platforms; otherwise use cross-platform formats for other types of files.

❏ Save your files in formats the other platform can read.

❏ Save files with the right options for the other format.

❏ Don't use characters in the file names that the other platform can't read.

❏ Don't make file names longer than the other platform can read.

❏ Use the correct extensions for all files destined for Windows PCs.

Sending Email Attachments

Even if you never have to actually touch a PC, at some point you'll probably have to email attachments to one or you'll receive files directly from a Windows machine. In transferring files from Macs to PCs and vice versa, attachments can cause lots of headaches. Most of the painful experiences can be avoided simply by paying very careful attention to preparing your files before attaching them and by knowing the quirks of your email software. In this chapter, we explain how attachments work and what you need to know so your files flow back and forth easily and cleanly.

Preparing files as email attachments

Sending files by email is not always simple, especially if you and the person at the other end are using different types of computers. You can increase the chances that your files will arrive safely by first following all the guidelines below for *preparing* cross-platform files.

Before you attach a file

Before you worry about how to properly send an attachment, make sure the file itself can be read once it gets there. Many of the following check points were discussed in the previous chapter on transferring files, so if you're not quite sure about any of these, please refer to its page.

- Talk to your intended recipient. Make sure they have the *correct* application to open your attachment. Ask which *version* of the application they have so you can change the way you've prepared your file if necessary.

- Save your file with the correct options. *(pages 306–307)*

- If you are sending an EPS graphic file from Mac to Windows, save the file with a Windows-compatible preview. *(pages 306–307)*

- Save the file in a cross-platform file format. *(pages 301–305)*

- Save the file with the extension that matches the file format. *(page 309–310)*

- Name the extension correctly (for example, .TIF, not .TIFF), and put a period before the extension, and nothing (not even a space) after it. It's best to stick to the "eight dot three" format; that is, eight characters for the file name, a dot (period), and the correct three-letter Windows extension. *(pages 307–308)*

- If there are external graphic files that are linked to the main document, be sure those graphic files are prepared properly, and send them along with the main file. *(page 304)*

- If you compress the file, make sure you use a compression that the receiver can uncompress. *(pages 321–323; this chapter)*

- Make a choice between compressing the file yourself or letting your email software do it, then adjust the settings in your email software appropriately. *(pages 324–326; this chapter)*

- Use the right email encoding method. *(pages 327–330; this chapter)*

When you attach a file

Make your cover email message informative. It can make a world of difference if you say, "The attached file is a Word 6/95 document which I've compressed with StuffIt 4.0 into a .SIT file." This is both polite and useful since it makes it so much easier to troubleshoot if the attachment doesn't open properly on the other computer system.

Compressing files for sending online

Files that are attached to email or sent directly over the Internet are usually compressed, which means the file is made smaller. Using special software (discussed on the following page), compress the file before you send it; the person at the other end must uncompress the file so they can read it. Compression is good for many reasons:

- Compression makes the file size smaller, which means it takes less time to send to the other computer and less time for the other person to download it.

- A file name is protected while it's part of a compressed file. If you download directly to a hard disk on either a Mac or a PC and uncompress the files, they'll appear on either Desktop without the DOS "8+3" truncation.

- Because they download quickly and are more compact, compressed files are less likely to get corrupted while sending. Corruption can be caused by a number of things, such as a bad phone line, an interrupted transmission, or a power surge. Compression doesn't prevent these things from happening; it just makes them less likely to affect your files.

- Compression can protect files in complex transfer environments. A growing number of people work in mixed-platform environments and can end up receiving email on a Mac one day and a PC the next. Combined with sufficient information in the cover email, a group of compressed files destined for a Mac can be successfully received in Windows, and vice versa.

- Compression is a good way to send multiple files attached to one email message because you can put several files into one compressed "archive." On America Online, you must compress multiple files into one archive because AOL can handle only one email attachment per message.

Word 6/95: **Refers to a file created using Word 6 on the Mac or Word 95 on the PC, or by a later version of Word but saved in the earlier version for compatibility. "Word 6.0/95" is a format option in the Mac Office 98 "Save As" dialog box.**

Compression software

When transferring compressed files between Macs and PCs, both sender and receiver must have compatible compression/uncompression software. The standard compression format on a PC is .ZIP—it's even more prevalent on Windows computers than the StuffIt .SIT or .SEA files are on Macs. Although Aladdin Systems, the company that makes StuffIt and StuffIt Expander (both of which can also uncompress .ZIP files), developed a Windows version of StuffIt Expander, chances are your typical PC user doesn't have it yet. (If you have control over the PC, you should get both StuffIt and the Windows version of StuffIt Expander called Expander, and install them on your PC.)

If the other PC user is not willing to change or add to their compression options, you'll need to invest in ZipIt, which is Mac shareware that makes and uncompresses .ZIP files on your Mac. You can download it from www.download.com or www.shareware.com.

Compressed files on America Online

If you are an AOL user and try to send multiple files with one email, the emailing software will automatically compress your files into one archive. That's great, except for one thing: you aren't given the chance to choose the compression type. Files emailed from AOL in Windows will always be compressed with ZIP and those from AOL on a Mac will always be compressed with StuffIt. Since there isn't any way to bypass this decision, you'll need to warn the person you're sending the files to that they'll need your system's uncompressor to open your files.

There are two work-arounds for this problem. You can send lots of individual emails, each with only one file attached. Or you can compress your files manually into one .SIT or .ZIP file. The AOL email package won't realize that the file you're enclosing is actually made up of several files, so it won't try to automatically compress them.

Compressed files on other email applications

Several other email packages (like Claris Emailer and Microsoft Outlook Express) also prefer to compress files before they send them, but unlike AOL they provide an option to turn automatic compression on and off (see pages 324–326). Make sure to turn off automatic compression if you're sending files to a non-Mac user.

Compression extensions

The extensions listed below indicate that a file is compressed. It helps to know which extension is meant for which platform so when you see one of these files you'll know where to begin to uncompress it. If your file has more than one of these extensions attached to it, it's been both compressed for size and encoded (see pages 327–330) to allow it to pass safely through the Internet. Although programs like StuffIt Expander can often handle both uncompressing and decoding, sometimes you might have to use more than one piece of software to get at the file. For example, a file called **candy.cpt.bin** was compressed with a utility called Compact Pro **(.cpt)**, then encoded as a Mac binary file **(.bin)**. To open the file, work from right to left: first use a program like BinHex 4.0 to decode the file and get rid of the **.bin**; then uncompress the file to get rid of the **.cpt**. Now you can open and use the file.

Macintosh compression extensions and how to expand them

Extension	What to use on a Mac	What to use on a PC	File type
.bin	StuffIt (all), ZipIt, ShrinkWrap	Aladdin Expander, MPack	MacBinary
.cpt	CompactPro, StuffIt (all), ShrinkWrap	Macunpack	Compact Pro
.dd	Disk Doubler	not possible	Disk Doubler
.sit	StuffIt (all), ShrinkWrap	Aladdin Expander	StuffIt
.sea	Will uncompress without extra software	Aladdin Expander	Self-extracting archive .sit
.hqx	StuffIt (all), ZipIt, ShrinkWrap, Compact Pro	Aladdin Expander, WinZip, MPack	BinHex

Non-Macintosh compression extensions and how to expand them

Extension	What to use on a Mac	What to use on a PC	File type
.exe	StuffIt Expander or Deluxe	Will uncompress without extra software	Executable file; self-extracting DOS/Windows
.mme, .mime	StuffIt Expander or Deluxe MPack, SunTar	WinZip, MPack	mime (page 329)
.tar	StuffIt Expander or Deluxe, MPack, SunTar, ShrinkWrap	WinZip	Tar Unix
.uu	StuffIt Expander or Deluxe, MPack, SunTar, ShrinkWrap	WinZip, MPack	Uuencode
.zip	StuffIt Expander or Deluxe, ZipIt	WinZip (and a host of others!)	PKZip

Disabling helper applications

Both Netscape Communicator's Messenger and Microsoft Outlook Express have a database of "helper applications" to automate file reading, compression, and uncompression. When the software sees a compressed file with an extension that matches one of the helpers, it automatically uses that helper to uncompress the contents. Most of the time this is a nice labor-saving device; occasionally, however, it just makes emailing very frustrating. If a Mac user compresses files in a typical Mac format, such as .sit, and sends them to a PC user whose email software, such as Messenger, automatically uncompresses attachments, the files lose their Macintosh Type and Creator codes, making them useless on any platform and impossible to repair. To avoid this nasty experience, disable the email software's automatic uncompression before receiving Mac files on a PC.

To disable the automatic file uncompression in Netscape Messenger

1. Open Netscape, then open the Messenger area.

2. From the Edit menu, choose "Preferences."

3. From the Category list on the *left*, click the "Navigator" triangle (Mac) or plus sign (Windows) to display its options (shown below), and also click "Applications" to display the application options.

4. In the Applications section you now see on the *right*, find the compression application you'd like to temporarily disable. Click to select it.

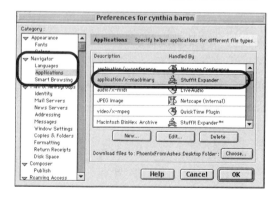

Macintosh Netscape preferences. Right now this dialog box tells Netscape to uncompress macbinary files with StuffIt Expander.

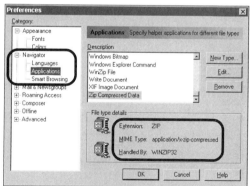

Windows Netscape preferences. Right now this dialog box tells Netscape when it finds a file that has an extension of .ZIP, to uncompress it with WINZIP32.

5. Click the "Edit..." button to get the "Edit Type" dialog box (below).

6. In the "Handled by" section, click "Save to disk."

Netscape will save the file to your hard disk where you can choose to uncompress it manually or move it to another computer. Netscape won't forget which application used to handle the uncompression (the one chosen with the radio button "Application"), so you can return to this dialog box and undo your choice at any time.

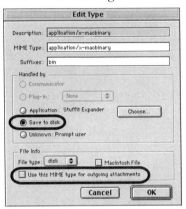

*To prevent Netscape from automatically uncompressing **incoming** files, click "Save to disk."*

*To prevent Netscape from automatically compressing **outgoing** files, uncheck "Use this MIME type for outgoing attachments."*

To disable the automatic file uncompression in Outlook Express

1. Open Outlook Express. You don't have to be online.

2. From the Edit menu, choose "Preferences."

3. On the *left* side of the "Preferences" dialog box, click "Receiving Files," then click "File Helpers" (shown below).

4. In the "File Helper Settings" section on the *right*, click the compression application you'd like to temporarily disable.

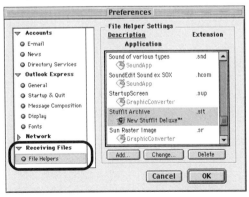

This is a Macintosh dialog box, but the Windows version looks almost exactly the same.

5. Click "Change…" to get the "Edit File Helper" dialog box, shown below.

6. In the "File Type" section, uncheck "Use for incoming."

7. In the "Handling" section, choose "Save To File" from the menu.

Outlook Express will save the file to your hard disk where you can choose to uncompress it manually or move it to another computer.

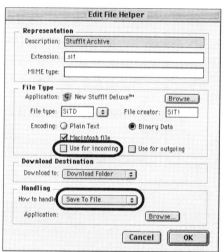

*To prevent Outlook Express from automatically uncompressing **incoming** files, uncheck "Use for incoming." In the "Handling" section, choose "Save To File."*

To restart automatic uncompression on new attachments, come back to this dialog box and choose "Post-Process Application" from the "How to handle" menu.

Understanding attachments and encoding

Email attachments are probably the most convenient way to transfer files across platforms—they're not limited by distance, they're almost instantly transmitted, and almost everyone with a computer has email. Attachments can also be very frustrating if files and transmission settings aren't correct.

Attachments can seem more complicated than they really are if you don't understand how they work. When you send a plain ol' email, it typically goes through the lines as "ASCII" text, which is text stripped down to the very basic characters, no fancy stuff like bold or italic or different typefaces. Since ASCII text is a universal format, email always comes through no matter what kind of computer you wrote it on.

To guarantee that attachments will arrive intact, all email programs transform attached files into ASCII, too. This transformation is called **encoding**. Once the file is encoded, the email program puts some information at the beginning of the file, called a "header." This header tells the receiving email program that everything it receives after the header needs to be decoded—put back the way it was so you can read it.

You probably won't be surprised to hear that not all email programs use the same method of encoding and, of course, the differences are mostly platform-dependent.

Uuencode (pronounced "you you encode") is the oldest form of encoding. It's native to Unix (UU is for "Unix to Unix"), so Uuencode is the standard method used by Internet shell accounts. For instance, if you get your email at a university computer by logging on to a central server, the email program on the server you use is probably Unix-based. You can tell that a file you've received has been encoded in Uuencode if it has a .UU extension at the end. Uuencode is being replaced by MIME.

shell: The "shell" is the Unix user interface, which is an unadorned command-line. Shell accounts are Internet connections without web browsers.

MIME (Multipurpose Internet Mail Extensions), sometimes called Base64, is the newest encoding method. It's meant to be cross-platform, and it was specifically developed for use over the Internet. Newer email applications can read and write MIME encoding; older versions can't. The MIME extension is .MIME or .MME.

BinHex is the Mac's favorite encoding method because it holds on to the all-important "Type" and "Creator" codes. BinHex was specifically developed for Mac-to-Mac transmission. Any email program that runs on your Mac is probably set to automatically encode in BinHex unless you have deliberately changed the defaults. A Mac BinHex file has an .HQX extension at the end.

If a file sent out with one kind of encoding is received by an email program that can't understand the header, the file will look like gibberish if you try to open it. It is possible to manually decode attachments that were sent via a different method, but it involves carefully editing out the headers in SimpleText or Notepad, saving the files with the right extension, and using a stand-alone decoder. It's easy to make mistakes in this process. Rather than go to this risky trouble, just ask the sender to resend the file using a different encoding method.

Encoding vs. compression vs. file format vs. application!

It's easy to get confused with all of these extensions, since some extensions refer to file formats (.EPS, .TIF), some refer to Windows applications (.P65, .DOC), some refer to compression schemes (.SIT, .SEA, .ZIP), some refer to encoding methods (.HQX, .UU, .MIM), and some files have several extensions, such as the Mac files that are labeled .sit.hqx. What to do? Check the chart on page 323, and be conscious. *You just have to learn to recognize the extensions.* Being able to recognize these abbreviations will prevent you from going mad!

Sending MIME-encoded files

Mac users who plan to send files to PCs should own an email program capable of sending MIME. Most current email programs have this option. You can find the encoding options in an email program's Preferences or Settings.

All three of the most popular free email programs—Eudora Light, Netscape Messenger, and Microsoft Outlook Express—let you change your encoding, but each offers distinct options and requires a different process.

Eudora for the Mac, although it can send and receive in MIME, doesn't have an attachment option labeled MIME in the Settings dialog box of the Macintosh version. This is a little misleading because Eudora does have AppleDouble which is even better because it's a combination of MIME and BinHex. It encodes in MIME so other computer systems can read the files, but it also sends the "Type" and "Creator" codes that the Mac needs.

To change your encoding format in Eudora Light or Eudora Pro

1. Open Eudora Light or Eudora Pro. You don't have to be online.

2. From the Special menu, choose "Settings." In the *left* side of the Settings dialog box, click "Attachments" (shown below).

3. In the "Encoding method" section, check "AppleDouble," and check "Always include Macintosh information." Click OK to close the Settings window.

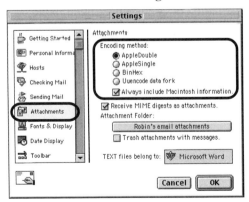

Outlook Express for the Mac calls its MIME option by the alternate name of **Base64.** Unlike in Eudora, you have to choose between maintaining the Mac codes and sending files in PC-readable format. If you usually send attachments to other Mac users, remember to change back to BinHex.

To change your encoding format in Microsoft Outlook Express

1. Open Outlook Express. You don't have to be online.

2. From the Edit menu, choose "Preferences." On the *left* side of the dialog box, click the "Outlook Express" triangle to display the options, then click "Message Composition."

3. Look for the menu labeled "Attachment encoding." Change this setting from BinHex ("Best for Mac to Mac") to "Base64." Click OK.

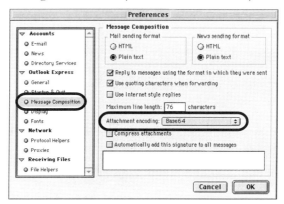

Netscape Messenger sends all files in MIME as the default. If you want to send a Mac file to another Mac user and retain the "Type" and "Creator" codes, you'll need to change Messenger's automatic compression settings to send .sit files instead of .mime.

1. Open Netscape Messenger. You don't have to be online.

2. From the Edit menu, choose "Preferences." On the *left* side of the Preferences dialog box, click "Navigator," then click its subcategory "Applications."

3. On the *right* side of the dialog box, find "application/macbinary," which defaults to StuffIt Expander. Click "Edit."

4. In the "Edit Type" dialog box, click "Macintosh File" and "Use this MIME type for outgoing attachments." Click OK.

Fonts

If you aren't a designer, you might think a chapter on fonts isn't very important to you. But transferring files, even word-processing files, involves more than proper naming and formats—your fonts need to transfer, too. Before you send a file cross-platform, there are steps you can take to improve the chances that the results will be legible, attractive, *and* print correctly.

Of course, it's always easier to work with fonts across platforms if you understand how fonts work on the Mac. You might want to read Robin's book, *How To Boss Your Fonts Around*, for a comprehensive look at fonts on the Macintosh and how to manage them.

Font technology basics

Following are some *brief* explanations of the terms used in this chapter.

PostScript Type 1 fonts

Mac PostScript fonts include two separate files.

PostScript fonts and Type 1 fonts are the same thing. (Type 2 fonts were never actually developed, and Type 3 fonts, which are also PostScript, are rarely used anymore.) PostScript fonts are created with a mathematical outline that allows them to be enlarged or reduced to any size without any degradation to the smoothness of the line.

TrueType fonts

This is the icon for a Windows PostScript font.

TrueType fonts use a mathematical outline (with a different math formula from PostScript fonts) that allows them, like PostScript fonts, to be enlarged or reduced to any size without any degradation to the smoothness of the line. TrueType is best when used on a non-PostScript printer, such as a desktop inkjet. Don't send TrueType fonts to high-resolution imagesetters, and try not to send them to PostScript printers.

On the left is the icon for a Mac TrueType font; on the right is the icon for a Windows TrueType font.

PostScript printers

A PostScript printer is really a computer. It has a CPU (the central processing unit), RAM (random access memory), and ROM (read-only memory). That's why they cost much more than non-PostScript printers. If your desktop printer cost more than $1,000, it's probably PostScript. It's best to use PostScript fonts on a PostScript printer.

On the Mac, both PostScript and TrueType fonts are often stored in these little suitcase files.

Non-PostScript printers

Desktop non-PostScript printers are simple, relatively inexpensive machines that print what they see on the screen or what a utility like ATM (Adobe Type Manager) sends down to them, such as "rasterized" PostScript fonts. If you have a color inket printer on your desk that cost less than several thousand dollars, it's not PostScript.

On the left is the ATM control panel for the Mac. On the right is the ATM application for Windows.

Adobe Type Manager and printers

Adobe Type Manager (ATM) takes a PostScript outline font and turns it into dots (rasterizes it) so the type characters display with smooth edges on the screen. ATM also sends the rasterized information to non-PostScript printers so the type will print with smooth edges. Without ATM, PostScript Type 1 fonts will look jagged on the screen and will print jagged on paper.

Windows and TrueType fonts

It's very easy to add and delete TrueType fonts in Windows. The font files get installed into a Fonts folder, just like on a Mac. The ease with which you can install fonts isn't necessarily a good thing because it can encourage you to install more fonts than your system can handle.

Unlike on a Mac, font information in Windows is written into several places in the system besides the Fonts folder. In Windows 95/98, the name of the font is written into the Win.INI file, which is a kind of text file that tells the system what all its components are. And a reference to the font with its full, long file name gets written into the "Registry." The Registry is what really controls Windows, so if something goes wrong within it, the whole operating system can crash—and stay crashed. Problems arise when you add lots of fonts because their names all go into the same place in the Registry, called a "key." Each key has a size limit of 64K. That's not a terribly large amount of text space, as you probably know from creating files yourself. When the key begins to fill up, the system slows down because it has to read all those font names. When the key gets completely full, the font list can become inaccessible to the system. If this happens, Windows can't even display its standard menus, so it crashes, requiring radical Registry surgery or a total system reload.

Knowing what can happen, you should keep track of how many fonts you have and ask yourself how many you really need loaded all the time. In theory, the Registry can handle about a thousand fonts before it gets into the danger zone, but many people have reported problems when it had only half that number. You're better off keeping your TrueType fonts backed up on a Zip or Jaz disk and loading them as you need them with a font management utility (see page 339).

Installing or deleting TrueType fonts

Technically, in Windows you can just drag TrueType fonts into the Fonts folder. Sometimes, though, this quick-and-dirty method doesn't write the font properly into the Registry. Instead of wasting time later trying to troubleshoot the problem, you should really use the method described below to install fonts.

GOUDY.ttf

This font is ready to be installed.

If your fonts have an .EXE extension, that means they're compressed. Before you install them, they have to be uncompressed: just double-click the icon. When your TrueType fonts are ready to install, they'll have an extension of .TTF, as shown to the left.

To install a TrueType font

Put the disk with the font into the machine, or if it's stored on your hard disk, make sure you know in which folder you stored it.

1. Open "My Computer."

2. Double-click the "Control Panel" folder.

3. Double-click the "Fonts" folder.

4. From the File menu in the Fonts window, choose "Install New Font..." (in Windows 95 or NT it will be "Install...").

Fonts

This is the Fonts folder in Windows.

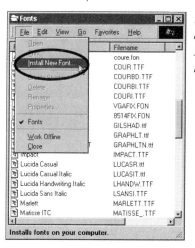

When you choose this menu command, you'll get the "Add Fonts" dialog box, shown on the next page.

334

5. In the "Add Fonts" dialog box, navigate to where you stored the TrueType fonts you want to install. Select them, then click OK.

The font is now installed and ready to use.

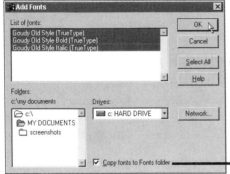

*If you want to install fonts from a network without copying them to your hard disk, **uncheck** the box "Copy fonts to Fonts folder." (You will only be able to access the fonts if you are online with the network.)*

To delete a TrueType font

1. Open the "Fonts" folder as described on the opposite page.

2. Select the TrueType font you want to delete.

3. From the File menu, choose "Delete." This puts the font into the Recycle Bin.

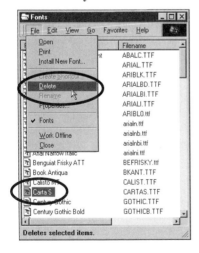

Windows and PostScript fonts

Actually, Windows doesn't deal with PostScript fonts at all. The only way to install a PostScript font into a Windows computer is with Adobe Type Manager (ATM), which is available for all versions of Windows. You also need ATM to display your PostScript fonts on the screen.

Installing or deleting PostScript fonts

Windows NT: Only ATM versions 4.0 and up (either the Light or the Deluxe versions) work with Windows NT.

You must have Adobe Type Manager to install or delete PostScript Type 1 fonts. If you've ever installed an Adobe product into Windows 95 or 98, you probably have ATM already. If you don't, when you buy an Adobe PostScript Windows font it comes with ATM because otherwise you couldn't install it.

If your fonts are in an .EXE file, that means they're compressed. Before you install them, they have to be uncompressed: just double-click the icon. When your PostScript fonts are ready to install, they'll have an extension of .PFB, as shown below.

When you look in a PostScript font folder (which you don't ever really have to do), don't faint if you see a pile of indecipherable files, like those shown below, left. The only file you need for installing is the **.pfb** file. To make it easier to see the .pfbs in the folder, use the View menu to change the view to "Detailed List," shown below, right. Then click on the heading "Type" to arrange the files according to what they are. You'll see a "PostScript Outlines" label for the actual font.

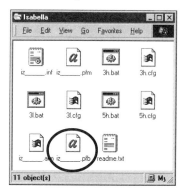 

This folder can be scary. But don't worry—Adobe Type Manager takes care of everything for you!

To install or delete a PostScript Type 1 font

Put the disk with the font into the machine, or if it's stored on your hard disk, make sure you know in which folder you stored it.

1. Launch Adobe Type Manager: if it's already installed, it's probably in your Start Menu, under "Programs," under "Adobe." If you don't find it there, do a search for "atmfm.exe," and double-click the icon.

2. In the left panel of the ATM dialog box (shown below) is a list of the fonts that are already installed. On the right side, navigate to where you stored the font(s). Fortunately, ATM will display the real name of the font, not the unintelligible DOS name.

3. When you find the font and it appears in the right panel, either drag it to the left panel and drop it in the list, or select it on the right side and click the "Add" button.

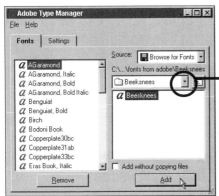

Use this menu to search for the fonts you want to install.

*If you want to install fonts from a network without copying them to your hard disk, **check** the box "Add without copying files." (You will only be able to access the fonts if you are online with the network.)*

Atmfm.exe
This is the actual program icon for ATM.

Tip: If you will be loading Type 1 fonts regularly, you might want to make a shortcut to the application: Right-click the .exe file (shown above) and drag it to the Desktop. From the little menu that pops up, choose "Create Shortcut(s) Here," then rename the shortcut to "ATM."

ATM
This is a shortcut (alias) to ATM.

If you buy and use Adobe Type Manager Deluxe, you can use it to install both TrueType and Type 1 fonts.

Viewing your fonts in Windows

To view **TrueType fonts,** double-click any of their icons in the Fonts folder (which is inside the Control Panel folder). You can enlarge the window that opens (shown below) by dragging its bottom-right corner.

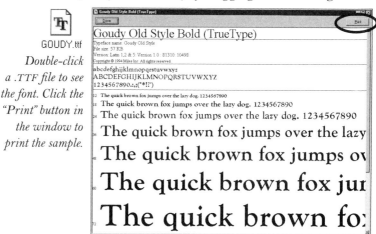

GOUDY.ttf

Double-click a .TTF file to see the font. Click the "Print" button in the window to print the sample.

When you double-click a **PostScript font,** it also opens to display the typeface (shown below), but it needs Adobe Type Manager to do so. Since you can only install and use PostScript Type 1 fonts if you have ATM, this isn't a problem. You can also double-click a PostScript icon directly inside of the ATM window.

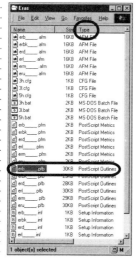

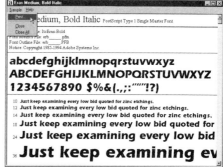

If you want to see which files are the actual PostScript fonts in your folder (shown to the left), view them in a detailed list (use the View menu), then click the "Type" heading to organize them by type. Look for the "PostScript Outlines."

Font management in Windows

When you put fonts into the Fonts folder, they load into Windows' memory. Every font in the folder appears in your font menu and, as you probably know, can create an extraordinarily long and unwieldy list.

Windows doesn't come with any sort of font manager or even a metaphor like the Mac "suitcase" to enable you to keep fonts in a family together. You can't even organize fonts into subfolders in the Fonts folder, nor can you turn off a font temporarily.

If you like to use lots of typefaces, you definitely need to invest in a font management utility, either **Font Navigator** from Bitstream (www.bitstream.com) or **Adobe Type Manager Deluxe** (www.adobe.com).

Both Font Navigator and ATM Deluxe allow you to create sets, or groups, of fonts for different projects or clients and then you can just open the individual sets. This keeps your font menu to a short, manageable list. You can store your fonts in a folder anywhere on your hard disk; you can have folders inside of folders so you can keep everything organized, and both ATM Deluxe and Font Navigator will still allow you to easily and quickly open and close the fonts.

ATM Deluxe will manage TrueType and PostScript Type 1 fonts (it sees Type 3 fonts as damaged).

Font Navigator will manage TrueType fonts. If you want it to manage Type 1 fonts as well, you must have a version of ATM (at least 3.02) also installed. Since you have to have ATM installed anyway so you can install, see, and print your Type 1 fonts smoothly, this shouldn't be a problem.

ATM vs. ATM Deluxe

ATM (Adobe Type Manager), the regular (light) version, is different from ATM Deluxe. You need the regular version (usually free with the purchase of another Adobe product) of ATM in Windows to install Type 1 PostScript fonts, to display them on the screen, and to print them to any printer, PostScript or not.

ATM Deluxe (which is not free) does everything ATM does, but in addition it lets you actually manage your fonts (as does Bitstream's Font Navigator) as described above.

Deluxe starts with version 4.0, so any version before 4.0 is the regular, or light, version. Recent Adobe products bundle the light version.

Know the font name equivalents

The Mac has always been typographically astute, and Windows has been trying to act like it knows what it's doing with type. There are a number of typefaces in Windows that emulate real typefaces on the Mac.

Here's a list of font equivalents:

This Windows font	is pretending to be this typeface
Arial	Helvetica
Book Antiqua	Palatino
Bookman Old Style	Bookman
Century Gothic	Avant Garde
Century Schoolbook	New Century Schoolbook
Monotype Corsiva	Zapf Chancery
Monotype Sorts	Zapf Dingbats
Times New Roman	Times

These are font *equivalents*, not exact *duplicates*, and every program in Windows seems to have a different set of rules for dealing with them. Adobe Illustrator, for example, displays a warning dialog box listing every font that Windows doesn't recognize and then substitutes its default font (Times New Roman) for all the mystery fonts. Microsoft Word, however, automatically checks its font database and substitutes a font closest to the missing one, according to the database. If the equivalent font isn't installed, Word chooses another typeface; for instance, if a document was originally created with Bookman Old Style, Word would typically substitute Bookman for it, but if it can't find Bookman, Word will probably substitute Palatino.

When the original font is replaced by a substitute, the resulting text and headlines might be slightly narrower or wider than the original, which changes line endings, pages breaks, etc. If line endings, page breaks, and other typographic features are important to the document (as they would be in a newsletter with columns or a document whose text must fit on one page), open and carefully view the entire document onscreen with the substituted fonts in place before you print.

Don't use system fonts
if the file will go cross-platform

"System fonts" are those fonts created specifically for a particular platform, and the operating system itself uses them for the text in the menu bars, dialog boxes, etc. Don't use these system fonts for any documents that might (even remotely) need to travel to the other platform. If you do, everyone who gets your files had better really like Courier because that's what the files will display and print!

Fonts to avoid

Below is a list of the fonts that should never be used in documents that are going cross-platform because there is no equivalent font on the other platform. Many of these are bitmapped screen fonts that are not really meant to be printed anyway, and not one of these should ever be printed to a PostScript printer.

Macintosh	Windows
Chicago	Large Fonts, Small Fonts
Geneva	Modern
Monaco	Script
New York	Roman
Charcoal	MS Sans Serif
Mishawaka	MS Serif

Check your word processor or page layout program to see which font it uses as its default typeface. If the default is a system font, change it to a cross-platform typeface to prevent mistakenly creating documents that use Mac or Windows system fonts.

Installed fonts that are okay to use

Arial, Times New Roman (which is different from Times!), Courier New (which is different from Courier), and WingDings, along with a number of others, are Windows fonts that are now standard on a Macintosh as well, specifically so you can use them cross-platform. These fonts are installed in your Macintosh Fonts folder in the System Folder in Mac OS 8.5 and if you install Microsoft applications. If you don't have these fonts yet, you can download the Mac versions from the Microsoft web site (www.microsoft.com).

Separate your non-sharable fonts

If you are in a workgroup that shares files regularly between Macs and PCs, set up a group of cross-platform fonts and separate them from the rest of your fonts. If your company purchases a new typeface for general use, buy enough licenses to install it on every computer.

A font management program (see page 339) can make it easier to keep fonts separated. Specialty or expert typefaces that will only be used for certain projects can be isolated in their own suitcases or folders so they won't accidentally end up in any documents that will be handed off to Windows users.

Save your creative typography for documents that will be printed from your own machine, for headlines and buttons that are made into graphics for the web or CDs, and for files that will be sent as PDF files (Portable Document Format; see below).

Use Acrobat PDF files when possible

One of the least stressful ways to deal with cross-platform font issues is to turn documents into PDF files. PDF is a file format created by Adobe Acrobat Distiller and Acrobat PDF Writer. Acrobat creates an alternate edition of your document, turning graphics into bitmaps and embedding fonts into the document (making them a part of the file). Because the font information is in the document, none of the fonts that were used in the file have to exist on the other computer for the document to display on the screen or to print. As a result, if the file is properly prepared (see your Acrobat Distiller documentation), it will print like a dream and look the same as the original on any system that has the free Acrobat Reader installed.

If PDF is so great, why not use it for everything? The major drawback to this strategy is that once you've distilled a file, neither you nor the recipient can change it if all you have is the free Reader, which is all most people have. If you buy the Adobe Acrobat package, however, you can make minor changes like text editing, some typeface changes, color changes, etc. You can also apply separate notes which can be read on the screen or collected as a separate text file and incorporated into the original, undistilled file. This can create a lot of extra work on both sides, though, and is certainly not practical for files that need to be updated regularly, like spreadsheets, charts, or presentations.

Character sets

Mac and Windows fonts don't have identical sets of characters. Some characters can't be found at all; some exist on both platforms but in different places on the keyboard; others exist but in Windows you need to use the Character Map accessory (see pages 202–203) to find and copy them into your documents. Obviously, this can be a problem when sending text across platforms.

Every keystroke or key combination you type is represented by a numbered position. There are 255 of these positions in a character set. Of these, 127 are upper- and lowercase letters, numbers, punctuation, and certain foreign characters. These original 127 characters were standardized as a set called the ASCII set back in the days when everything had to be in raw text. Each of the 127 characters matches up in the same keyboard position on both platforms.

Then there is a group of characters we use regularly but that aren't part of the old ASCII set, like the bullet (•) and the copyright symbol (©). While both platforms have these characters in their fonts, the characters are not placed in the same positions so when text files are transferred, the computer has to substitute what it does have in its set for what it doesn't have in the document. Some cross-platform programs run an automatic translation feature to handle these problems, but they don't catch them all. That's why you'll sometimes get those irritating open boxes in a transmitted file instead of bullets or quote marks.

The worst situation involves a few special characters that are not part of the regular ASCII keyboard, but have been added as bonus items on either the Mac or the PC. In Windows, these characters include certain symbols, several premade fractions, and some (relatively) obscure foreign characters. On the Mac, the extra characters are the fraction bar and the fi and fl ligatures. These bonus characters do not transfer to nor print from the other platform even if you have the exact same font on both machines. So the Mac will display strange characters in PC-created foreign language documents or files that contain fractions, and PCs will display strange characters instead of ligatures in files originally created on the Mac.

If you know the file is going to go cross-platform, don't use platform-specific characters: build your own fractions instead of using the premade ones, avoid ligatures, and check all non-alphanumeric characters (anything besides letters and numbers) before you print.

ligature: Two letters that are created as one character.

flame fire
flame fire

The ligatures for the character combination "fl" and "fi" prevent the hook of the "f" from bumping into the top of the "l" and the dot of the "i."

fi = Option Shift 5

fl = Option Shift 6

Font style linking

A Macintosh understands fonts and allows type designers a lot of flexibility. Font families can include any number of individual font variations with multiple weights and alternate characters.

For example, this is what a partial list of the Univers family (which has a total of 57 variations!) looks like on a Mac:

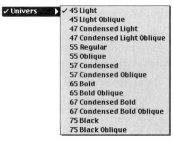

The Mac operating system doesn't care what a designer names a typeface or how many weights and variations a font family has. Univers was named with numbers instead of imprecise name descriptions, but the Mac understands that all the variations belong together.

Windows just doesn't understand fonts and wants to make all families squeeze into the same four-version box (Regular, Italic, Bold, and Bold Italic). If a typeface was designed with variations (like Heavy, Light, Condensed, or Expanded) the non-standard versions won't show up as part of the family in the font list. Instead, Windows separates the family into several packages, each with the standard four different versions.

Here's how the same Univers fonts above are arranged in a Windows font list. Notice the italics and heavier weights of the Univers family become "styles" instead of maintaining their own unique font names:

Oblique: The slanted version of most sans serif faces is called oblique; the slanted version of most serif faces is called italic. The term italic in a font name infers that the actual characters in the typeface have been redesigned instead of just slanted.

Windows font list	Style	True (Mac) name
Univers Light	Regular	Univers 45
	Italic	Univers 45 Oblique
	Bold	Univers 65
	Bold Italic	Univers 65 Oblique
Univers	Regular	Univers 55
	Italic	Univers 55 Oblique
	Bold	Univers 75
	Bold Italic	Univers 75 Oblique

The true-drawn italics and bolds are mapped to the Italic, Bold, and Bold Italic styles. In the Univers example above, you simply have to know (or learn by experimentation) which font variations are attached to which named typefaces. That is, you have to figure out that if you choose Univers Bold and apply the Bold style, you'll actually get Univers Black!

Why font styles are critical to cross-platform text

You have probably learned on a Mac that it's best to choose the actual italic or bold font from the font menu rather than use a keyboard shortcut or toolbar button to change the regular typeface into italic or bold. And you are correct. You have fewer problems and surprises that way, especially if you send your work out to a high-end imagesetter for final output.

But Windows, as we explained on the opposite page, is stupid about fonts. If you choose the font "Garamond Bold Italic" on your Mac and send that document to a PC that has the exact same Garamond family installed from the same vendor, Windows still thinks it doesn't have a font named "Garamond Bold Italic."

To solve this problem, in your Mac document you have to do the wrong thing: you have to set the plain "Garamond" text and use the keyboard shortcuts, the style menu, or the toolbar buttons to apply the bold and the italic styles. That way when the document gets to the PC, Windows can figure out the correct font to display.

If this is a problem because the final output of the document will be on a high-end imagesetter and you need to have the true font chosen, then do a search-and-replace on your Mac at the last minute—search for the italic *style*, remove it, and apply the true-drawn italic font.

What about the other variations that don't fit neatly into the four boxes, such as Univers Black? Experiment on the Mac and find the correct combination of font name plus style that lets Windows apply the correct typeface. If you can't find the correct combination, don't use that font.

It's possible in Windows to apply fonts that aren't really there. For instance, if a family variation only has two versions, Windows still offers four versions. You might install Garamond Ultra and Garamond Ultra Italic in Windows; there is no Garamond Ultra Bold and Ultra Bold Italic. But in the Windows font menu, you actually get the options to make Garamond Ultra into Garamond Ultra Bold Italic, which doesn't exist. Now, if you choose Garamond Ultra Bold Italic, it might appear on your screen (it will look a bit dorky and thick) and it might even print to a non-PostScript printer like your inkjet. But if you send that file to a Mac or to a PostScript printer, that fake style will disappear. **So in Windows, don't apply styles unless you know Windows really does have a font that links to that style.** How do you know? Look at the fonts you bought, look in the ATM dialog box, or try to print it to a PostScript printer.

Garamond ▶	Light
	Light Italic
	Book
	Book Italic
	Bold
	Bold Italic

Instead of choosing a font correctly through the menu, as shown above, it's actually best to use the shortcuts, like the buttons shown below, if your document is going to a PC.

fake italic
true (not fake) italic
You can tell by looking at most typefaces whether they are calling upon the real typeface or faking a style.

Converting fonts

If you need to use the same font on both platforms, you have two choices.

- You can **purchase** the font in both platform formats.
  This is the best, least troublesome solution and the one
  with the most satisfying aesthetic results.

- You can **convert** a copy of the font for use on the other platform *if
  your licensing agreement allows you to do so.* Some font vendors
  allow you to convert a font as long as you don't try to sell or
  distribute the font to others or try to pass it off as your own
  creation. But make sure you check directly with the vendor before
  you convert a font! Keep in mind that when you buy a typeface,
  you don't actually own the face—you own the right to use it on
  your printer. Read that license agreement! Ask before you convert!

The application Macromedia Fontographer, a high-end yet elegant
program, is the standard choice for all forms of font creation, manipu-
lation, and conversion. It's a wonderful, exciting, and fun program to use.

Converting fonts is the cheapest way to provide cross-platform
typefaces, but you should seriously consider whether this option makes
sense for your purpose. Most good quality fonts are optimized to look
their best on the platform for which you bought them. A lot of trouble
has gone into making letters space correctly and print crisply. When
you convert, some of the information that defines the font does not
transfer well. Although TrueType fonts tend to convert better into
PostScript than PostScript fonts do to TrueType, any font conversion
can produce dreadful problems in display and printing. Errors increase
when you change platforms *and* formats.

Converting font names

When you convert a font family to Windows, it's your job to rename
and reorganize the family into groups of four to fit the Windows format,
as described on the previous pages. Otherwise, Univers 45 Light and
Univers 45 Light Italic could turn into Univers 55 Regular and Univers
55 Regular Italic when you apply the bold and bold italic styles, and
then the rest of the bold or bold italic weights won't function at all
because Windows won't see any more fonts in the family.

When you have to convert fonts with more than four styles, figure out which weights you want to pair up before you start converting. It's not a problem if you have a family of weights that don't divide evenly by four. Just create a "family" with only one or two styles (Windows does it all the time). Try to stay close to the Macintosh name so you'll know what it is, but avoid exceeding 25 characters (including spaces) or your Windows font list will be too wide and hard to read. It's okay to shorten "Extra Bold" to "XBold," for example.

Fonts and DOS names

When you convert a font from Mac to Windows, you'll also have to deal with the DOS file name. If this file isn't named absolutely exactly right, fonts won't match up in transferred documents. Unfortunately, these names aren't at all intuitive. They hardly could be, with only eight characters to define them! The PostScript Type 1 font named **Univers 45 Light** on the Mac becomes **UVL＿＿.pfb** in Windows (that's two under-scores, by the way; if you only use one, the font won't reference properly).

If you are converting Adobe fonts (read your license agreement before you do!!), download the "Font Names" PDF file from their web site (www.adobe.com). The font names file is also found on "Type On Call" CDs. This very long file gives you the correct names of all fonts on the Mac and in Windows, plus the DOS file name equivalents.

Things that can go wrong when you convert

Remember that sometimes the best way to solve a typographic problem is to buy the typeface on both platforms or to create PDF files.

Windows Problem

- The font looks heavier than it should, particularly in body copy. The verticals seem too thick for the horizontal letter parts.

- The font looks a little taller or shorter than it was before, or the linespacing seems to have slightly tightened up so ascenders and descenders touch.

Reason

font metric data:
Information such as
character widths and
kerning pairs that tells
a printer how to draw
a font.

- *Font metric data* is different on Macs and Windows, and the converter has made some compromises about how the font should resize the shapes.

Windows Problem

- You copied the font to the Windows Fonts folder, but it doesn't show up in the font list.

- Your font might display and print correctly in its Roman weight (the one that appears in your menu), but not when you choose the italic, bold, or other weights.

Reason

font extensions: The
extension for a TrueType
font is .TTF, and for a
PostScript font is .PFB.
(Fontographer will apply
these for you
automatically.)

- You probably didn't name your font properly when you converted it. To install properly in Windows, a font must have the correct *extension*. For all of the various weights to work (such as light, bold, extra bold, etc.), the font's DOS and long file names must also be correct (see the previous pages for details).

Windows Problem

- Your font turns into Courier on the screen and the printer.

- Your font appears in the right typeface, but looks jagged.

Reason

- These problems usually mean that the PostScript outline didn't transfer or was corrupted in the process. Reconvert and try again.

Windows Problem

- Characters from other fonts are substituted in printouts or some characters "bounce" on the baseline.

Reason

- Font information did not translate correctly when converted. Try converting again, making specific character alterations in Fontographer.

The rules of using fonts cross-platform

Follow these general and specific rules to make sure your fonts will cross platforms without problems.

- **Use updated software,** both system software and application software.

- **Use the same version of the same application** on both platforms.

- **Buy and install the same font, the same technology (TrueType or PostScript Type 1), from the same vendor on both machines.** *Do not* assume that because you have a font called Garamond on your computer and the other computer also has a font called Garamond that those two Garamonds are the same thing! If necessary, delete the fonts that are in the machine and reinstall new ones to make absolutely sure they are the same.

- **Use simple font families** that don't have lots of extra members like condensed, ultra condensed, extended, etc., because Windows has a difficult time figuring out what they are. Stick to a good ol' basic family of regular, italic, bold, and bold italic for your cross-platform documents.

- **Instead of choosing the true-drawn version of the font** from the menu, choose the regular version and apply the italic and bold with the keyboard shortcut, toolbar button, or style menu. See pages 344–345 for details.

- **Don't use ligatures** (if you don't know what they are, you're not using them; see page 343). Ligatures are not built into the fonts for Windows and so they will turn into weird characters. The same with the Mac **fraction bar** (Option Shift 1)—it has no equivalent in a Windows font.

- **Make a trial document** to experiment with any special characters you need in the text to make sure the characters will travel back and forth. If you are sending files to and from the same version of the same application with the same fonts, it should work fairly well.

— continued

- **Don't use the system fonts** on either platform:
  - On a Mac, don't use any font with a city name (Chicago, Geneva, Monaco, New York), Charcoal, or Mishawaka. Don't even use Times, Helvetica, or Bookman unless you have installed the same font and same version from the same vendor on the PC.
  - In Windows, don't use MS Serif, MS Sans Serif, Roman, Script, Small Fonts, or Modern. Don't even use WingDings, Times New Roman, Arial, or Bookman Old Style unless you have installed the same font and same version from the same vendor on the Mac.
  - If the fonts don't have exactly the same menu name on both platforms, they will get confused!!
- If you have a really wonderful typeface for a headline and you can't get the typeface to the other platform properly, set the headline in your illustration program and **convert the text to paths or outlines.** Bring the converted headline into your document as an EPS graphic and make sure you print to a PostScript printer.

Color

Color is a really big topic with many different issues. This chapter deals only with the color issues that affect cross-platform graphics— in particular, differences between the Macintosh and the Windows system palettes (the collection of basic colors each system can display), color matching, and display brightness.

Macintosh images on PCs

You might be very surprised when you view an image on a PC that was created on a Macintosh—the image will appear much darker on a PC than on a Mac. And if the PC can only display 256 colors, the image will probably also look grainy, or very flat and *posterized*—like a bad psychedelic poster.

posterize: When you decrease the number of colors available in an image, the remaining colors can't blend smoothly into one another and so they create sharply defined areas.

You'll see these differences even if you are using exactly the same monitor and the same manufacturer's video card on both systems because the alterations aren't caused by hardware differences. To understand what's going on and correct for these problems, you need a little grounding in computer color and system palettes.

Computer "system palettes"

Many computer monitors are limited to only 256 colors. Of the millions of colors many monitors are *capable* of displaying—given the right hardware and memory combination—Microsoft and Apple had to choose *which* 256 colors their users would always have available, no matter what the limitations. This collection of 256 colors is called the **system palette.**

Microsoft and Apple came to very different conclusions about which colors should be included in the system palette. Microsoft viewed their palette as just a starting point for application developers, so they spent very little time designing it. Apple wanted to make sure that any image would look as good as it could on the screen even when there were only 256 colors to work with, so they created a more versatile system palette.

Dithered colors

Dithering is a technique that makes you think you're seeing a color that doesn't really exist in the computer's color palette. Imagine that you have a painter's palette without the color purple. If you paint really tiny blue and red dots close together in a pattern, the viewer's eye blends the two colors together and creates the *impression* of purple. To make a darker or lighter purple, you might change the pattern to add more or less blue, or bring in a third color.

Dithering is only as successful as the range of colors and shades available. If the right group of *hues* aren't available for a specific color, the result will look rough and textured. No matter how good a job the computer does at representing the color, if you look closely you can see the dithered pattern, as shown below, right.

hue: Basically, "hue" refers to the color itself, such as orange, green, or blue. Technically, it's a location on the standard color wheel.

The color in Browser's body is smooth and clean because the computer had this exact color in its palette.

Here, the color in Browser's body is "dithered" because the computer had to fake the original color by using tiny bits of colors from its own palette.

The Windows system palette

Windows doesn't *really* have a system palette; it only has a starter selection of colors. Any application written for Windows can throw out the Windows "system" palette and create its own group of colors, *except* for the first ten and the last ten colors in the palette (circled, below). The colors in these palette positions must *always* appear in these exact locations and can never be replaced. If you create an image using all 256 colors but don't include these twenty exact shades, Windows will throw out twenty of the custom colors from your image and replace them with these standard twenty.

The permanent colors in the palette include the purest primary and secondary shades (red, green, and blue, plus cyan, magenta, and yellow); these same six colors with their brightness reduced by 50 percent; black, white, and three shades of gray; and three additional pale colors (a blue, a green, and a creamy yellow). Most of these colors are not very elegant, although they're pretty good at displaying the Windows logo.

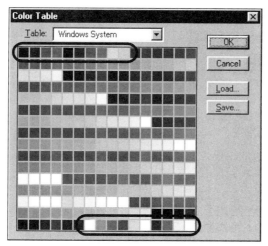

Circled are the twenty permanent Windows palette colors in the positions in which they will always appear.

The Mac system palette

To make a useful palette with enough colors to dither nicely when necessary, Apple devised a logical sequence that uses colors from the widest possible range of hue and *brightness*.

brightness: Refers to how much white is in a color, or the relative lightness or darkness.

The first part of the palette has an assortment of 216 different colors. The bottom portion of the palette has four sets of colors in even steps from light to dark—red, green, blue, and gray.

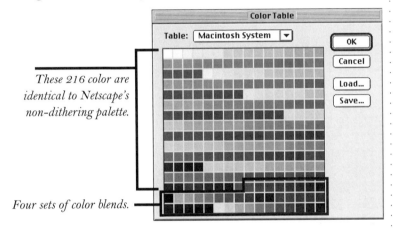

These 216 color are identical to Netscape's non-dithering palette.

Four sets of color blends.

Netscape and Adobe adaptations of the Mac palette

Remember, Windows has only 20 colors in its system palette; as long as those magic 20 don't change, any program can swap its own set of colors for the other 236 positions. So Netscape used the 216 Macintosh colors to create the palette for its Windows browser, with 13 other special colors for its own logo (which means 7 colors are left unassigned).

Adobe also uses the basic 216 colors of the Macintosh palette as the default in its Windows applications, which makes transferring graphic files from the Macintosh to Windows consistent and simple. However, the result can be a little surprising if you're expecting the Adobe default to be the Windows system palette, the way the Mac palette is the default on a Mac: if you set your PC monitor to 256 colors and then open Photoshop, you'll find almost every color in the table will be dithered because Photoshop has to "make" the Windows colors from its own default palette.

The Macintosh and Windows palettes compared

If you examine the Macintosh and Windows palettes side by side, you see they have a mere sixteen colors in common, and only some of these sixteen belong to the Windows must-have twenty. As a result, if your PC application uses the Windows default palette (as does the Paint accessory that comes with Windows), and if you have a PC that can only display 256 colors, then a Macintosh graphic will dither very badly on your PC monitor. (The more colors your PC monitor can display, the less of a problem you'll have with dithering.)

Another important difference between the Mac and Windows palettes is where they each put black and white. In the Windows palette, black is the first color in the palette and white is last; on the Mac, it's just the opposite. Black and white are among the twenty colors in the Windows palette that can't change their positions. Because of this switch, bitmapped images created on the Mac and brought over to the PC (for instance, to use as icons) often appear with their white and black areas reversed. There is no way to *prevent* this problem, which mostly arises in images with white or black chosen as a transparent color. You can *solve* the problem with Impact Software's Microangelo 98 (www.impactsoft. com), which opens bitmapped images and saves them for use as Windows icons or cursors.

Of course, these palette problems don't appear if both the Mac and the PC can display thousands or millions of colors because the system palette colors just become part of the larger group.

Macintosh color calibration

Every color monitor, scanner, or printer reproduces color in a unique way. Even if you have several peripherals from the same vendor, you'll still experience some color shifting. The only way to keep the color consistent is through a process called *color calibration*. Inexpensive color calibration software is available for both the Mac and the PC.

Color profiles

A color profile describes the range of colors a peripheral can process, what "color space" it uses, and the image brightness and colors of monitors. Applications that use color profiles attach them to files you create, allowing the next monitor or printer to read a file's color history and keep the colors consistent from different monitors to final output.

Most color peripherals sold today come with color profiles on a disk or have them available at their web site. To install profiles in your Mac in OS 8.5, drag the profile icon onto the System Folder.

Although monitors have standard profiles, Apple's ColorSync and similar Windows programs allow you to customize the monitor profile to correspond more closely to what you see on your screen. If you're creating images that will cross platforms, you'll improve the chances of color consistency if you customize your monitor profile.

If you don't have ColorSync 2.5.1 or later on your Mac, you can download it for free at the Apple site, www.apple.com.

For this process to work, you must have the *ColorSync* control panel enabled, as well as the *ColorSync Extension* and the *Default Calibrator* extension.

To customize a monitor profile

1. From the Apple menu, slide down to "Control Panels," then select "Monitors & Sound." If your control panel looks something like the one shown on the right, click "Color."

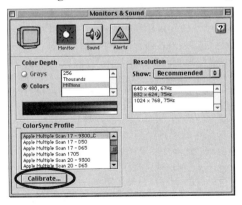
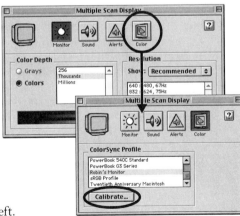

2. Click the "Calibrate" button on the lower left. This launches the "Monitor Calibration Assistant." —*continued*

3. Follow the easy instructions on the screen, read the informative explanations in each window, and click the arrow to move on.

4. You'll be asked to choose a monitor from a scrolling list, as shown below.

This bright triangle shows the range of colors your monitor can display. The more area the triangle occupies, the wider its color range.

This + symbol indicates your monitor's white point.

ColorSync profiles are stored in the System Folder.

There are so many profiles in this list that you should be able to find one that matches your monitor model or manufacturer. If nothing seems to fit, check the disk that came with your monitor to see if it includes a ColorSync profile. If it does, close the Assistant, drag the profile from the disk into the ColorSync Profiles folder in the System Folder, and start again.

5. You'll be given four possible choices of "white point." This setting determines how warm (yellowish) or cool (blueish) the color "white" will objectively appear. If you'll be switching back and forth between your Mac and a Windows monitor, the 9300 setting is a good choice.

6. Give your profile a name, then click "Create It." The Assistant will create your custom calibrated profile.

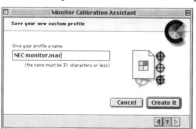

Type your new name here. Be sure not to duplicate a name that already exists. Click "Create It" and you'll go back to the control panel where you started.

7. Your custom profile will appear as a choice in the Monitors & Sound "ColorSync Profile" list. Choose the profile so ColorSync-enabled applications will attach it to your images.

Gamma

Technically, gamma is a measure of the contrast that affects the mid-tones (the midlevel gray values) of an image. You can adjust the gamma of, for instance, a photograph to change the brightness values of the middle range of gray tones without significantly altering the highlights or shadows.

On a monitor, gamma basically refers to the brightness of the monitor, which affects whether the colors on it look "right" to a human being. There is no one correct gamma, although there is a correct range. Macs apply a different gamma to monitors than other computer systems do, which is what makes the usual Macintosh monitor display look brighter than that of a PC.

These platform differences in gamma cause at least as many problems as incompatible color palettes. Many graphic designers like to use deep, rich, subtle colors, but a photograph or image created on a Macintosh with dark, subtle colors fades to black or gray on Windows. It's not safe to assume that the shadow detail you see on the Mac will be visible to everyone else — many images that look great to a Mac user will often look dark, gloomy, and indistinct to a Windows user.

Choose one

Avoid working on the same color artwork on two different platforms, particularly when using paint or color correction programs. Cyndi had a student who took a project from a Mac in the student lab to his own Windows computer at home. When he returned to the Mac lab, he repainted areas that seemed too pale. The result was an image that looked bad on both systems. The moral? Make a platform choice and stick with it. If you absolutely must switch between platforms during the project, change your Macintosh's gamma to match the PC before you begin (explained on the following page).

Adjusting gamma on the Mac

If you have to work with graphics cross-platform, the most sensible way to deal with gamma problems is to alter your Macintosh's gamma to match what a Windows user would see. Apple's ColorSync 2.5 makes gamma-setting easy; follow the directions below. Adobe Photoshop 5.0 also comes with a gamma control panel and a very easy assistant program.

To create a Mac monitor profile to match the Windows gamma

1. Follow the steps on pages 357–358 to create a new profile. When you get to the dialog box called "Select a target gamma," choose "2.2 Television Gamma." This is the correct setting to mimic a PC monitor. Your screen display will change to preview this new setting.

2. Continue following the directions on page 358. Name your Windows-compatible settings with a name that describes this profile, then click "Create It."

3. Both the Mac and the PC versions of your color profiles will appear in the ColorSync Profile box of the control panel. With one click you can change from Mac to PC gamma settings and back again.

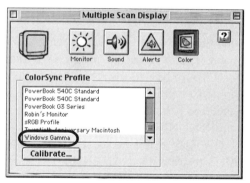

When you need to see how an image will appear on a Windows monitor, open your Monitors & Sound control panel and choose the profile you just made.

(Once you open the control panel, the actual name of it might be different from the one shown here, depending on which monitor you have attached to your computer.)

Setting a color profile in Windows 98

Windows 98 incorporated Apple's ColorSync standards and even uses the same color management module (the software that makes color consistent among different input and output devices) that Apple does. If your Windows system is color-calibrated to the same standards as the Mac, both systems will provide similar displays, and both will output similarly to the same color printer.

Windows 98 has a very extensive database of monitors, but new models are always being made. **If you have a very new monitor model,** you first need to install its profile into Windows' database:

1. Insert the disk that came with your new monitor. If there is an install program, use it to install any drivers or profiles.

2. If there isn't an install program, look for this file icon: Right-click it; from the menu, choose "Install Profile."

Once the monitor profile is installed in the Windows system folder, **make it the default profile** for your computer:

1. Right-click on the Desktop and choose "Properties" to get the Display property sheet.

2. Click the "Settings" tab at the top.
   Click the "Advanced button" in the bottom right.
   Click the "Color Management" tab (shown below).

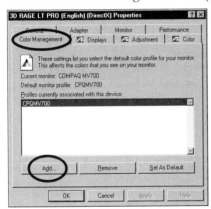

If your system has not already recognized your monitor type, the profile list will be blank.

3. Click the "Add" button to get the list of monitor profiles. If you've just installed your profile, it should appear in the list.
   Even if your manufacturer isn't listed, your monitor may

actually use one of the existing profiles. Many companies don't make all of their own monitor parts, so your monitor may actually be a Trinitron- or NEC-compatible. If you don't see a choice that matches your monitor, check the company's web site or call their customer support line to determine which profile to use. In the meantime, choose the generic Windows 98 profile: sRGB Color Space Profile.

4. Select your monitor profile, then click the "Add" button.

Once you have a color profile, it should be available to all applications. However, Windows Color Management depends on individual software vendors to implement its most important features, which means that older software won't recognize a new profile you've installed.

Look for an application's color management options in its File menu; if the application is using Windows' profiles, you'll see some sort of "Color Management" choice. It's also possible that your software has its own way to set color profiles. If so, it may incorporate the profile you've chosen into its own color management scheme. For example, in Adobe PageMaker, go to the File menu, and from the "Preferences…" submenu, choose "General…." Click "CMS setup" (CMS stands for Color Management System).

Gamma control in Windows 95/98

The Windows color management functions don't have a setting to alter a monitor's gamma. However, Adobe Photoshop and PageMaker both ship with a Windows control panel for adjusting gamma, as well as other monitor settings. This control panel is called "Adobe Gamma" and is installed in the Control Panel folder when the application is installed. We recommend using Adobe Gamma if you have either of these two applications. Otherwise, consider a third-party color management software program, like Sonnetech's Colorific.

Gamma control in Windows NT

Although a file called "gamma.cpl" comes with Photoshop 5.0, it doesn't do much in Windows NT 4.0. The gamma control panel works by talking directly to the hardware. NT really doesn't like software that tries to bypass the system, so this software won't actually install in NT even though it gets copied to the disk drive.

Advanced color topics

Here are a couple of advanced topics you might want to explore.

Adjusting levels

What if you have existing images, so it's too late to design them from scratch to accommodate Windows viewers? It is possible to adjust the images themselves to account for the brightness differences by adjusting highlight and shadow levels in Photoshop or other image editing software.

Warning: Don't try to make an image look better in Windows by just changing its brightness. The "Brightness/Contrast" control makes the whole graphic equally darker or lighter, so it will just wash out the image. Instead, use the "Levels" control to apply changes differently in highlights, shadows, and midtones.

Determine what your goal is: are you trying to create an image that will look acceptable on both systems or an alternate image for Windows only? If you must have one acceptable image for both platforms, be cautious. If you are creating a new alternate, you can afford to be bolder as long as you don't completely delete highlight detail.

1. Open your image in Photoshop. From the Image menu, slide down to "Adjust" and choose "Levels…," or press Command L. You'll get the Levels dialog box, which looks like this:

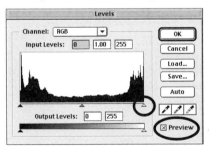

Make sure the "Preview" box is checked so you can see your changes as you move the slider arrow.

Tip: If you're accustomed to using Photoshop, you might want to make these changes on an "adjustment layer" so you have even more control. From the Layers palette menu, choose "New Adjustment Layer," choose "Levels," and click OK.

2. Move the right-hand arrow (circled above) one notch to the left. This should make the whole image a little brighter, but show more detail in the shadows. If the image must be optimized for Windows and is overall a little dark on the Macintosh, try moving the arrow one step further to the left.

Once you're satisfied with these changes, click OK, and use "Save a Copy" from the File menu to name your Windows version.

How color works on a monitor

Color on a monitor is extraordinarily different from color outside of a monitor. In your office, light comes from a source, like a lamp or a window; the light hits an object, like a red apple; and that light gets *reflected* from the red apple into our eyes. But on a monitor of any kind (television, video, computer), light is projected from inside the monitor straight to our eyes—it's not reflected off of anything.

In a monitor, there are three "guns" that "shoot" light to the screen; the guns shoot red light, green light, and blue light. When no light is sent to the screen, it's black; when the full value of the red, green, and blue lights are sent to the screen, it creates white. There are 256 intensity levels of each color, labeled from 0 (zero) to 255.

So color on a monitor is described as RGB, which of course stands for red, green, and blue. Every RGB color is composed of various combinations of the levels of intensity, so RGB colors can be "defined" by a number. For instance, if the red has an intensity of 199, the green of 243, and the blue of 62, you'll see a lime green color on the screen.

Because each of the three colors has 256 possible values, a computer monitor can theoretically display 16.7 million different color combinations (256 x 256 x 256). But to send all of that color information to every pixel on the screen takes a lot of memory. The larger the screen, the more pixels there are and the more memory it takes. When you change the monitor "resolution" to force even more pixels on the screen (such as 1280 pixels x 960 pixels), that takes huge amounts of memory. You may have noticed when you try to change the number of colors or the number of pixels, the numbers you choose affect each other; that is, if you want lots of pixels on your screen (which makes everything look smaller), you can't have as many colors. If you are willing to have fewer pixels on your screen (which makes everything look larger), you can have more colors. The limitation is from the amount of video RAM (VRAM) you have installed in your computer. If you have lots of video RAM, you can have both lots of colors and lots of pixels. You can add an additional color video card or additional VRAM to both Macs and PCs.

If an image is going to stay on the screen, as in a presentation or web page, it should be in the RGB mode. To reproduce a color image on a high-end printing press, its mode must be changed to CMYK (cyan, magenta, yellow, and black), but that's another book (specifically, *The Non-Designer's Scan and Print Book*, by Sandee Cohen and Robin Williams, from Peachpit Press).

Printing

26

Unless you do the type of work that never leaves the computer screen, eventually you need to print your documents. Printing in Windows itself is becoming more Mac-like (and thus easier) with every Windows revision. However, printing files created in one platform on a printer connected to the other one can still be a sticky proposition. In this chapter we look at how to set up and print in Windows, as well as what to watch for when you print files on a Mac that were created in Windows and vice versa.

Printers

*This is the Windows
Printers folder.*

Setting up a printer in Windows

Setting up a local printer in Windows 98 has become remarkably Mac-like in its simplicity. You plug the printer in, turn it on, turn on the computer, walk through a simple group of dialog boxes, and wait while Windows loads the right driver. All Windows versions come with an extensive database of printer manufacturers and models. You can install an infinite number of printers even if they're not currently connected to your Desktop (just like adding printer icons to the Chooser on a Mac).

To install a local printer in any version of Windows

1. Open the "My Computer" window, then double-click on the "Printers" folder. If there are no printers already loaded on your computer, the "Printers" folder window will look like this:

    *If you already have printers
    installed, you'll see their icons in
    this window. The "Add Printer"
    icon is always there, no matter
    how many printers you have
    installed.*

**Wizard: A ready-made
installer program built into
Windows. Many software
packages you install will
use the Wizard.**

2. Double-click the "Add Printer" icon to launch the "Add Printer Wizard."

3. Leave the default on "Local printer" in Windows 95/98 ("My Computer" in Windows NT), and click "Next."

(Windows NT users: Do steps 5 and 6, then step 4.)

4. In the "Add Printer Wizard," you'll see a list like this:

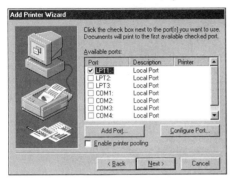

In Windows NT, this is what a typical list of available ports looks like. Check the box of your choice, then click "Next."

In Windows 95/98, there are no boxes to check; instead, click the name itself to select your choice, then click "Next."

5. To choose the correct port, you need to know if your printer is a serial (COM) or a parallel (LPT) printer. Refer to Chapter 3, *Setting Up Your PC*, if you need some guidance in identifying serial and parallel ports. Most of the time, your printer is connected to a parallel port; if it is, look at the back of the computer to see which parallel port it's connected to. Select the port from the list in the dialog box. Click "Next."

6. In the next dialog box, shown below, choose the manufacturer and model of your particular printer. Click the manufacturer's name on the left side, then click your printer's name on the right side. Click "Next."

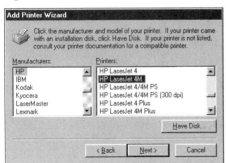

If your printer model isn't listed in this database and you have your driver software disk, click the "Have Disk…" button and follow the easy instructions for adding it to the database.

7. The next dialog box asks you to name your printer. Stick to short names so they'll fit neatly on a Desktop icon label. You'll also have to decide if you want this to be your default printer. Click "Next."

8. You'll see this dialog box in Windows NT only:

Sharing allows other users on the same computer network to see each other's hard disks and manipulates files on the other disks. It also lets everyone share devices like scanners and printers. Talk to your network's system administrator if you'd like to be able to share your printer with others. For now, choose "Not shared," and click "Next."

9. The Wizard gives you the chance to do a test print to make sure everything worked properly. Take advantage of this option: leave the button set on "Yes," and click "Finish."

10. The Wizard goes to the Windows system folder and looks in its database for the printer driver. If it finds the correct file, the Wizard quits and your test page is printed. If the Wizard doesn't find the correct driver, you'll be prompted to insert your Windows CD-ROM. Do so, and click OK. The Wizard will copy the correct files, quit, and print your test page.

Tip: **Sometimes Windows doesn't find your CD because the dumb system automatically tries to copy files from the D: drive, but the CD-ROM might be the G: or some other drive. If this happens, click the "Browse..." button in the "Copying Files..." dialog box and navigate to the CD.**

Locating the printer on the Desktop

Printers

The Printers folder is inside the "My Computer" window.

After you've loaded a new printer driver, its icon appears in the Printers folder. If you don't see the new icon, that's because Windows isn't smart enough to update the file icons immediately the way a Mac does. In the Printers folder window, go to the View menu and choose "Refresh." Your new printer driver icons will appear.

Any new drivers you added should now be available in this folder.

Printing a file in Windows

You can print a file in Windows just like you do on the Mac: drop a file on a Desktop printer icon or use the Print command (from the File menu) while the file is open in an application.

- If you print by dropping a file on a Desktop printer shortcut (see below), Windows launches the application, prints the file according to the default page setup, and quits the application.

  You can drag several files to the printer shortcut at once, even if they were created by different applications, but watch the memory! Although Windows can have different applications open at the same time, printing could be painfully slow.

- Once you're in an application and choose to print from the File menu command, the individual "Page Setup" and "Print" dialog boxes will vary as they do on a Mac, depending on the application and how it handles printing.

To make a shortcut of the printer driver

1. Right-click on the printer driver icon and drag it to the Desktop.
2. You'll get a little pop-up menu; choose "Create shortcut here."

The target printer

Perhaps the hardest thing for a Mac user to get used to is the lack of a Chooser. Instead, each Windows application includes a dialog box where you can change the "target" (chosen) printer. You might find it in the "Page Setup" box or in the "Print" dialog box, both available from the File menu. Look for an option with a drop-down menu, like these:

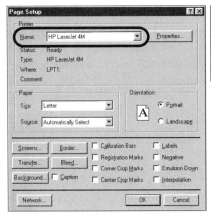

Canceling a print job

When you're in a hurry, it's easy to mistakenly send an entire document to print when you only meant to print a page or a selection. Canceling a printing job on a Mac involves one keyboard shortcut, the familiar Command Period. But this is Windows.

To cancel printing in Windows

1. Double-click the printer icon, either the one in the Printers folder or the shortcut on the Desktop. A window opens that displays all files that are in queue (lined up and waiting) for this printer.

2. Right-click on the name of the print job you want to cancel, and a pop-up menu gives you a choice between pause and cancel.

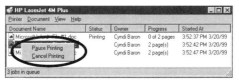

This is very cumbersome compared to the elegance of a keystroke, and it wastes paper as pages continue to print while you hurry through the steps. You can shorten the number of steps to cancel a print job with this easy trick: Double-click on your printer shortcut whenever you start up your computer; then it's always ready and available.

Printing a folder list—not!

Mac users are always hunting for a trick that will let us print a list of folder contents in Windows. When you're stuck with pressing the Print Scrn and Alt keys and printing the window snapshot that results, it seems impossible that there's not some solution to print the entire window buried in all those menus. Alas, your hunt ends here. The only "trick" to printing a list of folder contents involves writing an actual DOS batch file! Since even most Windows users don't know how to write batch files, you'll either have to live without this useful Mac function, or bribe a DOS techie to do the job for you.

General note on all cross-platform printing

If you're preparing Windows files for a Mac-based service bureau, or if you're a Mac user trying to print your files over an NT or Novell network, take extra care with all the little details. Begin by reading Chapter 24 on *Fonts* and Chapter 25 on *Color*, as well as Chapter 22 on *Transferring Files*. Many of the most frequent printing problems can be avoided simply by understanding the issues discussed in those chapters.

Windows printers and PostScript

If you use PostScript fonts or if you use applications that create Post-Script files, you may run into unfamiliar problems when you try to print. Unlike the Macintosh platform where almost every laser printer can output PostScript files, PostScript is often not available on PC printers or on high-volume laser and color printers attached to a PC network. Check the specifications of your chosen Windows printer before you try to print a file that contains PostScript.

Does your file contain PostScript information?

If you used Type 1 fonts, your file contains PostScript information. See Chapter 24 if you're not sure whether you used Type 1 or TrueType fonts. If you placed an EPS graphic, your file contains PostScript information (Illustrator, FreeHand, and CorelDRAW create EPS graphics). If you're using a page layout application like PageMaker, InDesign, or QuarkXPress, your file contains PostScript information.

Can your printer handle PostScript information?

If you send a PostScript file to a non-PostScript printer, it may print, but not always successfully, as described below. Non-PostScript printers can't interpret the PostScript information so they fake it. They print what they see on the screen. Here are typical symptoms of what happens when a PostScript file is printed on a non-PostScript printer:

- **The EPS graphics are bitmapped.**
  A non-PostScript printer prints the screen-resolution preview image instead of the smooth EPS information.

- **The EPS graphics print as gray rectangles.**
  If you saved your file without a preview, only a gray box prints.

- **PostScript Type 1 fonts look jagged.**
  The jagged type happens when no equivalent font lives in the printer's resident font library.

- **The type is smooth but it has uneven word and letter spaces.**
  The smooth but weird type results when the printer substitutes a similar font for the one you chose.

- **Page margins shift or graphics don't print completely.**
  Bitmapping a PostScript document takes a lot of memory. If you have a tabloid-size page or you're trying to print high-resolution pictures, the printer may simply run out of memory.

Troubleshooting printing with PostScript

If you know the target printer is PostScript yet you are still having problems printing, it might be that the printer is running with the wrong driver. Printer manufacturers make many slightly different models, and it's easy to load the wrong software from a long list. Most people don't know (or even care about) the difference between an HP LaserJet 4, 4M or 4M+. Since the printer often works fine with non-PostScript applications, no one realizes there's anything wrong. If you get bad quality output and you've been told the printer can read PostScript, follow the steps on pages 366–368 to add a printer driver, and look carefully at the list for printer driver alternatives.

If you're certain you've matched the right printer and driver, perhaps the driver itself needs an update. Before you give up, check the printer manufacturer's web site for their new printer driver versions.

If the problem is with the type, read Chapter 24 on *Fonts*.

The best alternative to output PostScript files to a non-PostScript printer is to get the full version of Adobe Acrobat and create PDF files (see Chapter 24, *Fonts*, for more about PDF files). The latest Mac version of Acrobat adds an icon to your Chooser. Choose this as your printer, and "print" to a PDF file. Or if you're in PageMaker, from the File menu choose to "Export" the document as an "Adobe PDF."

Saving EPS files for printing in Windows

If you've always worked on a Macintosh, you may never have noticed that when you save an EPS graphic there's an "Encoding" option somewhere in the application's "Print" dialog boxes or output options. This option becomes very important if you need to print Mac files using a Windows printer. Here are a few examples of the options:

- **Illustrator 7.0:** To set EPS encoding, from the File menu choose "Print...." Make sure your Print dialog box menu is set to "Adobe Illustrator." You can choose "ASCII" or "Binary" encoding (see below) from the "Data" menu.

- **FreeHand 7.0:** From the File menu, choose "Output Options...."

- **Photoshop 5.0:** Photoshop gives you the option to choose the encoding when you save a file as a Photoshop EPS, after you click the Save button.

Encoding EPS files properly

EPS files can be encoded in either "Binary" or "ASCII." Macs, Mac printers, and Apple networks prefer binary files. Binary files are very efficient on the Mac because they're much smaller than ASCII ones; unfortunately, they're worse than useless in Windows. PCs require ASCII encoding and when force-fed a binary-encoded file will usually spew dozens of pages of junk characters. This is also true for network operating systems like Novell and the servers that often regulate mixed-platform traffic to printers.

Note: "Encoding" is different from "exporting" as ASCII! Make sure you choose the "encoding" option.

If you aren't sure where your file will be printed, it's best to save your files with ASCII encoding. Macs and AppleTalk handle ASCII files without problem as long as they have enough memory to deal with these larger ASCII files.

Be very thorough when you change a file to ASCII. If an ASCII-encoded document has a binary-encoded file contained within it, you'll probably see ugly PostScript errors. It isn't enough to change the encoding of the page layout or the word processing file—you must make sure every EPS file you use in the document is also ASCII encoded. If they aren't, open them in their original applications, choose "Save As" from the File menu, and change their "Binary" defaults to "ASCII" (as described above). After you save this new ASCII version, replace the binary versions that were in your page layout, illustration, or word processing program.

Note: Even though you're saving the image as an ASCII file, be sure to add the extension ".eps" at the end of the file name because it's still really an EPS file.

Printing from a Mac to a Windows printer

Under normal circumstances, you can't output from a Macintosh directly to a Windows-only printer. The cables are incompatible, and in many cases a Macintosh version of the software driver doesn't even exist. You can get around this by purchasing Infowave Wireless Messaging's PowerPrint (www.infowave.com). They provide a cable with a parallel port connection on one end and a Macintosh ADB connection on the other, plus an extensive group of printer drivers. Once you've loaded these drivers and connected your Mac to the Windows printer, you'll be able to print normally.

Sharing a Windows printer

If you need to share a Windows printer between Macintosh and Windows machines, you can combine the PowerPrint solution (mentioned above) with a data switch box. This may sound scary and very technical, but the hardware part is surprisingly easy if you're a person who's comfortable with Macintosh upgrades and installations. Just use the guidelines in the "hybrid solution" section of Chapter 1, *Preparing to do Windows,* for sharing a monitor between a Mac and a PC, but substitute "printers" where it mentions "monitors," and "printer cables" for "monitor cables."

Printing Mac files to a Windows printer over a non-Macintosh network

Mac files will output on a Windows network printer as long as these two circumstances apply:

- The Macintosh has software on it that allows the file server to recognize that the Mac is there. Speak to your network administrator about making sure you have this software on your Mac and for instructions on how to log on and print using the network.

- The network printer has drivers (printer software) that can be loaded onto the Macintosh. If it doesn't, you'll need PowerPrint Pro, which is the multi-user version of the PowerPrint software mentioned in the first paragraph.

Printing Windows files on a Mac printer

Sometimes the Windows computer you're working on doesn't have access to a printer or isn't connected to the type of printer you need, so you might want to transfer a file to the Mac for printing instead.

If a Windows file *was not* created with a PostScript application like Illustrator or FreeHand, and *does not* use PostScript fonts, you shouldn't have any problem printing it from a Mac.

If a Windows file *was* created with a PostScript application and you have that same application on both platforms, the easiest way to print it is to save the Windows file in the application's *native file format* before transferring it to a Macintosh. Then you can open the Windows file on your Mac and print it just as if it had been a Mac file originally (that's how many service bureaus handle Windows file output). Well-designed cross-platform software will prompt you to choose equivalent typefaces and warn you about missing graphics to help make sure your file prints properly.

If you create Windows files in their native formats, remember to include native file versions of your placed art as well. For more about native file formats, read Chapter 22, *Transferring Files.*

native file format:
The format that the application automatically saves in. A PageMaker file, a Quark file, a Photoshop file, etc. are all native file formats. EPS, TIFF, or WMF files are not native file formats.

"Print to file"

If you have to work in Windows software that has no Macintosh version or doesn't have any cross-platform file formats, you can't use the usual printing and file transfer strategies. You might decide to take the Windows file to a service bureau for printing instead, only to discover that many service bureaus are still Macintosh-only or have a more limited range of applications on their Windows computers than they do on their Macs. Or you might be using software, like QuarkXPress, that doesn't *really* place images into files, but only creates *links* to the originals; that means even if you have the same application on both platforms, you still have to transfer all of the images in the file separately and check all of your fonts before you can print.

Note: As a Mac user, you might think this process is the same as "print to disk," but it isn't exactly. It depends on the printer driver. In Windows, "Print to file" might create a PostScript file (.PS) or a .PRN file, which is an HP format used to print a non-PostScript file to a non-PostScript printer.

In any of these cases, you can use the "Print to file" option provided in many word processing or PostScript-based applications. With it, you create one file that doesn't need the original application and contains all of the font and image information to make your print.

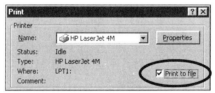

This is an example of one application's "Print" dialog box with a "Print to file" option.

When you "Print to file," your software goes through the same process it would if you were really printing—it finds all the file parts, translates them into the printer's language, and prepares the images—then writes all that work to a file on your hard disk with a .PS (for PostScript) or .PRN (for PRiNter) extension.

Creating a print file

Note: Once a printer file has been created, the service bureau can't go in and change it if they find a mistake. You'll need to fix the error yourself in the original document, make a new print file, and get charged a second time to have new proofs made.

To use "Print to file" successfully, follow the guidelines below. Although some of these suggestions are specific to making a print file, most of them are also good advice for anyone who uses a service bureau.

- Go through the Page Setup and choose the special settings carefully: color separations, printing emulsion down, printing at different percentages, crop marks, number of pages to be printed, which pages in the file to print, etc. Once you've made a print file, the settings in that file can't be added or changed!

- When you create the file, assign the correct driver *for the printer that the file will be output on.* This is critical! If you're sending the file to another computer to be output to another printer, you must assign the driver *for that other printer.* If you don't have the right printer driver because you're sending the file to a service bureau and you don't own the printer, call the service bureau and ask them to give you a copy of their printer driver. Follow the steps in "Setting up a printer in Windows" on pages 366–368 to add that printer driver to your computer.

- Use an interpreter like GhostScript (see below) to open and proof your print file carefully for changes in line breaks, headlines and columns, especially if you used your desktop printer's driver while working on the document. Your program could completely reflow the text if you create the document with your default local printer driver and then change to another driver when you make the printer file. Look for headlines that have been pushed to two lines, and check the ends of columns to see if text continues to flow the way you anticipated.

- Check the spelling in your text. Don't forget to check words in all caps, and always proof your headlines.

Keep an original

A printer file won't open in the original application it was created in because the file is no longer in the application's format. Always keep a copy of your original document after you've made a printer file.

Printing the print file

The computer from which you're going to print needs a small, compact program called an "interpreter" that reads the file and completes the process you began by sending the file directly to the printer. Aladdin Enterprise's GhostScript, which is free and has versions for every major platform, is the best-known interpreter. It comes with a user manual and also works as a PostScript file previewer and graphics viewer. Aladdin Enterprises (not Aladdin Systems, who makes StuffIt) can be reached at ghost@aladdin.com. If you want a simple Mac utility that doesn't take up much space on your hard disk, try Bare Bones Software's freeware called DropPS, which prints the file when you drag it onto the DropPS icon. You can download DropPS at www.barebones.com.

Summary of printing files

Before you try to print a file cross-platform, use this quick checklist:

- Use native file formats to transfer files across platforms whenever possible (see page 375 or Chapter 22, *Transferring Files*).

- Check your fonts to make sure you have the same ones on both platforms and that you styled them correctly for cross-platform work (see Chapter 24, *Fonts*).

- If your fonts are not exactly the same on both platforms, carefully proof your file on the platform from which you plan to print (see Chapter 24, *Fonts*).

- Make sure your graphics have been saved in a cross-platform format (see Chapter 22, *Transferring Files*).

- Save EPS files (and any graphics that were placed in the EPS file) as Binary for Macintosh printing, and as ASCII/DOS EPS for Windows printing (see page 373).

- If your file contains PostScript information, make sure the printer you plan on using is a PostScript printer (see pages 371–372).

- Use "Print to file" (see pages 376–377) or Adobe Acrobat (see Chapter 24) to make file transferring easier across platforms.

Part Six
Extras

The technologies that have had the most profound effects on human life are usually simple.

—*Freeman Dyson*

Multiple Users on One PC

If you're the only person using your computer, you can make radical Desktop changes and install applications all over the place. But what if you share the computer with others? In Windows, creating individualized Desktop environments for each person is easier than you might think. If you have a personal account (a unique log-in identity on your Windows computer), your customization can be part of a "personal user profile," or collection of preferences, that can be saved. Once your profile is saved, you can log into it whenever you want. If your company server is set up to accommodate personalized access, you can even bring many of your changes with you to a different computer.

User profiles maintain your Desktop settings

There are several kinds of computer user accounts. The most familiar one to Mac users is the network account. The network administrator determines how much access you have to servers and their data. Generally, you have very little control over your network interface.

Windows is different from the Mac in that it offers a local log-in feature. If you have full access to your "local" computer (the one on your desk, as opposed to the "remote" server that's somewhere else) you can customize your Desktop and set up log-in accounts for others who use it, like your ten-year-old nephew. Once you do this, your nephew can cover his Desktop with Star Wars themes without having any affect on the way *your* personal Desktop looks. This special log-in account is your **user profile.**

If your computer is part of a company network, speak to your system administrator before you try to add user profiles, install applications you don't want to share with others, or customize the Desktop in any way. Be sure to ask if you have enough privileges to make local changes (that is, changes to the individual machine you work on, not to the network); if you do, you can turn on user profiles yourself—just read the following step-by-step instructions. If you don't have local privileges, any changes you make to your Desktop will vanish the instant you log out if your computer doesn't have user profiles enabled.

A note about creating a password

When you log in to a user profile, Windows asks you for a password so other people can't log in under your name, either deliberately or by mistake. Windows passwords are "case-sensitive," which means it matters big time whether you type the password as capital letters (uppercase) or small letters (lowercase). For instance, if you set up your password as "Swizzle" with a capital "S," then the word "swizzle" with a lowercase "s" wouldn't let you in. When setting up your password in the first place, make sure the Caps Lock key isn't pressed unless you *want* your password to be in all capital letters.

Conf P,N
 # P39 2788955 - 0/26/2006/10:14:39

http://www.varsitybooks.com

501 South Gladiolus Street
Momence, IL 60954-1799

Your order of January 09, 2000 (Order ID 1896668)

Qty	Description	Author
1	WINDOWS FOR MAC USERS	WILL

THANK YOU FOR SHOPPING AT VARSITYBOOKS.COM!

ice

SOLD TO:

SHIP TO: Jennifer Groseth
          29 North Park Street
          Oberlin OH 44074

	List Price	Our Price	Total
IAMS, ROBIN	19.99	11.99	11.99

Books Total	11.99
Shipping	4.95
Order Total	16.94

t reflect this discount. To view a receipt for
ge and enter the order number listed above.

Create Desktop profiles (Windows 95/98)

Before you create new user profiles in Windows 95/98, you have to change one Control Panel setting.

1. Open the window for "My Computer," then open the Control Panel folder.

2. **Right-click** on the "Passwords" file to get the "Passwords Properties," as shown below. Click the "User Profiles" tab.

3. Click "Users can customize their preferences and Desktop settings." Once you click that button, the bottom half of the dialog box, "User profile settings," becomes active:

Passwords

This is the Passwords control panel, found in the Control Panel folder.

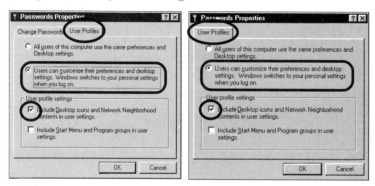

Windows 98   *Windows 95*

4. Under "User profile settings," check the first box, "Include Desktop icons and Network Neighborhood contents in user settings."

   You'll want to carefully consider the second option, "Include Start Menu and Program groups in user settings," because it has more bad points than good. By including the Start Menu and Program groups in the list of items a user can customize, you make it possible for one user to load a program that no other users will know is there. Anyone else wanting to use that program would have to manually add the program to their version of the Start Menu, or launch it by finding its icon on the hard disk. This might be useful for some situations, but make sure it's useful to *you* before you click.

5. Click OK to close the window.

Now you can actually create the users. Although the general idea behind adding users is the same in both versions of Windows, the dialog boxes you follow are different.

To create new user profiles in Windows 98

1. Open "My Computer," then open the Control Panel folder.

2. In the Control Panel folder, double-click the "Users" file to open its dialog box.

Users

This is the Users control panel icon in the Control Panel folder.

This is what the "User Settings" dialog box looks like when no users have been set up yet. Users will appear in the user list after you create them.

3. Click "New User" to launch the "Add User Wizard." In the first dialog box, click "Next."

4. The next dialog box asks you for the new user name. Enter it, and click "Next."

5. You can either give the user a password or not. Unless you're on a network, passwords in Windows 98 are a joke—anyone can delete your personal profile or change your Desktop settings without knowing your password. Since user profiles in Windows 95/98 are just a convenience, you can leave the "Password" line blank. When you're finished here, click "Next."

6. Check "Desktop folder and Documents menu" if you plan to change the Desktop. The other options aren't necessary if you are simply creating a new profile so you can customize the look and feel. When you've made your choices, click "Next," then click the "Finish" button on the next screen.

If you check "Favorites" and "Downloaded Web pages," each person who uses Internet Explorer will be able to keep their URLs, shortcuts, and downloads separate from everyone else. If you check "My Documents," every user will have a separate place to keep their files.

To create new user profiles in Windows 95

1. From the Start Menu, choose "Shut Down." In the dialog box that appears, choose "Close all programs and log on as different user." Click "Yes."

2. You'll be asked for a user name and password. This has two purposes:

   - If you are already a user, type your information, click OK, and the computer will log you in.

   - If you enter a name and password that the computer doesn't recognize, it will ask you to confirm the password. Once you confirm it, Windows will create the name you entered as a new user.

     (If you choose "Cancel" at this point, you'll just be returned to the Desktop as the general "default" user you've been all along. You can always log on as a general user even after you've created new users, and the Desktop you see will be the same one you've had until this point.)

3. Windows will ask you to retype the password you entered in the previous dialog box. It does this to confirm that you typed it exactly as you want to remember it. After you enter the password, Windows logs you in as the user you just created. You'll be that user until you choose to log off by going to the Start Menu and choosing "Shut Down" again.

Now there's an intuitive feature—to create a new profile, you choose "Shut Down."

To create new user profiles in Windows NT

1. Click the Start button, click "Programs," click "Administrative Tools," then click "User Manager."

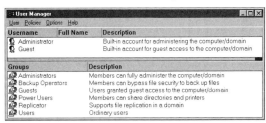

If you've never changed or added names to your list of users, the "User Manager" dialog box will look similar to this one.

We recommend you make new users rather than change the existing ones. In particular, avoid changing the "Administrator," at least until you feel very comfortable with administering your local computer. "Administrator" is the only default group that can do everything, and if you change its name and password by mistake you could lock yourself out of your own computer!

2. From the "User" menu, choose "New User" to get the dialog box shown below. Fill in the blanks as indicated, substituting your own name in the "Username" and "Full Name" fields. Obviously, you can make up your own description.

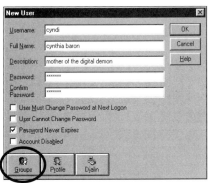

If you don't want to be bothered with a password, leave both the "Password" and "Confirm Password" lines blank. Just remember that having no password means anyone can change your Desktop defaults (and lots of other things, too).

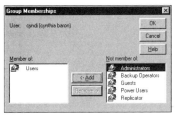

3. Click the "Groups" button in the lower-left corner of the dialog box (circled, above left). The "Group Memberships" dialog box will appear (shown to the left).

4. As the primary computer user you'll want to have full computer access, so click "Administrators" in the list on the right, then click "Add."

Windows NT has six different "Groups." These Groups represent different security access levels to the computer workstation. Only four are important to you unless you are a network administrator:

- **Administrators** have full control of the computer and can change other users' access rights. If your computer has a system administrator, this person will probably have blocked your access to this level by making you a "Power User" or "User" instead.

- **Power Users** can't access or control Administrators, but can make minor system changes (like resetting the computer's time clock), set up sharing on their computer, and create other users at their level or below. In a corporate setting where you are the primary user on your computer, this is one of the two access levels you probably have.

- **Users** can use the computer and its programs, but can't set up sharing or make computer system changes. This is the "average" level that administrators give to users.

- **Guests** have almost no access rights other than the ability to log into the computer. They can access only what the Administrator or Power User allows.

The last two access levels are for networks only:

- **Backup Operators** are the people who come in at night to backup and restore hard drives.

- **Replicators** aren't really users. Replication is a computer function that lets the person sitting at the workstation download master files from a server.

If you're going to create other users, you might want to limit what they can do. Read the extensive help menus to figure out which of these levels suits you best and choose the group whose privileges seems to fit. (You can always change the user's access level later.)

5. When you're done, click OK. NT will take you back to the "New User" dialog box. Click OK, quit the "User Manager" (click the X in the title bar or press Alt F4), and you're done.

Logging on as a different user

There are some ways in which Windows isn't very intuitive, and logging on as someone else is one of those ways. In all forms of Windows, the only way to change users is by shutting down the Desktop and bringing it back up again for the next person.

To log on as a different user in Windows 98

1. From the Start Menu, choose "Log Off." The name of the current user will show up as part of the "Log Off" line, as shown in the example below.

The sin Windows 98 gives you a clue as to which user is currently logged on.

2. A dialog box will appear and ask if you're sure you want to log off. Click "Yes."

3. The Desktop will go blank, and the "Log In" dialog box will appear. Just enter the new user's name (and password if there is one) and click OK.

To log on as a different user in Windows 95 or NT

1. From the Start Menu, choose "Shut Down."

2. In the dialog box that appears, choose "Close all programs and log on as a different user." Click "Yes."

3. The Desktop will go blank, and the "Log In" dialog box will appear. Just enter the new user's name (and password if there is one) and click OK.

Deleting user profiles

Eventually you'll probably need to know how to delete a user from the log-in list. Sometimes you make a mistake when you create a user, or perhaps a user is no longer using your computer and you want to free up disk space.

It's much easier to delete a user account than to create one, so don't delete unless you're really sure. Once you've deleted a profile, there's absolutely no automatic way to get all of the customized features back, even if you create a new user with exactly the same name and password —all the user's Desktop preferences will need to be created from scratch.

To delete user profiles in Windows 98

1. Open the window for "My Computer," then open the Control Panel folder.

2. In the Control Panel folder, double-click "User" to open its dialog box. From the list of Users in the property sheet, select the user or users you'd like to delete.

3. Click "Delete." You'll get a warning dialog box:

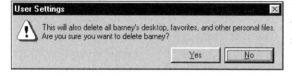

This is the only warning you'll receive.

4. Click "Yes" and the user is history.

To delete user profiles in Windows 95

The only way to delete existing users is to throw away their entire user profiles folder.

1. From the Start Menu, choose "Find." Search for the name of the user you want to delete. You should find it in two places: as a .PWL (profile) file in your Windows folder, and as a folder with the whole user name.

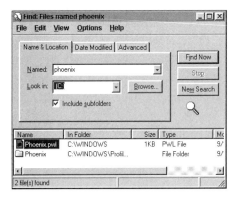

2. Drag both items right out of the Find box to the Recycle Bin.

To delete user profiles in Windows NT

1. From the Start Menu, click "Programs," click "Administrative Tools," and click "User Manager."

2. In the "User Manager" window, select the user you wish to delete, and press the Delete key. The very wordy message you get next reminds you that deleting a user is a very serious act. Click "Cancel" if you change your mind; click OK to proceed.

   You'll get one confirmation dialog box if you proceed:

3. Click "Yes" and the user is removed.

Preventing Problems

While computer problems are never fun, self-inflicted ones are by far the most unpleasant. Computers can freeze even when you've been a perfect user, but when you're careless or rushed, the odds are much greater that you'll create a truly nasty problem. Windows is less tolerant of messy behavior than a Mac is and is harder to nurse back to health once a serious crisis erupts.

Be ready for inevitable problems by anticipating them. This chapter provides some preventive medicine to minimize your Windows' downtime. Follow even half of these suggestions, and when (not if) a problem arises, you'll be irritated, but not devastated.

Read this before you crash

On a Mac, you can wiggle out of almost any situation besides hardware failure by booting with the system CD. This doesn't work in Windows because PCs can't even see that they have a CD until its driver loads. CD drives are just some dumb extra hardware to a PC, not an integrated part of the computer as they are on the Mac. Not only can't you boot from a CD, you can't use a CD as your operating system disk either. This could make it difficult to save files *after* a crash.

Emergency disks

Assuming your system is running well right now, you should make emergency disks so you can recover your data if the computer crashes and stays down. Unlike a Mac emergency disk which starts up the Mac OS, allowing you to save your files and troubleshoot the problem that crashed the system, this emergency disk won't even launch you into Windows. It will stop at DOS, where you'll have to run the startup disk's utility programs to help resurrect your system.

Windows NT doesn't let you boot the system from a startup disk, so if you are using NT, look at the section called "NT repair disk."

Making a startup disk for Windows 98

Note: Making a startup floppy disk in Windows 95 is rather technical. If you have startup trouble, make sure you have a Windows-savvy tech friend handy.

When you install Windows it gives you the option of creating a startup disk. You may have rushed right past this installation screen, or perhaps your system came pre-loaded so you never saw the option. Either way, if you don't have a startup disk already, you need one right now. Begin with an empty, newly formatted, floppy disk.

1. Put the disk in the drive. Find your installation CD and insert it.

2. From "My Computer" or the Start Menu's "Settings," open the Control Panel folder. Double-click "Add/Remove Programs," then click the "Startup Disk" tab.

3. Click the "Create Disk…" button. If you haven't put the CD in, Windows will remind you to do so. Once the CD is in, Windows will copy information from the CD to the disk. You now have a Windows startup disk.

Using the startup disk

We'll be delighted if you look back on the process of creating a startup disk as a pointless exercise. That's OK. However, should your system ever refuse to wake up one morning, we know you'll be relieved that this startup disk exists. Here's how to use it:

1. Turn off the computer. Put the startup disk in the A: drive, then turn your computer back on. Floppy disks are slower than other media, so wait patiently. Pretty soon, you'll have a black screen with a prompt on it that looks like this:

    A: \ >

2. There'll be a flashing cursor waiting for you to type. Type the following line exactly as you see it below, with the space between "dir" and the drive name. Don't forget that colon (:) either!

    dir c:
    Then hit the Enter key.

    You've just asked DOS to take a look at your hard drive (C:) and read what's there. A long list of files and folders should scroll up your screen. If it does so, there's nothing wrong with your hard drive itself, and your files are still okay.

    Warning: If you don't get a list, or if you get an error message telling you that the drive doesn't exist or can't be found, you need to consult someone who actually knows something about computers. There are just too many possible problems—from viruses to a dead hard drive—that can make the drive disappear.

3. We assume that your list looks okay, which means there are two broad possibilities for what might be wrong:

    - There are bad sectors on the drive.
    - One or many of your system files are corrupt.

4. To check for bad sectors, do this:

    - Type **dir a:**
      Then hit the Enter key.

    This returns you to the disk where your utility programs are.

    - Type **scandisk c:**
      Then hit the Enter key.

    ScanDisk is a utility program which will check your disk for errors and fix them if it can. *—continued*

5. Unless ScanDisk finds lots of errors (in which case you should go back and read the warning about not finding the C: drive), run one more utility to renew your hard disk.

- Type **sys c:**
  Then hit the Enter key.

This copies the basic setup files to your hard disk which will enable it to boot up and launch Windows again.

6. Once the files are copied, eject the disk and restart your system. If everything doesn't boot correctly, you'll need to reload files from your Windows disk or even reinstall it completely. As long as you followed our directions for adding CD-ROM files to this startup disk, you should be able to access your Windows CD and do exactly that.

Backup Windows 98 system files

Besides making a startup disk, it's a good idea to create a backup disk of your most important system files. If you ever have to reload Windows from scratch (a long and unpleasant task!), these files provide a template of how your system used to look.

Use a clean floppy disk (*not* the one you used to create the startup disk). Find the following files on your PC and copy them to the floppy disk:

1. From the C:\ root drive, copy:
   autoexec.bat
   config.sys
2. From the C:\Windows folder, copy:
   system.dat
   user.dat

This backup disk is also a good place to put duplicates of any hardware drivers, like the one for the CD-ROM drive. How do you know which files are drivers? Look again at your **config.sys** for any line that begins with **DEVICE=**. The text that follows **DEVICE=** contains the name of any driver files your system needs.

NT repair disk

NT doesn't make a startup disk. Instead, you need to create a "rescue," or repair, disk, which should allow you to return to the state your computer system was in just before it crashed.

To make a repair disk in Windows NT

1. Click the Start Menu, and choose "Run." You'll see this:

2. Type **rdisk** in the "Open" edit box, then click OK. You'll see this:

3. If you've added software or hardware since the computer was first installed, *and* if your NT station is functioning well, click "Update Repair Info." This will alter the information in the repair directory to make sure all of your changes have been accounted for and will be written to the disk you're about to make.

   Don't click that button if you are worried about your system because it will only ensure that your worries continue! Instead, click "Create Repair Disk." This will make a repair disk based on the old system information, which is probably just what you need.

4. You'll get a dialog box reminding you that updating the repair disk will erase the old information; confirm that you want to do this by choosing "Yes." When you agree to the update, a small status bar appears, followed by another dialog box asking if you want to create an emergency repair disk. Click "Yes," and have a floppy disk ready in the A: drive.

5. After NT finishes, make sure to label, lock, and save your repair disk.

As you add software or change settings and properties, you should repeat this process. Don't keep using the same disk, though—it's always a good idea to have a copy of the last time your system was in good working order. The next time you update your repair disk, use a different floppy disk and hold onto the previous repair version just in case. Wait for a third update before you reuse the first disk.

Important warning:
If you're already experiencing serious problems with your computer, you run a risk of transferring these problems to the rescue disk you make. Instead of creating a repair disk, back up all your important data, then find a knowledgeable Windows NT computer person and beg for help.

Back up your files

Of course you backup files on your Mac, don't you? You don't want to lose everything you've drawn, written, or calculated because of a silly disk crash. It's even more important to backup regularly in Windows. You can't boot a Windows computer with a CD, and a floppy startup disk won't let you access your removable hard drives—even if they're built in Zip or Jaz drives—to save your big files after a crash.

Macs don't usually need to be backed up before you install hardware or load new applications. Windows computers do. Drivers and applications write information to many places inside the system. In a worst-case scenario, these newly written files can corrupt systems that were running happily before. One of the major complaints about the Windows 98 upgrade is its tendency to write over files that other company's software needs to run. Many consider this to be a serious offense.

Until very recently, most PC backup devices have been tape drives, so the backup software bundled with Windows 95 and Windows NT is designed for tapes. Now that Iomega and other companies make cartridge backup devices, tapes are becoming less prevalent. Tape backups are very dependable, but they're also very slow and you can't reuse the cartridges for any other purpose.

The nice thing about automatic solutions is they always remember to backup even when you don't—or don't feel like it. If you're on Windows 95 or NT, don't have a tape drive, and can't invest in a cartridge and software backup package, you should at least manually back up your most important data files daily.

Using Microsoft Backup in Windows 98

Although the backup programs that are bundled with Windows 95 and NT are pretty lame, Windows 98 comes with a really good one called Microsoft Backup. It's based on a commercial program created by Seagate Software called "Backup Exec," which Windows 95 or NT users might want to consider.

No matter which method you choose, don't wait. Backup on a regular basis because at some awful, catastrophic point you'll wish you had.

To use Microsoft Backup, go to the Start Menu, choose "Programs," choose "Accessories," choose "System Tools," and choose "Backup." It's very self-explanatory. If you want to backup onto your Zip or Jaz disk, insert it before you run the program.

If you don't see "Backup" in your Start Menu, it may not have been loaded when Windows 98 was installed (this may mean your system was *upgraded* from Windows 95 to Windows 98, since a clean install would have loaded the Backup software automatically). Find your Windows 98 installer CD and insert it in the CD drive, then open the Control Panel folder and double-click the "Add/Remove Programs" file. Choose "Install," and the Wizard will walk you through installing Backup. For more details on installing from the original Windows CD, see Chapter 16, *Installing and Using Applications.*

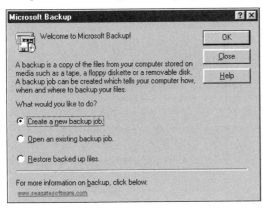

You'll find it easy to backup using this utility.

Fragmentation and disk errors

Every version of Windows includes tools to defragment drives (described below) and hunt down disk errors, but some of these tools are more effective than others. Two particularly useful ones come with all Windows 95/98 versions: **Disk Defragmenter** and **ScanDisk.** If you've used the Optimize and ScanDisk modules from a program like Norton Utilities on the Mac, you know what these tools do. Running both of them should become part of your regular routine.

Defragment your hard disk

As you install, uninstall, create, modify, and delete files, your disk drive (if you could see inside of it) begins to look like a crazy quilt. Even though the computer tries to put things onto the drive in a logical way, it can't predict how big a document might be, especially after the file has been altered and replaced several times. It may start a file in one place, discover that the next holding space (sector) on the drive is already in use, and send the rest of the file to the next blank disk sector, which could be very far away from the first part. After a while your drive begins to slow down as the computer system wastes time trying to find all the scattered little file pieces. The result is called **fragmentation,** and it's very bad for computer performance.

Fragmentation is even worse for a PC than it is for a Mac, due to how PCs handle memory. If you read Chapter 16, *Installing and Using Applications,* you know that Windows grabs a piece of the hard disk and uses it as virtual memory; this piece is called a "swap file" because Windows swaps data in and out of it. As the drive fills up and fragments, so does this swap file. Eventually you'll get application memory errors and very slow, painful waits while Windows works.

To defragment your drive in Windows 95/98, go to the Start Menu, to "Programs," to "Accessories," to "System Tools," and choose "Disk Defragmenter." Select the drive you want to defragment and the rest is self-explanatory.

Use this Disk Defragmenter about once a month.

Check for disk errors

Disk errors aren't only caused by fragmentation; there are physical problems that can plague a computer. Disks can be damaged by moving the computer while it's turned on or by the zap of an electric surge. Sometimes disk problems show up immediately after the damage is done; other times they lurk until the next driver or utility is loaded so the problem is misdiagnosed. If you start getting strange Windows errors, find document files that won't open, or experience very slow performance on what used to be a fast system, run ScanDisk.

To run Windows ScanDisk

1. Open "My Computer." Right-click on the disk you want to scan, and from the pop-up menu choose "Properties."

2. Click the "Tools" tab. Click "Check Now." The ScanDisk dialog box will appear.

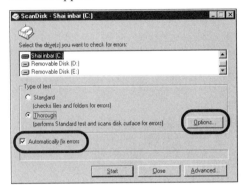

3. If your computer seems to be working well and you just want to run a quick check, choose "Standard."

   If you've been experiencing incomplete software installations or you suspect PC damage, choose "Thorough." This option will also check the physical sectors on your disk. Minor bad sectors will be walled off so the system no longer tries to write to them. Doing this clears up nagging problems.

4. Check "Automatically fix errors" (circled, above).

5. Click "Options" to get the "Surface Scan Options" dialog box, shown on the following page.

— continued

6. Check "System and data areas" to find out if there are any problems on your hard disk that might lead to a system crash or failure.

Leave "Do not perform write-testing" unchecked.

Check "Do not repair bad sectors in hidden and system files." Since you checked "System and data areas," you want to prevent ScanDisk from making system repairs before you have a chance to backup important files. When a disk scanner finds a bad sector, it takes the information contained there and moves it to someplace safe. Problems can crop up when the bad sector information is part of the system, which is what most hidden files are. And some programs go looking for system pieces in specific disk places and won't work if they can't find what they're looking for.

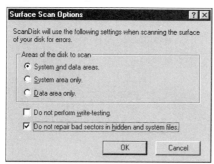

Click OK to return to the ScanDisk dialog box.

7. Click the "Advanced" button to get the "ScanDisk Advanced Options" dialog box. You'll want to change a couple of the settings in this dialog box (explained on the opposite page).

Very briefly, here is what each advanced option does:

- **Display summary** provides a list of what ScanDisk found. Choose "Only if errors found" unless you are in training to be a PC geek.

- **Log file** archives the display summaries. If you start seeing problems, choose "Append to log" so you can provide tech support with a copy.

- **Cross-linked files** are files that fight to occupy the same space on the disk. This is a bad conflict that usually happens because of a system crash or an improper shut down. ScanDisk prefers to copy each cross-linked file into a separate space and delete the overlapped area. Usually, one or both files are damaged already, but "Make copies" at least gives you the chance to look at and maybe salvage information before you delete the files.

- **Lost file fragments** are caused in the same way as cross-linked files. They are often pieces of application temp files and are usually not worth keeping. If ScanDisk finds any lost pieces of files, use Find to search for files with a .CHK extension, so when you find them you can trash them all.

- In **Check files for,** uncheck "Invalid file names." As a Mac user, you may have some file names on the Windows computer that use invalid characters. If you plan on opening these files in Windows, you should change their names, but if they're just temporarily on your Windows Desktop you might not want to slow down the scanning process by having Windows locate them.

- **Check host drive first** should be unchecked unless your system is using Drive Space, a compression program that causes more problems than it solves.

8. Click OK. Click "Start," and walk away. When you return, you'll see a readout of what ScanDisk found. Unless ScanDisk found bad sectors (see the sidebar), you can just click "Close."

A useful thing: Windows 98 bundles both Disk Defragmenter and ScanDisk into a customizable "Maintenance Wizard," also in the Start Menu under "System Tools." Once you've played with these utilities and are comfortable with what they do, you can automate the process of running them using the "Maintenance Wizard." You can set either or both utilities to run at specific times, like late at night or at lunch time.

If ScanDisk found problems in the system and hidden files that you told it not to repair, the bad sectors are still on your disk and bound to cause you problems. Backup your hard disk immediately so all of your data will remain intact. Then consult a knowledgeable Windows person.

Defragmentation and disk error tools in NT

Windows NT's system diagnostic options are surprisingly bare. It does have defragmentation and error checking tools, but you can't customize them as you can in other Windows versions. The error checking tool is called "Check Disk."

To use "Check Disk"

1. Open "My Computer." Right-click on the icon of the disk you want to check, and in the pop-up menu choose "Properties."

2. In the property sheet, click the "Tools" tab.

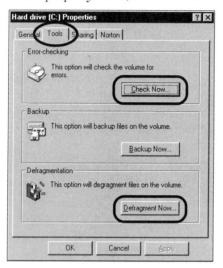

3. Click the buttons to launch and run the error checking and defragmentation options.

This tool is better than not having anything at all, but if you're using NT you should buy a third-party disk utilities program. These kinds of programs are not very expensive, and they handle the job of keeping your system in tune far more efficiently than the tools that come with Windows NT.

Keeping the disk trim

Because Windows hides so many files from you, it's easy to fill up a hard disk without realizing you've done so. The memory swap file (see page 233) requires a certain amount of space, and if Windows doesn't get it because your hard disk is too full, your applications will either crash regularly or they won't run at all. To keep your disk trim, delete unnecessary files; then defragment (page 398) to reclaim space and efficiency.

- **Delete .TMP files.** All programs make "temporary" files, and some programs never seem to get rid of them. You'd be surprised how many temp files your disk may have and how large they are. Use Find's wild card to search for ***.TMP**, then drag the whole list to the Recycle Bin and delete the files. **Warning:** Trash the temporary files when no applications are running (you wouldn't want to dump a .TMP file while it's in use!).

Jayva.tmp

- **Uninstall programs you no longer use.** In Windows you can't just *delete* programs because they leave system droppings everywhere. These leftovers will cause the system to do weird and disturbing things, like it may try to launch the phantom files and throw incomprehensible error messages at you. Use the "Add/Remove Programs" control panel to correctly uninstall program files (find it in the Control Panel folder, which is in "My Computer").

Add/Remove
Programs

- **Dump cache files.** Do you use a web browser? Every time you go to a new site, web pages and graphics get downloaded to your computer. Depending on your browser's default cache settings, you could have surprisingly large amounts of disk space taken up this way. Search for the "Cache" folder in Netscape, or the "Temporary Internet Files" folder in Internet Explorer. Open them up, and drag the contents right into the Recycle Bin. Don't forget to empty the Recycle Bin (right-click on it and choose "Empty Recycle Bin").

cache   Temporary
         Internet Files

  You can go into the Preferences or Options in your web browser and change the amount of disk space you are willing to give to your browser for its cache.

Viruses

Viruses are little bits of code written by really nasty people intentionally to destroy data on computers. Viruses usually piggy-back on legitimate pieces of programming, hidden from sight. Taking advantage of the things your computer and its programs do normally, viruses turn these natural processes against your system. Some attach to the "boot sector" of a drive so they activate whenever you turn the computer on. Others are application-specific and only do their damage when you use the application they're attached to. Many viruses can jump from disk to disk, so if you put in a floppy disk that contains a virus, it can jump onto your hard disk. Then when you put another floppy disk or Zip disk into that computer, the virus jumps from the hard disk onto that removable disk. And so ad infinitum. People who write viruses are miserable wretches and are heaping seriously bad karma upon themselves.

While there are very few and relatively benign Macintosh viruses, there are thousands of PC-based viruses already in existence and new ones are discovered every week.

Where do viruses come from?

There are many ways to become infected with a virus.

- **Downloading software from the Internet.** This is the fastest way for viruses to spread. Have you ever considered where the software utilities you download came from and how well protected the server is that they're stored on? See page 406 about protecting your computer.

- **Using a computer lab, especially one in a school.** Schools frequently don't have the personnel and resources to keep anti-viral programs up to date. They're also home to many young programmers who think that creating viruses proves they're cyberjockies. Actually, it proves they're superjerks.

- **Sharing programs, particularly pirated ones, over a network.** Some virus creators have a strange sense of ethics in that they will modify an illegally-copied program and anonymously offer it to all comers so it infects the hard disk of anyone who takes them up on their offer. Their thinking is that if you're immoral enough to pirate someone else's software, you deserve to be punished.

- **Sharing disks.** Most people spread viruses inadvertently, just by putting an infected disk into several different computers. There are viruses that infect computer hard disks as soon as the disk mounts on the Desktop, even if you don't open any files.

- **Sharing Microsoft Office files, even between Macs and PCs.** Microsoft has done such a good job at cross-platforming its Office suite that it's now becoming possible to attach malicious code that travels between platforms. This is a brand-new problem. Fortunately, this doesn't happen often because most viruses are still trapped on their initial platform.

- **Installation software or CDs in magazines.** Yes, even commercial software can be infected before it's shipped.

- **E-mail attachments of a certain type.** Until recently, infected email was the Internet equivalent of an urban myth. Contrary to the periodic messages that well-intentioned people may send to you, there is no such thing as a "Good Times" virus or any other infection that can be spread merely by opening up and reading a text-only email message. However, email with attachments that have self-starting Java code can actually transmit a virus. The Melissa "virus" of 1999 that was sent through email didn't actually infect computers with a virus or harm anyone's personal hard disk—it wreaked havoc with mail servers by overloading them with automatically sent messages.

How can you tell you've got a virus?

There isn't any one symptom of a virus infection. You can be sure of a virus problem if nasty or obscene messages periodically flash on your screen. Another sign is a disk that seems to have filled up far too quickly for no good reason, or a rash of files that come up with disk errors or open with scrambled data. Problems that only happen when you use a specific program might be virus-related, as well as things that happen on a schedule—like a disk that tries to connect to the network every half hour or a program that won't launch on Tuesdays. The worst symptoms are the ones you aren't aware of until the damage is done: corrupted system files and erased disks.

What can you do to prevent a virus?

Your best prevention against a virus infection is to own a really good anti-virus program *and keep it updated.* On the Mac, virus protection software packages have changed versions very slowly because they haven't had to respond to many new and different situations. In the PC world, updates are frequent. When a new version comes out for your software, get it. Also, in this case it's not a good idea to depend on shareware anti-virus programs because individual programmers or small groups often don't have the resources to respond quickly to new infestations.

virus definitions: Files that are specific to an anti-virus application that tell the application how to recognize a virus and what to do about it.

Download new *virus definitions* for your software at least once a month. More is better. The large, commercial anti-virus vendors have web sites that let you update your computer's definitions while you're connected. After you download a new set of virus definitions, use the software to scan your hard disk for new viruses, especially if you do a lot of down-loading. A new virus might have found its way to your computer in the time between one update and the next.

If you find a virus on your hard disk, scan all of your other cartridges and disks! Chances are great that the virus has spread.

Part Seven

The Stuff at the End

The Index

About the authors

Cyndi Baron

I have an eclectic background that started in literature, jumped to theater design, and segued into typography. Along the way I picked up an MBA because I figured it would be the last thing anyone would expect. I teach graphics and run a busy bunch of labs with too many PCs and not nearly enough Macs at a large art department in a very large university. Bad at saying "no," I write about design for a magazine, about computer topics in books, and about life in poetry. I think every problem short of death can be conquered creatively. That's probably why I enjoy *New York Times* crossword puzzles, computer crises, and travelling in countries whose language I don't speak. My home is an old Victorian just outside Boston where I live with my husband (a scientist and gourmet cook) and the cat who owns us.

Robin Williams

Well, I must say that after working on this book, my opinion of Windows has changed—it's worse than I thought. I've written lots and lots of books and articles and columns about computers and design and typography and the Internet and the web, many of them cross-platform although I do happen to have a strong bias toward the Mac, in case you didn't know. I live on 2.5 acres outside of Santa Fe in the middle of a short, stubby, piñon forest whose trees don't get in the way of the sunrises and sunsets. I live with my adorable sweetheart John and have only one child now left at home. For those of you who have been keeping track, Ryan is now a Navy SEAL, Jimmy has graduated from high school, and Scarlett is a teenager. I don't know how they got older and I didn't. See you at UrlsInternetCafe.com.

About the book

Colophon

Cyndi, in Boston, wrote the text on a Power Mac using Microsoft Word 6.0. For screen shots, she used Flash-It on the Mac, TechSmith's Snag-It on the PC, and Adobe Photoshop 5 on the Mac. She sent text files to Nancy.

Nancy Davis, in Buffalo, did the first-pass editing and sent the text files to Barbara.

Barbara Sikora, in Cazadero, laid the text into PageMaker 6.5 on a Mac G3, cleaned up screen shots in Photoshop 5, then sent the files to Robin.

Robin, in Santa Fe, edited and added in PageMaker 6.5 on a Mac G3, created screen shots on the Mac using Captivate Select, screen shots on the PC using ScreenThief, cleaned them up in Photoshop 5 on the Mac, and did final production and layout in PageMaker. She sent hard copy to Nancy and to Cyndi.

Nancy Davis, back in Buffalo, did final editing and sent her copy to Lisa, and Cyndi did a final pass and sent files back to Robin.

Lisa Brazieal, in Berkeley, checked the pages for potential production problems and sent the pages back to Robin.

Robin, in Santa Fe, cleaned up all the odds and ends, generated the table of contents and created the index in PageMaker, had PageMaker gather all the necessary files and fonts for final production, and sent electronic files off on a Zip to Peachpit Press and really final hard copy to Nancy. Nancy and Robin made last-minute changes.

Lisa, at Peachpit Press in Berkeley, did a final production check on the electronic files, received the final hard copy from Nancy, and sent the package on to Edwards Brothers in Ann Arbor to be printed.

Robin and Cyndi have never met.

The fonts used are Bell from Adobe and Monotype for body copy; **Index**, designed by Tim Glaser and Josh Darden, available from GarageFonts, for the heads and subheads; and AlleyCat from EyeWire for the chapter heads.